THE RISE OF CHARLESTON

CONVERSATIONS WITH VISIONARIES, LUMINARIES & EMISSARIES OF THE HOLY CITY

W. THOMAS McQUEENEY

THE History PRESS

Contents

city and region to heal racial differences. A long and troubled history of racial animosity kept Charleston from realizing its potential, and I knew that until we squarely faced and met that challenge, real progress would not be possible. It was not a question of replacing some people at the decision-making table; it was a matter of making the table bigger and giving everyone a place. We certainly have much more work to do, but I am proud of how far we have come and what a difference this racial reconciliation and inclusiveness has made to the real accomplishments in every facet of life in Charleston since the late 1970s.

I also wanted to help Charleston regain its economic footing, to revitalize the downtown business district and to spread this new growth and progress to our suburban neighborhoods. We started with a plan and followed it through many challenges. The King Street shopping district, truly unique, is one of the most successful downtown spaces in America.

Tourism has become a major industry in Charleston, but we devote as much time to tourism management as to tourism promotion. It is a delicate balance that must be maintained, for it would be fatal to tip the balance in either direction.

I realized that a central city like Charleston had to be able to grow to provide the services that were expected and provided for the entire region, and in the past thirty-five years, the physical size of the city has grown from ten to more than one hundred square miles, from Daniel Island to Johns Island, from Bees Ferry to the Battery.

Public spaces define a city and its values, and Charleston has worked hard to build on its tradition of an inspiring public realm. From the Waterfront Park on the site of burned-out docks on the Cooper River to the brand-new recreation complexes across the area, the public realm has grown geometrically and been enhanced by new parks that take advantage of this area's beautiful natural resources in both North Charleston and Mount Pleasant.

Sports venues—from our beautiful baseball stadium with its river views to the fabulous Family Circle Tennis Center—help attract new residents and entertain those of us who are already here. The phenomenal growth of higher education in Charleston—the College of Charleston and the Art Institute in particular—provide opportunities for higher education and for jobs.

Charleston has experienced in the last few years an enormous explosion as a center for the arts. Spoleto Festival USA, the Moja Festival and the growth of the visual arts have made possible the restoration of the Dock Street Theatre and the planned renovation of the Gaillard Auditorium into a world-class performing arts space.

Charleston is truly cosmopolitan, the result of its long history as a thriving port, carrying goods from one part of the world to another. This trait, coupled with the efforts to make our public realm as beautiful and user-friendly as possible, have helped to land Charleston high on most national or international lists of best places to live. It is important not to forget that Charleston's situation on the water is what made the city and the area great places to live. Shipping and related activities have long been a key component of the local and state economy.

While the built environment is critical to a region's success, nothing is more important than the people who make it all happen. The people you will read about in this book are many of the talents that make this community so successful. Their diversity shows the hundreds of strands of effort and inspiration that have contributed to making Charleston an incomparable place to live. And they all share in common the realization that we must never rest on these laurels. There must always be more to do.

Joseph P. Riley Jr.
Former Mayor, 1975–2016
City of Charleston, South Carolina

Acknowledgements

Oh, and by the way…”

That seems to be a thematic part of everyone’s life in the Holy City. In Charleston 1960 as in Charleston today, it was a way of saying, “Did you know that so-and-so is the first cousin of this person who married that person?” Interjections like “Well, I declare” or “Isn’t that grand?” were always a staple part of the lexicon.

With natural growth from the home roots, coupled with the ivy and jasmine that came from yonder, many of the connect-the-dots relationships have disappeared. It is not the same garden it once was. Nonetheless, there were verdant associations that characterized the rise of Charleston. My personal associations with the personalities comprising this effort are not unlike those of others of my era who have intertwined their last handful of decades here.

For instance, Arthur Ravenel regaled me at family reunions. He is a true people person. My mother and Alicia Rhett were two of the dozen local artists who started the Charleston Artist Guild in 1953. I met Tim Scott through mutual charitable causes before recruiting him as the Charleston County Council chairman to assist me in other community work. Fritz Hollings had been president of the Hibernian Society of Charleston; my roles there have brought me in contact with the venerable senator. Joe Riley went to my high school and my college ten years ahead of me. I knew him well enough in the aftermath of Hurricane Hugo in 1989 to bring the president and CEO of State Farm, Ed Rust Jr., to his office. Mike Veeck and I built a friendship out of his humor and my appreciation thereof. Dr. Charlie Darby invited me to a Ray Charles concert several months prior to Charles's death in 2004. Darby is a distant cousin. Reverend Anthony Thompson finished Bishop England High School with me in 1970. Les Robinson may be among a handful of my very best friends ever. I've known Major General Cliff Poole since he took over the interim presidency of The Citadel in 1995–96. Judge Sol Blatt is father-in-law of Tee Hooper, a fellow member of The Citadel Board of Visitors. He is also an active member of the Hibernian Society. Senator Glenn McConnell gave me a copy of a wonderful speech he gave in 1980. Our interaction in the interim has given me an appreciation of his academic excellence and his political leadership. Fisher DeBerry has been my golfing partner since his retirement. Former governor Jim Edwards was my childhood dentist. Frank Abagnale's wife, Kelly, insured her wonderful fashion shop on George Street, the House of Sage, through my insurance agency. Abagnale is a most impressive moral example to all of us. Bobby Harrell and I have been solid friends for more than thirty years through our mutual association with State Farm. Michael Duffy and I have shared the laughter of the Irish for forty years. I met Bobby Cremins through his friendship with my father thirty-five years ago. Anita Zucker has been a neighbor and friend who can always be counted upon. Vietnam veterans Tommy Baker and Tommy Condon are not just my buddies but gentlemen I deeply respect. Bernie Puckhaber has been a personal mentor to me. Henry Berlin is a fine acquaintance and a Charleston institution. Others I met along the way or made my way to meet them as I considered them quite important to our mutual community. Charleston certainly lends itself to lasting friendships and social interactions.

To undertake this project with the given spectrum of topics, personalities and events would be all too ambitious without the assistance and support of several individuals. It is impossible to bestow the volume of appreciation I feel for those who lifted me and made my life so much more meaningful. Just knowing them is a special honor.

It was Mrs. Angie LeClerq of The Citadel library who first gave me the inclination to pursue this comprehensive assignment. She was never given any specific role in this enterprise. Yet she became my public relations liaison, my catalogue of creativity and my earnest advisor. My aptitude and attitude for the project were both elevated by her genuine friendship and support. She and her husband, Fred, are mainstays of the Charleston community by the sheer dedication and implementation of their devotion to our culture—and especially to the art of floral gardens.

The History Press is a most professional organization with a home office in London and the convenience of a regional office right in the downtown area of Charleston. They were recommended to me by a fine Irish interest author, Donald M. Williams. Like me, Donald has a day job. He is a lawyer. Jessica Berzon took me on as a novice and made me a novice first class. She arranged the happy coordination of photo editor Annie Martz and manuscript editor Diane Parham. Both have been delightful, informative and—most of all—patient. Diane, especially, has taken the time to make me seem coherent and insightful. It was a considerable task!

There are other appreciations to acknowledge for any potential sense of accomplishment I might incur. As an English major at The Citadel, I was quite inspired by the entire department to include several mentoring professors, some of whom have passed away. As Major General Cliff Poole indicated, one would be hard-pressed to find a better collection of dedicated professors than those who had gathered at The Citadel—for me, in the early 1970s—to enlighten my entire life. No one professor taught me more than my friend James A.W. Rembert, who gave me the desire to travel and "see the literature" in future years. I did so. I went to Ireland's County Sligo to see Drumcliff Churchyard and the grave of William Butler Yeats; to Canterbury to feel the cathedral of Geoffrey Chaucer's pilgrimage; to Denmark to walk the walls of Hamlet's Kronborg Castle; and to Bath to experience the scenes of Jane Austen. I went further yet—to Italy, France and Greece. The chase for historical and literary culture found me in Spain, Turkey and Russia and then in Germany, Scotland and Malta—more than fifty countries in all. I related so much of my travel to the mental pictures that words conjured forty years ago. Much of my travel stayed centered upon literature and art. This impressionable Charleston boy—late of bare feet, bumbling brogue and hand-me-downs—had never had the slightest sense that what was out there was incredible. Professor James Rembert and others adjusted my vision. My passion for travel was further developed through The Citadel's famous English department.

I would like to thank those whom I had the tremendous fortune to interview. Every one of them could have found something better to do than to sit down with yours truly for perhaps an hour. Knowing that their time was more valuable than my own, I earnestly studied the person and jotted down six questions. Why six? It left space on a single sheet of paper for the answers, and it limited the time to meet the parameters promised—well, almost. I anticipated that if I couldn't establish insights within six questions, then my enterprise was not worthwhile enough to pursue. I always reserved the right to call back and clarify an answer. It was not necessary. I also gave each interviewee the editorial license to read my draft and correct or even delete information. This happened infrequently. I know what you're thinking. I was surprised, too!

There was a point when the experiment had its moment of "Eureka!" I felt it as strong as it must have felt that late August day in 1886 when the earth shook down much of Charleston's former splendor. I was in the private chamber of Judge Solomon Blatt Jr.—by appointment, thank God! He came over to his chair and sat down to tell me a wonderful story of his formative years. I was there—listening and jotting notes—when that monumental emotional shake occurred. It came to me. I realized I was having so much fun doing these interviews that it should be a vice or a sin. Who else had ever had this unique experience, this dynamic privilege or this fantasy exchange of question, tale and insight with this select group of personalities? Few, if any, have—and none could possibly have had the inspirational lift this experience gave to me.

There I sat, not a published author, without an editor or a promised publishing house or any sense to my interviewee that they, their friends or family would ever see this as printed word. The only promise I had was a handshake and the trust of friendship. They believed in me. It took several interviews into the project before I even believed in me.

I wrote in exhilaration. The energy of my now-determined mind carried me forward from appointment to interview, essay draft to essay. By the time I had established that I had only a handful of other subjects with whom to schedule interviews, I had more than forty essays. Oops! The project approached four hundred pages. It was on my son Billy's thirty-fourth birthday, July 26, 2011, that Jessica Berzon of The History Press called me to tell me that their board had accepted my manuscript. My elation was that of a child with a balloon, a Popsicle and a yo-yo.

If God took me tomorrow, I would have no quarrel for the experience this book has given me. The scope of the book being even less than regional, I have had no pretensions of its popularity, only its edification for what it is—a chronicle of the people that made up a time. I only hope the book makes the people of the city I love all the more human and yet wonderful to the generations that follow us. Yes, I claim to be a part of their era, though only an insignificant scribe enjoying their experiences.

All in all, it was the people who are in these pages who indemnified the project. They are inexorable parts of this great city. They comprise what we are and from where and whence we came. They are "the rise of Charleston."

Introduction

Charleston is alive. It breathes, it sweats, it cries and it laughs aloud. It is suspended by the syncopation of a clock that does not keep time correctly. It matters not. The time in Charleston is unique unto itself.

Had there not been a devastating earthquake or an inferno that destroyed a swath across the city, there would not be the sense of conquest over the elements. Had there not been a revolution, an uprising, a misnamed "civil war" and a reconstruction, there would not be a foreboding sense of destiny. The anticipation of divine providence defines the attitude of the populace. It is grandiose.

The city's natural attributes are considerable. The temperate climate gives its inhabitants more than our fair share of good outdoor opportunities. The deep harbor is what its founders coddled for a maritime future. The sun-drenched beaches remain pristine, unpolluted and expansive. There are mineral resources that have been excavated, like phosphates, clay, limestone, sand and gravel. There remain the renewable loblolly pine forests that surround Charleston, but it is more famous for its grand live oaks and palmetto varieties. The soil is rich. It produced the worldly wealth of antebellum planters with the production of rice, tomatoes, snap beans and indigo. Our creeks and sounds are the incubators for Atlantic shrimp and blue crab. Offshore and inshore fishing is plentiful.

The grid work of even newer maps does not find Charleston as a major crossroad or junction. It is a literal destination. One needs to have the goal of arriving here as opposed to happening upon the city on the way to another destination. That segment of traveler does not exist here. Many of the old Charleston crowd might consider the destination status as an asset. Perhaps so.

The surge of rampant growth—as in Atlanta or Houston—would not have played well here. Instead of four or five million inhabitants, the entire metropolitan area population is less than seven hundred thousand.[1] That's proven to be manageable. Yet the city has all of the benefits—and more—of the megacities. The ambience remains. Charleston has world-class restaurants alongside posh boutiques and top national hoteliers. The event schedules list a wide assortment of enjoyable festivals, expositions and cultural affairs. The downtown center has been preserved, and the historical architecture is beyond any city in the Western Hemisphere. There are negligible traffic concerns and no air pollution. Crime control and fire protection are rated among the best in the United States. The outlying formal gardens are lauded as the best of their kind anywhere in the world. Outdoor activities are the envy of other competitor municipalities—golf, tennis, fishing, sunning, sailing, swimming, touring and retail therapy. The city market is a popular vestige of more than three centuries. The city exudes culture. The indoor activities are equally enticing—great museums, theaters, galleries and spas.

Inevitably, it is the people that define a city. Charleston has been heralded as the friendliest city in America, the best-mannered city in America and the best place to live in America by multiple magazines multiple times. It is not by chance.

My humble but ambitious supposition is that it took the people who lived here for a generation, who came here for a time or who have impacted Charleston even more recently to rush helium into this large and bright balloon that is Charleston. It is these individuals whom I have identified and cornered. They have told me much that, as a Charlestonian born and raised, I did not heretofore know. They are the reason that we have become "us."

The places stage the people, and the people allow the places to come alive. The stories herein are about real events, real venues and real voices that make up this little sprit of heaven between two rivers. They are well known and unknown heretofore. They comprise the essential parts of a lifetime, and they elicit the sentimentalities of a time in my life. It has been my heartfelt privilege to know most of these personalities in varying degrees from acquaintanceship to close friend. I have long admired each of them for what they have meant to our city—and in many cases to our country.

I am a seeker of sunsets. They are each excitingly different. I've photographed them many times, but I have found my favorite sunsets to be the ones I earn by positioning my lens from the best angle, however difficult, with the best view. It is compelling to sit and admire these for the short time they appear on the horizon. They will not come in the same hue ever again.

There is layered joy in seeking the small pieces of mortar that built a grand wall. Those genuine personalities with Charleston stories to tell repointed the mortar anew. They were engaging, insightful and passionate. That mortar of storytellers had a forensic sense that made the view from atop that wall seem wider, further and brighter. I am glad that I had the experience and that you have taken the time to climb the ladder to meet me for the sunset I have imagined over a lifetime. It highlights our Charleston.

This book was originally published in the fall of 2011. Since that time, much has occurred within the life stories of those interviewed herein. The passage of time has moved the publisher, The History Press, to request a second edition. I'm humbly honored to do so.

Sadly, several of those interviewed have passed. Those include a personal mentor, Bernie Puckhaber, and his great friend Cam Burn. The list is lengthened with the names of Alicia Rhett, Judge Sol Blatt Jr., former South Carolina governor James B. Edwards, Carl Cannon and the wife of Reverend Anthony Thompson. Myra Thompson was one of the nine people brutally murdered in the Mother Emanuel Church on June 17, 2015. Solemnly, I attended services and events honoring each of the deceased persons above.

There are several other chapters that require the injection of contemporaneous detail. Five years changed much, and Charleston continues to evolve. In that vein, John Tecklenberg was sworn in on January 11, 2016, to succeed Joseph P. Riley Jr. as mayor of Charleston. It was the end of a political era—the transition both daunting and anticipatory. Joe Riley had performed masterfully. Much is expected of John Tecklenberg, a fine man in his own right. Joe Riley left him shoes that might fit Paul Bunyan.

The two leading travel magazines of our times, *Condé Nast Traveler* and *Travel & Leisure*, have both placed Charleston as the world's number one travel destination over the last five years. The 2016 rankings have them both placing Charleston number one in the United States, although they differ on the current world list. *Travel & Leisure* has Charleston as the number one world destination. *Conde Nast Traveler* has placed Charleston either number one or number two worldwide over the past five years. The competition? Sydney, Australia, and Florence, Italy, seem to push the Holy City consistently.

Burgeoning issues of the day in the Charleston area are presented as traffic congestion, cruise ship "mania," bicycle paths and the need for newer schools. Many here lament the rapid growth. But it cannot be stopped. It should be embraced and—importantly—strategized.

Since 2011, Volvo has committed to open its American plant just up Interstate 26 into Berkeley County. Mercedes-Benz will build its popular Sprinter vans here. Others, like Google and Boeing Inc., have expanded their workforces. The world has found us!

The Charleston International Airport has finished its upgrade renovation just in time to be considered obsolete. That's my prediction opined. Growth and popularity go hand in hand.

The hotel and restaurant industries have repopulated much of the downtown peninsula. The Bohemian and the Spectator are late additions. Entrepreneur Michael Bennett will open Hotel Bennett, a five-star luxury hotel on Marion Square, by September 2017. I suggested to him that he call it "Bennett House" a few years ago. I still like my name better, but my friend Mikey is the one paying the bills.

The Dewberry opened in 2016. That hotel was once the L. Mendel Rivers Federal Building on Marion Square. It was a lamentable 1960s architectural eyesore previously. John Dewberry worked a miracle.

The Restoration on King Luxury Hotel, a condominium conversion, has been named one of the top hotels in America. In a bit of irony, I was one of the original owners of that magnificent project and lost my shirt. Timing is everything. It was beautiful when we developed it and even more beautiful to the subsequent investors.

Bicycles have made their way into a city built for horses and carriages, never mind automobiles and delivery trucks. Bikes are the next iteration of mobility, experiencing a popular resurgence. They are fuel-efficient, healthy, quiet, non-pollutant and convenient. They are also dangerous for the cyclist and a constant obstacle to normal driving conditions on narrow streets already encumbered by horse-drawn tourist carriages and pedaling rickshaws. Bring on Uber!

The influx of new residents to the Charleston area was recently reported at forty-one people per day. Where will we put them all? Massive building permits are being issued, especially in the corridor from Summerville to Goose Creek. New schools cannot be built fast enough. We need teachers, coaches and administrators.

Only one cruise line regularly ports at Charleston. A new cruise terminal is in the works. Cruise ships have a tendency to look odd in Charleston because of the city's inherently low profile. They obscure our steeples. Years ago, I suggested in a published editorial that the cruise terminal be placed on the Mount Pleasant side of the harbor. Nobody listens to me. That simple juxtaposition would have helped both Mount Pleasant and peninsular Charleston. In other shipping news, the harbor is to be dredged to allow for the "Panama Class" ships that will frequent Charleston when completed. The designers of the Arthur Ravenel Jr. Bridge (2005) had already anticipated these enlarged vessels. The South Carolina State Ports Authority will grow accordingly.

With all of the growth, crime has been kept, relatively, in check. It's an attestation to the police chiefs and the mayors of the surrounding communities. Future rush-hour patterns will need to be discerned and the traffic nightmares of yonder cities averted.

The rise of technology brings the world closer. Smartphones are cameras, voice recorders, schedulers, encyclopedias, route planners, music caches, journals, flashlights and much more. They are phones, too. The technology that makes us more productive, smarter, wiser and instantaneous has made us more communicative, as well. Instagram, Twitter, Facebook, LinkedIn…I'm on all of them! But I call them the four horsemen of the media apocalypse. If you cannot spell "apocalypse," its not the end of the world! I stand by my assertion from a few years back: social media can be an affront to the cordialities to which we are accustomed—a smile, a pause or a simple handshake. It places a burden on the old Charleston societies to encourage personal interaction. In a few years, colleges will offer courses on the art of eye contact!

We've changed. Some may suppose it is because of a bridge or a hotel, a factory or a festival. My books portend otherwise. It is because of the "beenyas" and "cumyas," the innovators and the entrepreneurs. Newly arrived personalities gave benefit to characters already here. The old societies are stronger than ever. We ooze the old standards of our prior generations—that of decency and dignity.

Now, everyone knows about Charleston! The jig is up. We've been found.

My Childhood Charleston

The shadow of two large buildings blocked the morning and evening skies from my childhood. Our little pink home was surrounded by the large white dominance of St. Francis Xavier Hospital on one side and the signature red bricks of the Medical University of South Carolina on the other. We only had one residential neighbor, Mrs. Anderson. I mowed her grass for a dollar. There were tenants that came and went over the years from the small apartments my grandparents depended upon for income. In fact, the little pink home I lived in was rented from my grandparents.

Being the fourth of eight children (a ninth was born after we moved), we had the expanse of the property to live large outdoors—where my mother wanted us anyway. The pink house was diminutive. Originally, there was a total of only four rooms on two floors. In time there were partitions to create more privacy, plus a bathroom. Built in 1835, the bathroom was a retrofit that did not really fit. There was no den, living room or study. There was a small kitchen area with a dining table and sideboard. There was no dishwasher, washing machine, dryer or air conditioning. Clothes were washed from my grandmother's back porch, hung on a clothesline and ironed as needed by the person who wore the clothes. We also had an old chest freezer in our dining room. With a lace doily and a candlestick atop, it still did not pass for furniture. It held frozen, day-old bread and a variety of saved food items from innumerable sources. We did not go hungry.

That pink house was a haven for bats. They lived in the boarded-up chimney flues. It was not unusual for one or two to find a way into our bedrooms at night. A midnight bat yell is distinctive. It is much louder than a nightmare. I was the designated bat killer, because my lack of fear towards bats was, looking back, brazen stupidity. Who knew what diseases they may have carried? I dutifully waited for a wall landing before whaling them with a broom we kept behind the door for such occasions. We flushed their ugly carcasses down the toilet and went back to bed.

Bat killing is character building.

Summertime nights in Charleston were oppressive without air conditioning. We left our screened windows open—hoping for that predominant breeze that wafted mercifully from the Southeast. On particularly humid evenings, my father would allow us the advantage of electricity by plugging in an oscillating fan. The motor was heavy, and my mother had trouble lifting it. The fan was loud enough to nearly overpower the sounds from beyond our open windows. We heard the city buses, barking dogs, church bells, the odd-houred chatter from the change of nursing shifts and—worst of all—the sirens. Ambulances had no concern for the dead of night. It must have been in their manual to turn on those shrieking sleep-stealers together with the invasive, red, flashing lights. Yet, owing to my Catholic school instructions from the Sisters of Saints Cyril and Methodius, I blessed my forehead in bed each time I heard one. It was a sign for my God to assist an unknown soul in the urgent distress of life. I may have unknowingly been complicit in saving dozens of teetering lives over the years. Only God has that scorecard.

Our best sleep came after the frequent Charleston thunderstorms. My father asserted to us that lightning could not ignite our brick home. That made momentary sense. Those storms that raged through our summer nights had louder and more convincing voices than the nightly assurances of my father. Otherwise, we became oblivious to the sounds of the night.

The upper floor had the two bedrooms and the only bath. There was no shower—just a claw-footed iron tub. It was large enough to wash two children at a time. Baths were commanded daily with the threat of corporal punishment. I do not ever remember my father issuing a second warning.

My parents slept downstairs in the wood-paneled room that was never meant to be a bedroom. The lack of a bathroom facility downstairs made the home most inconvenient, I'm sure. Yet I do not remember that there was any inconvenience ever detailed or discussed. It was what it was. I slept on the Ashley Avenue side of the house with five other brothers. Six boys. One room. One fan. Later in life I joked that the oscillating fan gave us a rhythm of night breathing. You only breathed in when the air was on your side of the room. Who knows? That might well have been true.

My two sisters slept in the smaller bedroom, away from the noise of the street. They were in the room that the bats liked the best.

We were blessed with the best of all worlds. We had hand-me-down clothes and toys. The cowboys only suffered minor injuries from the Indian attacks. It's good that the hospital was across the street. We had other children from other large families around in our half-block yard. We had imagination, energy and each other. There were no dull moments—save for the early years when my mother made us take naps by turning on Art Linkletter's show and *Queen for a Day*. Real cowboys didn't nap. We faked naps. At least, I think we did.

The prologue to the new Charleston that describes the makeup of my family life was clearly consistent with other families around us. I know, because my mother shuffled us off to others from time to time. I think it was a ploy so that her sanity could return. Our seemingly disheveled family life was full of energy, activity, creativity and respect. It had little supervision. I tell you about our home, our activities and our resources because it positions the mindset of what was to come.

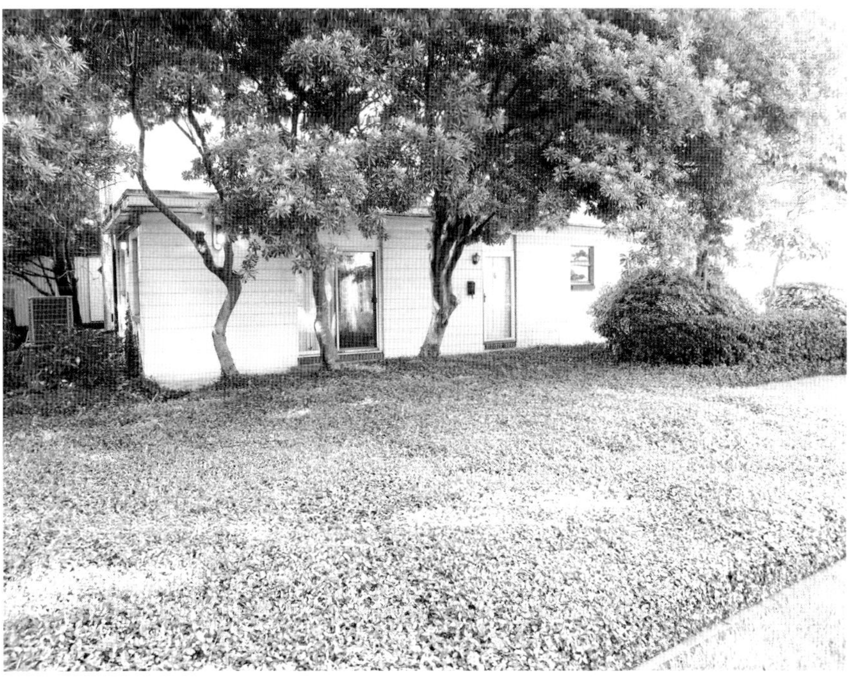

141 Ashley Avenue was built circa 1835 as a servant's quarters. The one-floor front section was added in 1960. The house is nestled among a preponderance of imposing medical structures. *(Kathryn McAltman)*

We thrived in those hospital shadows.

There was a time when the sustenance of my childhood yard elevated my belief in Eden. We had five pecan trees, two fig trees and a jujube bush. All were seasonal. We had to beat the squirrels to the pecans and the june bugs to the figs. The jujubes were unopposed. These grape-sized delicacies were related to the date family. They were the taste of sweet apple. We buried the seeds in hopes that more would grow. Jujubes were eaten in two states—green and red. The red ones were softer and sweeter. My siblings and I usually ate them in the harder green state, owing to our mutual impatience. The smell of the jujube bush was strong enough to rival the honeysuckle that grew wild in our downtown Charleston yard. One could easily snack on the figs, pecans and jujubes, especially in late summer and fall. The honeysuckle was a bonus.

An unscheduled wooden handcart rolled down Ashley Avenue. We were excited to hear the calls from the vendor.

"Butter beans, tomatoes, cukes and melons! Bananas, sugarcane, sweet corn!" The vendor sometimes had okra and cabbage as well.

In the time before the infamous Bay of Pigs incident, ships from Cuba frequented our port. Cuba was a regular supplier of sugarcane. You could buy a stalk for fifty cents. My grandfather would sometimes buy the sugarcane and cut it into six pieces so that we could voraciously ruin our teeth for hours. It was my favorite treat ever.

There was other free sustenance delivered.

My uncle Tom, a personable, white-haired farmer, would stop by our home on Ashley Avenue from time to time and bring us a bushel of snap beans or a pile of watermelons. We all got excited to see Uncle Tom's pick-up truck roll into the yard. Tom White was not a blood relative. He was married to my grandfather's older sister. He had a heart of gold and a sincere interest in each of us.

When I graduated from The Citadel in 1974, Uncle Tom came to my grandmother's home after the event and gave me a Cross pen-and-pencil set. He smiled when I opened it. He then proclaimed, "The pencil is for planning that which could be erased." He continued, "The pen is for writing checks and making promises. Both should be taken to the bank."

That profound statement never left my conscience. I still have that Cross pen, and I have adhered to the principle he advocated to me that day. The pen was symbolic. The real gift was his devoted mentorship.

It was not until years later, at my uncle Tom's passing, that my father told me about Uncle Tom stepping forward to offer one thousand dollars to help pay for my Citadel tuition. He did so when my earnings, combined with my student loan money and what little Dad could offer, fell short. I was only a sophomore. I wish I had known about that magnanimous gesture so that I could have thanked him personally. But Uncle Tom never did anything for thanks. He did it because he cared.

Others cared as well. There was a full community of adults that had a singular focus of ethics, morality and the proper reverence of elders. Every address to any adult was respectful. A "sir" or "ma'am" was in every sentence. My father would not even allow a first warning on that matter. Any deviations from the laws of respect were reported. In return, the many adults of my childhood went mostly out of their way to be stewards of the community in the upbringing of our generation. They rewarded effort. They extended a hand and gave sound advice freely. It seemed that everyone knew my father—or my aunt or my uncle. My conduct was monitored well within the bounds of the peninsula. The lifelong lessons I received extended well beyond.

I mentioned my father in terms of his discipline. There was no mistaking his iron hand. Yet I had seen his discipline in all matters of his responsibility, service and spirituality. A World War II veteran, he enlisted at the age of seventeen from a fractured home. He came back determined. He succeeded by strength of will. He loved sports and taught us boxing, football and baseball. His own athletic prowess was in basketball. At six feet, three inches tall, he was the star of his high school team when he left prematurely for a bigger team—the United States Navy. My father fostered three avenues of dedication—our Catholic parish, our academic pursuits in a parochial environment and competitive sports. He played to win. It took until I was twenty-eight to finally beat him in a game of golf. He gave no quarter.

My father ultimately became responsible for thirty-three meals a day. I mentioned his fractured home. It was worse than that. His mother died accidentally when he was a young teenager. His father—my grandfather—used to nap at our house sometimes at midday. He was a pensioned World War I veteran. He was also an alcoholic. It was not until we were grown that we understood his need for midday naps.

Dad sold trucks. Big trucks. He had advanced through the various levels of salesmanship that comprised International Harvester Company. He started in the parts department and graduated to farm equipment sales. The trucking industry in the United States was hitting its stride when he took his amicable smile and gregariousness to this new venue. He sold trucks for the next thirty years. There was no interstate highway to Charleston when he

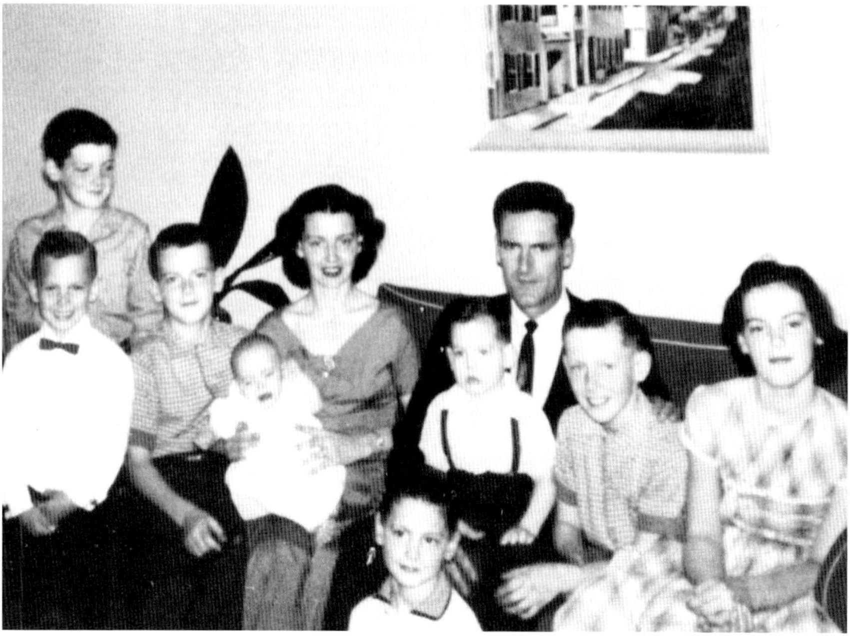

Left to right: Tommy, Ritchie, Danny, Sharon, mother Charlotte, David, Larry, father "Bully," Charlie and Gail McQueeney. *(Agatha Aimar Simmons)*

started. Indeed, the bigger trucking companies needed a good map. One would think that Interstate 26 was built so that these entrepreneurs could get to see my father more often. He became known for his energy and integrity. The eventual climb to consistent sales and a very healthy income happened for him in the years leading up to his retirement.

He and my mother were both Charleston born and bred. They would have been from different sides of the tracks if we'd had a train. (We may have had a train, but I never heard it above the barking dogs and sirens.)

My father died when the azaleas were in bloom, on March 24, 2011. He passed both slowly and suddenly. He had suffered several strokes over seven years that had taken the sight of an eye, his manly strength, much of his speech and, finally, his legs. As much as I loved my father, I found his slow demise that much more difficult to manage. His exuberance for life had turned into his own prayer for death. A heart attack stopped his suffering. He was finally at peace. My father was my hero, my confidant and my finest companion. After all, he had daily challenges in that little pink house. He never missed the opportunity to be responsible.

My mother was a career housewife. (She still is, but her duties now are to fight the ravages of cancer and accept our unyielding love for her.) The word "housewife" never defined her. She was a professional artist and sold paintings on a regular enough basis to supplement primary family needs. Mom also sewed and did minor repairs—even plumbing. She was the perfect fit for a family of nine. She handled the family finances, maintenance, landscaping, procurements, rations, appointment schedules, medical duties, attire and laundry. She exhibited the hands of a surgeon and the demeanor of a saint. She was unruffled by the everyday occurrences that would alarm others. Her fluid and paced temperament also meant that she didn't handle discipline. She simply gave an evening report to the Gestapo.

Mom came from a sophisticated old Charleston lineage. Her parents boasted of ancestry that predated the country. Her mother was a genteel southern lady, complete with the commensurate listing of the prerequisite pedigree. Her maiden name was prominent upon the signage of the marked-for-history mansion house she managed from her heirloom dining table. The three-story edifice was built by a banker to entertain the wealthy planters of 1830s Charleston.[2] Only the gilded gentry would emerge from such a castle. "Granny" was a member of the Garden Club of Charleston, the Preservation Society of Charleston, the Charleston Library Society, the French Huguenot Society, the Daughters of the American Revolution and, most importantly, the United Daughters of the Confederacy. The UDC had so much significance in 1960s Charleston that only the elites of the peninsular ladder climbers were invited to join. That right of arrival meant—by bloodline—that my brothers and I were all to be members of the Sons of the Daughters of the Confederacy. There were no permutations I know of beyond that spinoff. I guess we outlived it like childhood asthma. I was never offered cognac and a sword.

The post–World War II baby boom repopulated the Charleston peninsula. The McQueeney family? We certainly did our part. But others were hugely responsible. The large single houses with sweeping piazzas were rejuvenated with children and bicycles and dogs. The six degrees of separation were only taken to the second stage in Charleston. Essentially, everybody either knew everybody or they knew of everybody. The children played, and the barriers fell. There existed a unity of purpose. Religious lines were starting to dissipate. The Catholics, Episcopalians and Jews were on basketball teams together. By the mid-1960s, the African Americans were a part of the resurgence. Indeed, several Charleston schools did not wait for a checkered flag to start the process of desegregation. This generation built—albeit subconsciously—a singularity of purpose. The dormancy stage that hosted my described childhood was the gestation period of the New Charleston. Birth was near.

If the rabble-rousing, barefoot mass of McQueeneys could emerge with store-bought shoes and their own teeth, then Charleston could not be a gaveled sentence, but rather what is always was—a hope and an opportunity in transition.

Charleston was the familiar enchantment of ivy and wisteria alleyways. It was the faint chorus of evening crickets. It was art vendors on the street and a policeman that occasionally gave out dimes. It was a group of wide-eyed children staring up at an expansive planetarium at a dilapidated old museum on Saturday mornings. It was a milkshake at the counter at Oakman's Drugstore. There were grocers at every third corner. The playgrounds were all reached by bicycle. The doctor you visited had the best aquarium you ever saw and a poster of Disneyland on his wall. My brothers and I would push flooded cars through the waters the equinox tides brought to Ashley Avenue. We did it as a public service. It was not unusual that we left home for hours with one bus token. With "transfers," we could tour the entire peninsula. We explored the city dump one day and the old jail the next. We imagined we saw ghosts. My brother Charlie even swam in Colonial Lake, not by his own choice.

It was the knot of friendships, the proctoring of parents and the posturing for greatness that compelled a community forward. Niceties were the norm, manners the makeup. We were all becoming Charleston.

Growing up in Charleston was growing out and growing forth.

Those behemoth hospital buildings never blocked the noontime hour or the warmth of my Charleston childhood.

The Second Coming of the Holy City

The Holy City presents a misty and mysterious energy. Charleston is a melodic rapture, a silent meditation and a magnetic inducement all at once. The city of my birth has undefined sensory powers that evoke euphoria. The city graces a peninsula of heaven, embraced by the nourishment of two rivers and the expanse of a mighty ocean. What would distinguish our mortal paradise from the scriptured paradise only entails life and death—and the lack of pearls upon our gates. It is by no stretch of history that I brazenly proclaim the truth about my beloved hometown. It is the only place on the globe that has been discovered twice without the benefit of a cataclysmic burial in between.

The first discovery in 1670 is well documented. Its historical rise to a lofty tower of culture, charm and dignity had heightened my childhood perceptions of who I was. Surely good fortune had cast me unto a place that must undoubtedly be the center of the universe. Was it like Babylon, Pompeii or Troy? Was it archeologically or biblically anointed and then dispatched?

In time, our ancestry of worldly citizens curried the urgency of demanding their rights of self-determination. The idea of the sovereignty of states' rights won all arguments. This regressed to a bloody and devastating incendiary—the first shots of the War Between the States. All had changed. Four years of horror ensued, with victims of this city and others waylaying the great promise of a burgeoning society. In short, our chivalry wounded our pragmatism, and the infection lingered.

The second time of discovery is less pronounced to the non-Charlestonians. (Yes, there exists a group of people from outside of the gates.) It is in the prologue to this second discovery that I was privy to the realities and seemingly mundane dormancy of this great city. I grew up in the caldron of what the wizards, witches and warlocks concocted.

To recount the misinformation disseminated to the misinformed could be the primary service of this enterprise, but it is not. We were not in a vegetative state. We had not intermarried and produced an "idiocracy." We had not regressed to illiteracy and impertinence. On the contrary, our sense of decency arose. In time, we became one with our determination and resourcefulness. Charleston, like the rest of the South, was defeated, but never beaten. To wit, one would think a major fire or devastating earthquake or this nation's worst strife would bracket the end of the first "Age of Charleston." Not so. To be sure, Charleston was the second-largest city in the South prior to the Civil War, only bested by New Orleans. It had the polished finishes of its utopian strategy—the arts, the architecture, the society and the prosperity like no other. The ocean currents that brought Europe and Africa to America also brought the diversity that inspired the city's allure. But the end of that seminal event—"the recent unpleasantness"—was a measure of our strength, not our weakness. Our real character was born.

You see, we came from better stuff.

John Locke's 1669 work titled *The Fundamental Constitutions of Carolina* gave the religiously oppressed of Europe an open and free respite. The upstart rice and indigo plantations built international trade from a natural deep-water port. The unfortunate collaboration of old-world servitude with new-world needs fostered slavery. The artisan craft of those wretched souls lives well past the lifetimes of their oppressors. It is seen in the classical ironwork, the Flemish-bond brickwork and the expertly wood-carved mahogany furnishings. Though the vestige is the bookmark, the book is weighty. A war washed away the practice and brought on a time called Reconstruction. That period was not the next beginning, either. It was simply an unspecific time ushered in by a specific time. We were not told when Reconstruction was to end, if indeed it ever did.

My childhood in Charleston enveloped the transitional phase that made the second discovery of Charleston possible. The familiarity of that experience was not so different than that of the other children who grew up here, symbolically rooted in the pluff mud. We did not know the world, but we knew each other. And thus we became the new foundation for a great city.

We identified ourselves within the mission of who others were. They were our parents and grandparents. They were also nonrelatives who were related by the austerity of our commonalities. There was a promise that grew from one generation to another through the sheer incentive of what we could be.

I can relate this in my own experience. I saw the warmth within. I felt the pride and the dignity. I lived within the inherent expectations of our city's second coming.

In solemn reverence, I can explain the events leading to the eventuality.

It was in the late 1980s that I first noticed that the license plates on Calhoun Street were a growing assortment of "cumyas," a common term better enunciated as "come heres." They were from Indiana, Missouri and Maine, among others. Every contiguous state seemed to be well represented. They were all coming here. It was as if the world's largest electromagnet had been turned on. Our fulfillment was beckoning. They were coming to see the phenomena and mystique of the golden peninsula. We had a role to play as hosts. Those commensurate "yes sirs" and "yes ma'ams" of our collective upbringings coddled even more visitors. We were touted as the friendliest place in America—and we were just being ourselves.

There were reasons other than our natives that enticed the hordes. God provided it. There was agreeable weather to share. Our beaches were wide strands of gullies, blanched shells and driftwood. Our storied live oaks still lined the horse-cart passages to our lingering plantations. The selfless perspectives of our ancestry gave us gardens beyond the expectations of all but the angels. They were large and nationally famous or small and quaint, but always with appeal. The waters brought the masses, too. Sailors, surfers, swimmers and boaters were all players in the "aquafest" that bathed Charleston within its rediscovery. The salt marshes spawned the shrimp. The shrimp baited the fish. The fish came to the local restaurants fresh from a farm we called the Atlantic Ocean. Yes, God played a role.

Other restaurants emerged as the license plates multiplied. A world-class city of fine cuisine was established. Connoisseurs contend that Charleston restaurants now rival only New York and San Francisco in their variety and quality of American fare. All of those magazines told readers how to get to Interstate 26.

My childhood friends and the others of that second degree of separation were mostly responsible for those restaurants. They developed much of the hotelier culture as well. Boutique hotels became not only a pleasant option, but also every bit as popular as the restaurants. Staying on the peninsula became chic to the cumyas. They brought another variation of gold—Visa, American Express and MasterCard.

There had to be a maestro for these efforts. In 1975, Charlestonians elected one of our own to orchestrate the transition. We could previously have been described as a sleepy backwater, a yawning afterthought or a pale point on a pallid map. In fact, we were in a self-contained laboratory with activity that would rival the split of the atom. The right man to lead presented himself as selflessly as the rest of us were presumed to be. That man was our mayor for nearly four decades. It was with his prophetic leadership that the new discovery of Charleston materialized. An Irish-lineage American, Joseph Patrick Riley Jr. will be remembered for untold generations as the Charlestonian most responsible for the second discovery. There were others, to be sure. I will explore their contributions as well. But it was a visionary that gave us all vision.

And so it is that the second coming of Charleston is the propitious advent of one man within the exuberance of our generation. It was like Genghis Khan appearing from his childhood tent or Douglas MacArthur wading ashore at Leyte in the Philippines. There was a sense of purpose that Joe Riley represented.

The mayor was constant in his passion for the city's reemergence. He filled our calendar with festivals that became the envy of other municipalities. There is Spoleto Festival USA, the most significant old-world arts festival ever attempted in America. The Southeastern Wildlife Exposition is perhaps the most outstanding event of its kind on the globe. International sailing races and land-based sporting events followed. The old traditions became magnified into components of a new society in a new age of an old culture.

The mayor achieved a first-rate infrastructure boasting police, fire and residential services and an attitude of quality growth. Businesses did well to avoid the boxed-in marketing of the malls in order to experience the outdoor ambience of our unique retail establishments. Walking on King Street became a pleasure that transcended shopping. You knew the merchants and many of the customers from other walks. It became evident that King Street was the place to expand your social horizons while deflating your wallet.

The prominent societies that celebrated old-world diversity emerged as integral parts of the weave within the city's fabric. They were what the currents had brought generations ago—the Scottish, the Germans, the French, the Africans and the Irish. Belonging to the present was edified and celebrated by the sense of the past. Charlestonians belonged to Charleston, and that most enriching experience, described in my personal childhood, is exponentially expressed herein.

Being a Charlestonian was a sacred right of those born within our hospitals. The second coming of our formerly private heaven has made it so that our certified birthright was meant to be shared. The new Charlestonians are welcome. They bring much and take very little. I suppose that they won't mind if we old natives wink at each other knowingly from time to time.

We owe a great deal to the generations before us—so much that cannot ever be adequately measured. The most recent rating of world cities in *Condé Nast Traveler* has placed Charleston near the top of all cities. It is ranked fourth in the entire world, ahead of London, Paris and Rio. *Travel & Leisure* places Charleston as the number-two travel destination in America. The custodians of this peninsula and beyond dedicate this city upon the world stage as it was always intended to be. Bow to us, Toronto and Singapore! May it always thrive in reverence and respect, beauty and humility. Come to think of it, I'll leave the humility up to the next generation!

Charleston, from Others

The following pages represent a time in Charleston that is epochal, not literal. That epoch stretches from the Charleston of the 1950s and 1960s to the present day. In that time the metropolitan population more than doubled. The city had previously been in a bottomless decline. Ironically, the post-Revolutionary Charleston of 1790 was the fourth-largest city in the new United States, behind New York, Philadelphia and Boston.[3] The winds of change prevailed, and the seminal event of the American War Between the States moved the Holy City to the windless doldrums. It was not until the generation represented in this book came along that the forward wind was refreshed. A time was lost and a vision gained. The city moved to the forefront and is now considered a "must see" by every major travel source. Charleston has surely risen.

The essays are representative of so many personal insights and recollections of those interviewed. Each has made an impression on many others around them, whether it's been a lifelong commitment to public service, a role as a mentoring influence or simply a personality that has inspired the best of our citizenry. They are all of the notion of celebrity.

There were many others that were considered for this effort. For a number of discordant reasons, a limit was established to seek, interview and complete the thematic tapestry. There are so many wonderful people of great substance and deserving recognition in the Charleston area that additional books on the matter could easily fill a library. Please accept the humble apology of the author for any unintended omissions.

The oldest of those interviewed, artist Alicia Rhett, is ninety-six. She was also the first to be interviewed. Others were more than cordial in the benevolence of their time. The interviews were completed in the old-fashioned way, by pen and paper. Those interviewed were contacted again upon completion to ascertain accuracy and to simplify the editing process. Every person interviewed in this production has been someone the author has known well enough to call and ask for an interview without the credentials of a known writer. For that, there is profound appreciation.

The enterprise of essays is meant to capture these celebrated Charlestonians in print during their times, for all times. It is a loosely bracketed historical account in that regard, but it is a living and contemporary dialogue in a completely different approach.

It is hoped that the reader will enjoy these pages in even a fraction of the enjoyment gained by the interviewer in conversation and subsequent correspondence associated with this venture. It has been an entertaining, jovial and wondrous journey that I will cherish forever.

Permanent Attaché to the Peninsula Proper

Thomas F. Hartnett

If Tommy Hartnett were to witness a hit-and-run accident, his abilities to vividly recall the crime would be surreal. He would not only rattle off the color, make, model and license tags of the vehicle that left the scene but would also likely include a report on the remaining tread life of the tires.

The accident that happened in Charleston lasted one hundred years. The details linger. It was a city that had to "make do." To those who did not witness the accident, the testimony—at least to address the effects and aftermath—becomes crucial. It is in these details that Tommy Hartnett becomes bystander, observer and spectator. He saw it all, recorded the meaning and cheered the "cheerable" moments.

"I understand that less than 20 percent of the people in Charleston today are originally from Charleston," Hartnett said. "So those that did not see the things those older-generation Charlestonians like me saw may think this city was just like any other. We know it wasn't. What I remember growing up was something that was part fairy tale and part harsh reality."

Hartnett is unrestrained, enlivened and yet comforted. He loves to talk about the city he adores and the friends he has appreciated for so many years. He was barely twelve days removed from heart bypass surgery when interviewed, though insistent that the interview be conducted presently. He received the full poker hand of reinstalled arteries. Yet his vigor belied those facts. Charleston is his favorite subject and, for him at least, a better therapy than a ward full of rehabilitation specialists.

"It's sobering to think that those of my vintage are the last generation of old Charlestonians—those that knew from where we came, how our grandparents and even our parents struggled. Yet we were all a very happy group of children," Hartnett reminisced. "We had the paper routes and the ball teams, and we did odd jobs and mostly stayed out of trouble. We used to gather in the summer at Colonial Lake to fish and because there was always a breeze there, or we would have a pick-up game of baseball at the Horse Lot (a vacant field between Chisolm Street and Ashley Avenue). My whole universe was Charleston south of Calhoun Street. You pretty much knew everybody. There were perhaps as many as eighteen corner grocery stores south of Queen Street. They were mostly Greek proprietors. There were no supermarkets, so you just hopped down to the corner.

"My paper route was south of Broad," Hartnett continued.

His lovely wife, Bonnie, interjected, "Tommy was everything described in Pat Conroy's book *South of Broad*. He had known so many of the people Conroy described; he had that particular paper route and was the same age."

Bonnie Kennerly Hartnett and Thomas Forbes Hartnett have been married for forty-six years. She is petite, personable and engaging.

"She's right. I should get character royalties," Hartnett offered. "Even in Conroy's book, you got that sense that Charleston was special. And it was. We bicycled to the theaters on King Street, to the ballparks and to school. There was no real traffic to be concerned with. The four-way stops had what we called a 'dumb policeman,' a concrete hump lower than eye level that had the word 'stop' painted on it and was installed in the middle of the street. These were all over the South of Broad area before they installed octagonal stop signs."

There is a certain sentimentality and homage paid to a time and place that intersected the past. Hartnett's nostalgia had the effect of bringing one to a Moultrie Playground Little League game or, next to it, Colonial Lake, a small tidal pond, a palmetto-lined rectangle of concrete surrounding it. No traffic concerns of horns or sirens or city buses would spoil the sensory moments, because those intrusions were virtually nonexistent. The prominent sound was of seagulls and pigeons and children playing.

"There were service stations that courteously pumped gas and did repairs at Meeting and Chalmers, Tradd and New, Tradd and King, Ashley and Wentworth and, later, Rutledge and Calhoun," Hartnett recounted. "There were a half dozen parochial schools and parish churches and only a handful of small high schools—Murray Vocational, Charleston High, Bishop England, Rivers and Burke. There was Porter Military Academy and Ashley

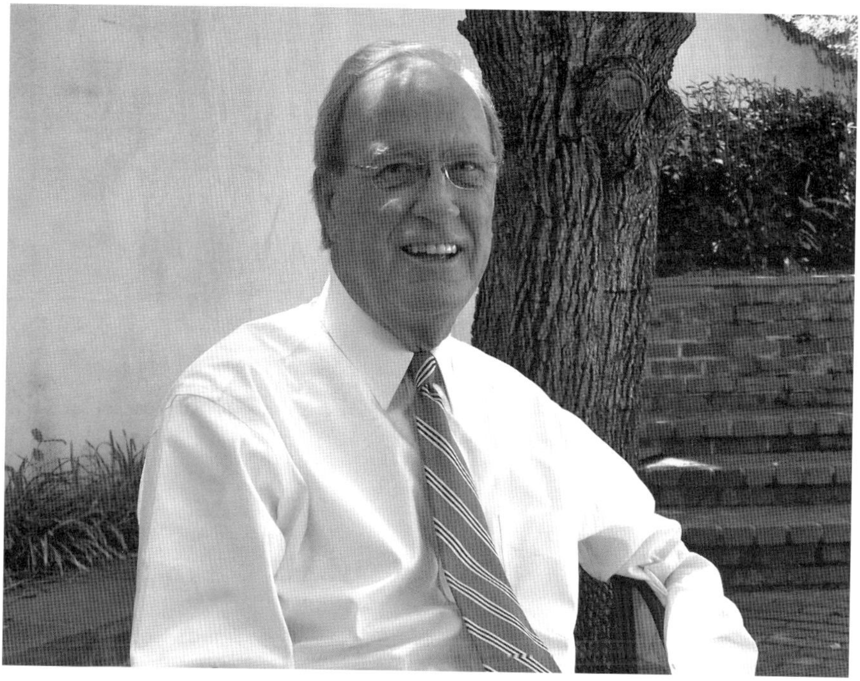

Tommy Hartnett has served his constituents in Charleston in the South Carolina House and Senate, along with three terms in the United States Congress. *(Bonnie Hartnett)*

Hall—both private with boarding students. Only Burke and Ashley Hall remain on the peninsula from those mentioned."

Hartnett recalled the drugstores and florists, the candy stores and the few viable retailers that were on King Street.

"There were always a few wholesalers on Meeting Street, most near where Charleston Place is now, and you really didn't have much in the Market area except sailors and merchant seamen. Market Street was a place for booze and tattoos, not a nice area whatsoever," Hartnett remembered. "And there really weren't any restaurants near the quality of what is here today. We could choose between the Colony House, Henry's and Labrasca's. The restaurant business grew with tourism, and now we're recognized as among the best for cuisine anywhere in America. There were extremely limited choices before.

"There were very few hotels—the St. John's, the Timrod, the Argyle, the Francis Marion and the Fort Sumter," Hartnett recalled. "And many of the homes and businesses were actually duplexes. The setting of Charleston then was the sight of children everywhere. I grew up on Rutledge and then moved to Tradd. The vacant lot at the intersection of Rutledge and Tradd Streets had a huge billboard sign owned by Turner Outdoor Advertising—Ted Turner's father. Can you imagine a billboard in the middle of a residential neighborhood south of Broad Street?"

There were children playing that would be leaders, and adults abound who served them as valuable mentors. The Hartnett generation would transition to lead the upsurge of peninsular Charleston.

Hartnett paused to talk about one of his boyhood friends, Joe Riley. "I have known Joe Riley all my life. He was a groomsman in mine and Bonnie's wedding. Our group of friends would play basketball in Joe's backyard almost every afternoon after school. Many mornings, after he got his driver's license, he would give several of us rides to Bishop England High School. Joe was interesting always, serious minded and a really fine student. As young married adults, we lived next door to each other and even served in the state legislature together.

"There were mentors we all had back in the day that we appreciate so much more now," Hartnett stated. "Joe Riley Sr. was a great man, a truly civic-minded, generous soul and a mentor of mine. He had a heart as big as Charleston. Father Louis Sterker, a priest at the Cathedral Church on Broad Street, was fantastic. Two of the nuns that taught us at Cathedral School, Sister Mary Agatha and Sister Mary Rosaire, were exceptional women who cared about their students and were especially good to me and challenged me as a student. Bobby Molony is still a great man of Charleston. J.C. Long was a developer who called himself an 'operative builder.' His wife Alberta's mother was a Hartnett. J.C. Long was bigger than life and owned some eight hundred properties in Charleston County alone.

"My parents, especially my mother, because of my dad's physical condition, had to work harder than most," Hartnett stated with insight. "My dad once ran for political office but lost. His career was cut short by a stroke that paralyzed him on his right side at the young age of thirty-one. Although physically handicapped, he was a fine role model. He was very bright and read everything. He loved baseball. He was the one who pushed me to run for public office the very first time.

"Fritz Hollings was another person who influenced me and so many others along the way," Hartnett added. "Senator Hollings counseled me when I first ran for public office. He also gave me one of my first campaign contributions. I remember him yelling from his office in that loud and distinctive voice to Patty Igoe, his assistant, 'Give Tommy Hartnett a hundred dollars for his campaign.' Patty was to tell me later that there was barely two hundred dollars in his checking account back then. And I can remember I only had enough money for one live commercial during the local news hour. I told them my name and stressed that I was a member of the Cathedral of St. John the Baptist Church. Hollings called me the next day and, believing I was trying to appeal to the Baptist vote, repeated my words in humor with an inflection on 'St. John the *Baptist* Church.' In those days, in South Carolina, being a Catholic was not a political asset."

It was ironic that the closest of Senator Hollings's six senatorial races was the one against Tommy Hartnett in 1992, a narrow 2 percent victory for Hollings.[4] The two former political adversaries remain great friends today.

"Hollings is still a man I admire greatly," Hartnett stated.

Hartnett, a retired, three-term United States Congressman from South Carolina's First Congressional District, spent much of his adulthood in public service. He served four terms in the South Carolina House and two terms in the South Carolina Senate. He served in the U.S. House during the first six presidential years of Ronald Reagan, 1981–87. He was elected president of his freshman class of fifty-one new U.S. House members on January 3, 1981. But even after leaving public office, he continued to serve, spending twelve years on the State Ports Authority Board of Directors. He is currently a member of the South Carolina Legislative Audit Council. He recently was among a small group of Charlestonians who started Harbor National Bank, where he serves as board chairman.

Hartnett has been a long-term fixture in the Charleston real estate and appraisal market. He remains active in the business his mother and father founded in 1947, the Hartnett Realty Company, Inc. Given his recent and difficult surgery, he is happy to remain active in everything.

"In 1964, when I was first elected to the South Carolina House, there were eleven seats from Charleston—all 'at large,'" Hartnett recalled. "That was very good for Charleston then. We could get much done by working together. The move to single-member districts changed all that. Now we're too parochial—more concerned with what benefits each smaller area instead of the city as a whole. Back then, the school board was appointed by the legislative delegation. It worked better. There were no political agendas."

The state aspect of governance was but a microcosm to the national stage. That changed as well.

"In Washington, incivility took over. Extreme partisanship became the rule. I came in a few years after the legendary Mendel Rivers," Hartnett noted. "And my greatest responsibility was to hold onto what Rivers had achieved and build back as we needed. Mendel Rivers devoted a lifetime of toil that brought much to Charleston. His powerful House Armed Services Committee had Charleston in the budget every year, it seemed. There was the air base, the navy base and navy yard and other auxiliary military depots. As a member of the Armed Services Committee, it was my job to keep the bases open and find funds to repair or even replace buildings that were so vitally important to Charleston. With the cooperation of others, I was able to do just that."

The late L. Mendel Rivers chaired the high-profile House Armed Services Committee from 1965 until his death three days after Christmas in 1970.[5] Rivers had been the First District congressman from Charleston since 1940.[6]

"Now it's all hardball politics. Not as much gets done, I'm afraid," Hartnett lamented. "Some things will have to change in Washington to get us back where we can operate across party lines in trust."

Coming back to the Charleston he once knew was almost impossible. By the time Hartnett retired from Congress in 1987, much was changing.

"There were a handful of things that came to mind in the transition from the Charleston I described to the Charleston we know today," Hartnett explained. "First and foremost, Joe Riley becoming the mayor was the biggest thing. Joe Riley was a perfect complement to the needs of Charleston at the time. At some point in time, he will be hard to replace. His successor will have big shoes to fill. Joe appointed Reuben Greenberg as police chief. The chief was great for Charleston, and crime rates dropped dramatically."

Hartnett gave other insight. "Two things that seemed bad might have been good. Closing the shipyard, I think, was a long-term benefit. It diversified our economy and got us away from being a navy town with all of the potential downside that implied. When Hurricane Hugo came in 1989, the community came together in ways that I would not have imagined. And some of the old, scrappy, 'tear-down' buildings went away. And everybody had a new roof."

Hartnett continued, "You could say the opening of Charleston Place in 1986 was so very important. Of course the Spoleto Festival and the Southeast Wildlife Expedition are huge events that help put Charleston on the map as a tourist destination. But in the bigger picture, it was the industry of tourism that changed Charleston. Tourism took Charleston away from Charlestonians and gave it to the world. The busy streets with horse carriages, the crowded restaurants and retailers are all a part of the ramp-up of tourism. I suppose it's been a good thing, overall."

Hartnett seemed invigorated by it all. The mental acuity he has always displayed was most prominent in his lively and rich recollections. He deftly explored the small town he admired as it was, to become the world city that it is. One cannot imagine what a wonderful conversationalist Tommy Hartnett is whilst under a doctor's care. He will be back at work soon. Charleston needs him. Friend Joe Riley should appoint Hartnett as "Attaché to the Peninsula Proper."

The cobblestones, wisteria vines and Spanish moss–adorned oaks remained. The old alleyways, Charleston brick fences and rush of springtime azaleas became ever more eminent. The weekend harbor regattas and formal society banquets cycled anew. The life that was Charleston is forever Charleston. It is Joe Riley's Charleston, as well as Tommy Hartnett's Charleston. Hartnett's detail of the nostalgia gives it the pungency of a South Battery wine cellar—in a variety of pleasant reminiscence.

A Fly on a Charleston Wall

Henry Berlin and Bernie Puckhaber

Two octogenarians meet for breakfast at Saffron's on Mondays and Fridays without fail. They are both in their mid-eighties. Both are quick-witted and accomplished community citizens. They have served as inventors of some of the most uproarious pranks ever played on fellow Charlestonians. Astonishingly, they both still work full time in their respective careers. One is a retail clothier and the other a stockbroker. They are living proof that laughter is healthy. Lots of it is healthier yet.

Henry Berlin and Bernie Puckhaber both attended the High School of Charleston at nearly the same time. They became close friends following World War II by playing softball for the same team, the Budweiser Buds. They are both World War II veterans of the United States Navy.

"I fought in the great battle of Times Square. It was every man for himself," Puckhaber disclosed. "I was just finishing training at the navy facility at Bainbridge, Maryland, when the war ended. You'd be surprised how many other people I saw from Charleston at Times Square."

Berlin, a helmsman, was on duty at virtually the same time, guiding his U.S. naval ship through a horrible storm in the Pacific. The storm, Typhoon Louise of 1945,[7] was terrifying, and, indeed, the navy lost ships—a full dozen sunk in addition to thirty-two other vessels grounded or damaged beyond economical repair. Winds were approximated as high as 150 miles per hour. Berlin played an essential role in his ship's survival.

"We lost more ships in that storm than we did in battle," Berlin recalled. "The captain put me at the helm, and I was actually tied to it. I fought that storm for thirteen hours straight. When I got through, the first lieutenant sent me to get some sleep and made an announcement that anyone who woke up Berlin would be put on report. He was serious."

If you had not been in Charleston long, you would not understand the verbal brogue these two Charleston icons were exchanging at breakfast time. An onlooker might have thought it was a foreign language or that they were speaking in tongues. It is pure Charlestonese.

Both Berlin and Puckhaber were college sports stars. Berlin was a baseball player at The Citadel when World War II broke out. He had once pitched a game against—and beaten—the powerful University of South Carolina. When he came back from his Pacific duty with the navy, he finished his undergraduate degree at South Carolina and continued his previously interrupted baseball career. In a role reversal, he pitched against The Citadel and won that game, becoming perhaps the only pitcher in history to beat each of those teams while pitching for the other.

Puckhaber's expertise was on the basketball floor, where he was a flashy guard for the College of Charleston Cougars, then nicknamed the Maroons. Early in his career, he scored a nearly full-court shot at the end of a game against Presbyterian College. A fine player in his own right, he and his running mate, Ernie Nelson, were considered top-notch guards for any college.

"Ernie Nelson was an all-state selection for two years," Puckhaber humbly recalled. "Now that's in competition with the Clemson and South Carolina players, along with a dozen other state colleges back then."

What the humble Puckhaber never mentioned speaks volumes of his humility. Puckhaber was also an all-state selection. Puckhaber is in the College of Charleston's Athletic Hall of Fame.

Both Puckhaber and Berlin served as president of the Exchange Club of Charleston, the largest civic organization in the United States. They are two of the twelve members whose memberships date back more than fifty years. Both are active members of the Hibernian Society of Charleston, the oldest benevolent Irish Society in America (1799).[8] Neither was a founding member, as their cronies jokingly suggest. Both are accomplished senior tennis players with hundreds of old Charleston stories, wide grins and sparkling blue eyes. They are a comedy team in almost every sense; their brand of humor is half vaudeville, half *Saturday Night Live*. They are fully recognized as legends of the Charleston community.

"I have never shuffled when I walked, because my mother told me that I should always walk fast through life or I'd miss something," Berlin was overheard saying. "I did just what she said. Three weeks ago, I was about forty years old. So I missed a half century."

Henry Berlin, almost eighty-seven and slightly older than "Pucky," has served as a Charleston city councilman and as the first chairman of the Downtown Revitalization Committee. He commanded a lead role in the development of the property that became Charleston Place in 1986. It was but one of his many volunteer contributions to Charleston. His clothing store, Berlin's Menswear at King and Broad Streets, has anchored that corner since 1883. Berlin once attended USC law school for a year. Ever the comedian, he was caught mimicking his professor to the amusement of his classmates. The professor was the only audience that Berlin may have ever had that didn't think he was funny. Berlin left law school to continue the family's haberdashery business at Berlin's Menswear—becoming the third-generation Berlin in Charleston's finest clothing store. Berlin is amicable, talkative and brilliantly astute. He has a marvelous singing voice and has emceed dozens of local charitable events. He is an Orthodox Jew and attends Brith Sholom Beth Israel Synagogue. He and his wife, Terry, have been married for fifty-six years. He is "Mr. Charleston."

"Gentlemen, I had something important to say, but I'm having a 'Berlin,'" Puckhaber stated in jest. "I can't remember if it was important, but I do remember my brain was half engaged. A 'senior moment' is to others what a 'Berlin' is to anybody else in Charleston."

Bernard F. "Pucky" Puckhaber is perhaps the city's best practical joker—ever. He has remained athletically fit, is a formidable competitor, coached college basketball and, with his wife, Anne, forms perhaps the most active dancing couple at any gathering that includes a live band. That takes in dancers of all ages. He and the former Anne Stender tied the knot fifty-eight years ago. Puckhaber served as president of the Hibernian Society of Charleston and has been the driving force behind decades of social functions at that National Historic Register hall, the last vestige of the 1860 Democratic National Convention. His oratory and literary skills are well known. His sense of humor is well beyond the peninsular heaven. "Hilarious" is the initial adjective used to describe him. He wears a coat and tie daily and reports to his downtown brokerage firm, Wells Fargo Advisors, where he serves as a senior vice president. Neither his Barre Street home nor his Meeting Street office is too many blocks from where he grew up. He's a devout Catholic who attends daily mass. He's a member of St. Mary's Church. He is that one person in Charleston that can surgically dismantle even the most serious and cautious target with a well-planned hoax. The only way he is ever caught is by the same means detectives use to arrest a famous cat burglar—by the correct supposition that nobody else could have pulled it off.

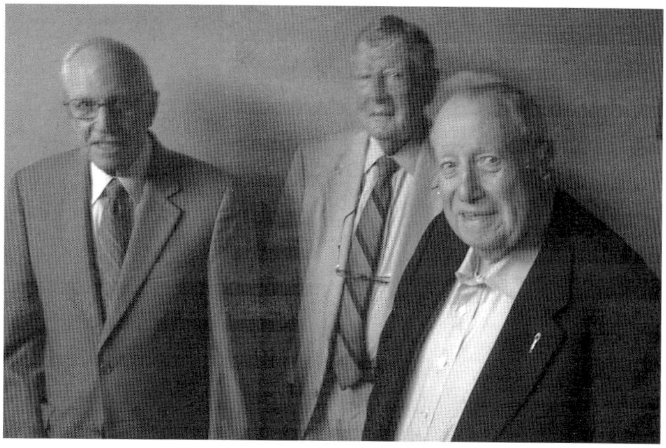

Bernie Puckhaber, Cam Burn and Henry Berlin (*left to right*) get together often and reminisce. Sometimes, they do a little "planning," too! *(W. Thomas McQueeney)*

The Charleston chapter of the American Cancer Society put on a fundraiser production at the Dock Street Theater for twenty years titled "A Step in Time." It was bulwarked by Berlin as emcee and Puckhaber, who claims he was the choreographer and talent scout. The memories of this distinctly Charleston event represent just one of the many combined experiences that recall the fun times these two gentlemen have enjoyed. There is no room for melancholy. The trappings of euphoric laughter supersede all else. So it is that the retelling, complete with embellishment, exaggeration and diminishment of each other's importance always heralds the moment.

"He was the emcee, because he lacked the talent to perform," Puckhaber noted. "Everyone else showed up with some contribution of entertainment except Berlin. Since he looked so goofy and had a frog's voice, they made him the emcee."

"They don't remember Pucky. They remember me," Berlin countered with a devilish grin. "Pucky took up tickets for a while, escorted dignitaries to their seats, emptied the trash and swept the stage afterwards. He had no talent whatsoever, and if he said he had good looks, he'd be lying."

The event raised not only "monster" funds for the cancer society but also awareness. It remains the premier eleemosynary Charleston variety production event of its day. The two "semi-professional comedians," plying trades in other endeavors than their natural comedic array, captured Charleston's funny bone.

Cam Burn, another octogenarian and a breakfast regular, has been, perhaps, the most persecuted persona of the Puckhaber-Berlin schemes over the last fifty years. Burn is the owner of Hughes Lumber Company, a hardware and building materials supplier to the peninsular Charleston community for

125 years. It's on Mary Street near the Charleston Visitor Center. Hughes Lumber Company was started in 1888 and purchased by Cam Burn's father in 1910. Burn usually meets Berlin and Puckhaber at the Friday breakfasts.

"What I like best about Cam is that he's an easy target!" Berlin said. "He's just such a trusting soul. Thank goodness we have him, because we couldn't possibly pull off some of these things on each other."

"He's the perfect patsy," Puckhaber added. "He's the greatest target ever. You know he's a boating enthusiast. We used to go out on his boat for years. One time we were tying up to a buoy out near Dewees Island. He did such a lousy job of getting me close to the buoy that I scraped my knuckles on barnacles. I had to get medical treatment and a tetanus shot. I starting calling him 'Captain Dum-Dum,' and the name stuck. I even think his children call him that today."

The rumble of ruses played upon the unsuspecting Burn has gained Puckhaber and Berlin reputations beyond their circles of friends. A few brilliant schemes have bridged years of laughter.

"It was back in the sixties, I suppose, that Cam and I both drove Chevrolets," Puckhaber explained. "We had met for lunch at Pirani's, a little blue-plate place that had fresh vegetables, at the head of Market Street. It was in the dead of winter, and it started sleeting outside as I left early. Not used to sleet in Charleston, my car was parked away, so I jumped into Cam's, waiting for the sleet to subside. Just on whim I tried my key into his ignition. It worked! I waited until I saw Cam coming out when I moved from the parking lot to wave at him, driving away in his car. He looked startled and yelled out to me, 'Hey, that's my car!' as I headed on back to work."

That was only the beginning of the story. It got better.

"Months later, I realized that, in effect, my key was also Cam's key. I went to a hardware store and had two more made—one for Henry Berlin and another for Harold Wolfe," Puckhaber recounted.

Harold Wolfe, now deceased, was another of the gang that came up with ribald tricks to play on others. He, Berlin and Puckhaber were considered Charleston's version of the Rat Pack.

"We hung around others, like Leonard Fulghum, Bobby Molony, Joe Griffith and Bobby Scarborough," Berlin remembered. "But they were too straight-laced. We needed devilish people with no conscience or manners. You can see why Bernie was such a perfect antagonist. He's the best, because he practices his dark side daily. Some unsuspecting people actually buy stock from him."

The devious personality of Puckhaber was brilliantly emerging.

"I just asked them to put the replicated key on their key rings and move Cam's car slightly whenever they saw it anywhere around town—at the post office, the grocery store, or wherever. So we'd move it across the street or a few parking places down whenever we saw it for months on end. We never got caught. Cam would come out and go to where he thought it was and find it across the street parked in another direction. His wife, Betty, accused him of drinking too much gin."

The triumvirate of car movers was never caught in the act. But they made the mistake of moving the car at an Exchange Club function when their always-suspecting wives were present. Cam's insightful wife, Betty Burn, knew right away what was up. The great car caper was over. Well, almost. The Burns were onto the scheme, but the perpetrators were now unaware that they knew. Burn then got the idea to get back at his prime suspect, Puckhaber. He went to Wilson Rumph, a local auto shop owner, and had him wire in an electric jolt to the driver's seat that would engage when the ignition was turned on. He was able to "buzz" Puckhaber. In fact, Burn witnessed the sight of Puckhaber loudly falling out of his Chevrolet onto the ground. The others got the word soon enough. They would have to come up with another angle to pull one over on the usually unsuspecting Burn. And they did.

A few years later, Burn had ascended to become the president of the Coastal Carolina Fair. In this position, Burn would evaluate not only circus-type rides and acts, but would have the latitude to rent the fairgrounds to groups and corporations for other uses for non-fair functions. This gave Puckhaber another opening.

"Cam is a wonderful guy, close to his family and his church. He's an upstanding, model citizen. That's what made the plan all that more enticing and entertaining," Puckhaber started. "I just thought it would be a great idea to put him in an embarrassing position as fair president. So I had an accomplice in Atlanta, Ed Mullan, send a fake letterhead as a 'Sunshine & Health' organization, asking to have a convention contract drawn to use the fairgrounds in 1970."

After an exchange of letters with Burn, another imposter letter (written by Puckhaber, sent by Mullan from Atlanta) divulged that the national convention was for nudists.

"This shook Cam's world," Puckhaber continued. "He was beside himself. He called a board meeting to get advice. He called the fair's lawyer, Joe Cabiness, too. By this time, I had clued in everyone but Cam! He was in a real panic. The imposter then offered to put a canvas covering completely around the fencing at his own cost to dissuade Peeping Toms. Cam reported this development to the board as a serious consideration, and it was all that Henry and myself could do not to fall out of our chairs in laughter right then. We laughed so hard we had tears. Still Cam did not catch on. It wasn't until we put an advertisement in the paper on New Year's Day of 1971 that poor Cam knew that he had been had. The notice simply said, 'To Our Friend Cam: May the New Year have in store for you many pleasant events as did Ye Olde 1970!'"

In the world of pranks, even Berlin had fallen prey to Puckhaber on occasion. During a 1960s remodel of the 1883 upstairs office and attic area at Berlin's Menswear, some old file boxes were found. Inside one was a set of handwritten dockets and bills of laden that predated the Civil War. Puckhaber could not resist.

"Cam Burn's daughter worked in Washington, D.C., at the time," Puckhaber said, grinning. "After Henry did some local footwork to see if he had valuable documents, I found a network through other means. Cam's daughter acquired stationery from a friend with the National Archives in Washington. I wrote a letter she had typed on the stationery and sent to Berlin postmarked 'Washington.' In the letter, I led Berlin to believe he was in possession of something of great value to collectors. All he could see then were dollar signs. He wrote back asking how best to store the now-valuable documents. This was too good to be true. The letter we sent back from Washington instructed him to place the documents into a refrigerator. He did just that! We'd meet for lunch, and he'd brag about the refrigerated documents and that he was waiting on an assessment from the National Archives. He had plans for the windfall of money already.

"Finally, I fabricated a letter to arrange a meeting at the Mills House. It set a place and time and a suggestion to bring the 'refrigerated' documents," Puckhaber added. "When Henry arrived, I hid behind a curtain to watch. Berlin had waited patiently for the man that would be changing his life and making him rich. Finally, I intercepted his waiter and handed him an envelope to give to Berlin. It said, 'Sorry I can't make it today, but I had a chance to play golf. I really have no interest in your papers anyway.' Henry was fit to be tied and was still fuming when he saw me saunter in like nothing had happened. We never let him forget that episode."

"I liked it better when we were working over Cam Burn," Berlin interjected. "It's not as much fun when you're the pigeon."

The banter in full swing, a young Saffron's waitress, recently engaged and familiar with their banter, presently took their orders. Berlin inquired about the waitress's boyfriend.

"He's in Canada for a month," she replied.

"Canada?" Puckhaber shot back. "Not Canada. You let a single guy loose in Canada? What were you thinking? My wife, Anne, never lets me go to Canada. Even she knows about Canada."

The young lady was at first concerned. Then she noticed the source—Puckhaber. She smiled in defiance and sneeringly took the breakfast orders. She gets lighthearted entertainment from them and their comrades twice a week.

"This restaurant is a great place," Berlin added as the waitress left. "They can make Alpo taste just like Puss 'n Boots."

Nobody is safe from Puckhaber.

Indeed, Pucky found a way to celebrate Charleston's biggest turkey every year on Thanksgiving Day. The Knights of Columbus Turkey Day Run is a five-kilometer event that routes past Berlin's King Street and Broad Street corner each year. It is the largest 5K in the state and boasts over seven thousand runners and walkers. Puckhaber had posters made with an image combining a turkey's body and Henry Berlin's smiling face. He posts them at prominent locations, such as store windows, along the route, especially on Berlin's own storefront windows. Typically, the caption beneath the Berlin "likeness" would read, "Happy Thanksgiving from Charleston's Biggest Turkey, Henry Berlin." The Berlin poster tradition continues.

But the Turkey Day posters were never as imposing as the bigger posters Puckhaber displayed back in the late 1960s. They were actual billboards. A client who owned the billboards leased a few well-placed, giant, up-lit advertising boards to the prankster. On them, he ran four words for ninety days that had those in traffic puzzled. The four words, navy blue on a white background, simply asked, "Who is Cam Burn?" Most of Charleston did not know what the advertising gimmick meant until the new billboards went up months later in the same placements. They had a rather uninspiring black-and-white photograph of Burn in a pose with a slight smile. The words below noted, "I are Cam Burn." The impact had a reverse and unintended consequence. Everyone seemed to view the surprised Burn as a celebrity after the billboards. In fact, Burn seized the opportunity to place a newspaper ad that included the billboard visual and added his address as "Hughes Lumber Company, 82 Mary Street."

"You could say that I put Cam Burn in the spotlight, I suppose," Puckhaber recalled. "I'd say that his grammar school English teacher cringed every time she saw him after that.

"You know his children won't go out with him in public," Puckhaber added in pseudo sympathy. "Can't blame them. It's really sad."

Henry Berlin and Bernie Puckhaber have other targets. One is former United States Senator Ernest F. "Fritz" Hollings. They have played tennis with the venerable senator for decades.

"He's a pretty good player. He's tall and rigid," Berlin said. "But he doesn't move around much. His nickname in our tennis group is 'the Washington Monument.'"

They have other sociable conversation on other people they have admired.

"Joe Riley is the best thing that ever happened to this city," Berlin attested. "No question."

"I remember when 'Big Joe' (Joe Riley Sr.) used to bring little Joe around to the Hibernian Hall," Puckhaber added. "We tried our best to corrupt him, but it was no use.

"Arthur Ravenel—now that's another guy," Puckhaber continued. "We were classmates with Jim Edwards at the College of Charleston. All three of us graduated in 1950, me ahead of time, those other two bringing up the rear! Arthur was a fine historian and had a great deal of knowledge. Smart guy. He was the only student I have ever seen that would argue about history with a history professor. He'd get away with it."

"Mayor Joe Riley had a scheduling conflict one time, and I had to show up to a convention in town as his substitute to welcome folks to Charleston," Berlin recalled. "Arthur Ravenel was to speak after me. My Charleston Gullah accent is strong enough, but nowhere near that of Arthur's. At the end of my remarks, which I'm sure most people there couldn't quite understand, I introduced Arthur by saying, 'And now Congressman Ravenel, who speaks perfectly enunciated English, will explain to you everything that I just said!'"

"Jim Edwards was at the College of Charleston, too," Puckhaber added. "He was a little quieter than me, but then again, who isn't? Jimmy Edwards was the greatest delegator I have ever known. He'd find the right person for the right job and match them up. In this way, he was a brilliant politician and statesman. Had I figured that out like he did, I would have been president!"

Berlin noted, "Edwards was an excellent dentist. He was my dentist, and my teeth have outlasted other parts of me, so he did a good job."

The two men recalled some of Charleston's seminal moments.

"Building the Mills House [1970] prior to Charleston Place [1986] was a big deal," Puckhaber said. "They were finishing when I was serving as the Hibernian president. It was during Charleston's tricentennial celebration. I can remember that they wanted us to paint the sides of the Hibernian Hall, because we are the next building over. We never thought to paint the sides and figured it was an unnecessary expense until then. Nobody saw the

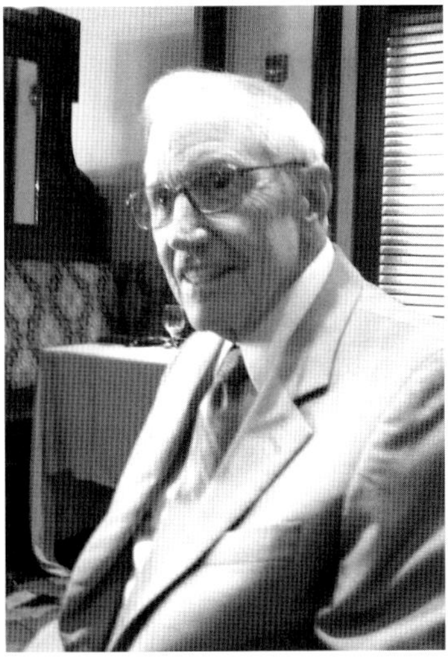

Bernie Puckhaber works full time for Wells Fargo Financial at the age of eighty-three. His impressive physical energy is surpassed only by his magnificent sense of humor. *(W. Thomas McQueeney)*

sides, so why waste the money, we thought. Nobody could remember when those old walls had ever been painted before."

"Charleston was really, really different back then," Berlin added. "You could only find decent food at Perdita's and sometimes Henry's on the Market was good. If you wanted a steak, you had to cross the Ashley Bridge to the Cavallaro Restaurant on Savannah Highway. The Cavallaro had music, too. It was a real night out."

"I seem to recall going all the way to Savannah just to get a steak at Johnny Harris's Barbecue and Steakhouse," Puckhaber noted in remembrance. "Can you imagine you really couldn't get a good steak in Charleston?"

"Market Street was derelict," Berlin offered. "Sailor bars, dive night clubs. The Octagon Lounge I remember. Melvin Berlinsky hid a friend's car there between two trucks while they were at the bar in the Octagon. I think that was where Pregnall trucking was then—right there on the Market. It took that poor guy hours to find his car."

"My older brother made ten dollars a week working for Pearlstine's then. They were around the corner on East Bay Street," Puckhaber recalled. "My mother made him cough over eight dollars of that ten dollars, so he was really just making two dollars a week."

Pearlstine's Beer Distributors has been a Charleston legend. The original I.M. Pearlstine's manufactured Confederate Army uniforms in 1862. Through five marketing regenerations, Pearlstine's is still family owned and has been a wholesale beer distributor since 1900.[9] The major brand of beer distribution is Budweiser. The Pearlstine family has endeared itself to Charlestonians well beyond beer. They have been extremely generous community citizens for 150 years.

"Two dollars was a lot of money," Berlin shot back. "I went to school with a nickel and with that bought a container of milk and a johnnycake for lunch and had a penny left over."

All in all, the city has positives of the past missed now by those who lived it.

"I miss the movies downtown," Puckhaber confided. "And I still enjoy walking everywhere. The geographic area of the city is not that big where you can't just walk. Anne and I both walked to grammar school, to high school and to college. Not many married people today can say that."

Just about everybody walked everywhere then.

"There were not a lot of cars in Charleston," Berlin added. "Nobody had that kind of money, and there really wasn't a lot of need for local transportation. You walked to school, to the doctor, to the corner grocer and to the movies. Now everybody has two cars, one to drive while the other's in the shop."

Though much of the past is lamented, there is more to offer in today's Charleston.

"You really can't compare our downtown restaurants now," Berlin said with insight. "They are world class. They are simply wonderful. There are people standing out on the sidewalk waiting to get in. Look at the boats in our marina. They're crowded with these high-priced yachts. You can't move around on our beaches these days. The retailers have everything from across the globe. Charleston has so much more now to offer everybody. You better believe we've come a long way."

The days have not passed these two gentlemen by in any sense. They are sharper than a pair of thirty-year-olds. They have the advantage of knowing what's important in the scope of a lifetime and what's only important for the moment—like splitting the check and the generous tip for a young waitress getting married with her whole life ahead of her.

The scope of a lifetime finds the importance of friends gathering to enjoy friendships. They have lived more than 170 years between them. There are many more pranks to plan and heady banter to be enjoyed by all who come around them.

They are inexorably and forever Charleston's own: Berlin and Puckhaber.

Bernie Puckhaber passed away on December 26, 2014, at his residence. Ironically, he passed away within a few hours of his friend and college classmate, James B. Edwards—both on the day after Christmas. Bernie's dear friend Henry Berlin celebrated his ninety-second birthday in August 2016. He remains active. Their mutual lifelong friend Cam Burn died on April 20, 2013. Their rollicking pranks remain an integral part of Charleston's lure and lore.

A House in Order

Speaker Bobby Harrell

When Robert William Harrell was born into a Rockingham, North Carolina, family, there was no knowing where the road ahead would lead. He became, with his mother's passing from complications during childbirth, an orphan. His father had died before he was born. It was precisely the road ahead that would define his life.

Bob Harrell Sr. died on September 3, 2010. The road ahead may have been one he had built—in more ways than one. Part of that road has become familiar to all of Charleston and the State of South Carolina.

His son, Robert William "Bobby" Harrell Jr., had become the Speaker of the South Carolina House of Representatives. In a state that has distributed influence in odd proportions, it may be that the House Speaker exceeds even the sitting governor in the everyday ability to administer the needs of the state's infrastructure, services and capital improvements. It's an incredibly responsible position. Bobby Harrell learned about responsibility from his father.

"Daddy learned to handle life dependent upon himself. He was orphaned at a young age in the face of the greatest depression this country has known and was raised by his maternal grandparents," Harrell noted. "I imagined that his early years always had the specter of him being orphaned again."

He must have influenced his children—Bobby, Lea and John—in the hardships of life. They listened well. And Speaker Harrell, perhaps among the most sensible of politicians, found others to listen as well. They listened to common sense.

"I was upset over taxes in 1992. I was also concerned about the lack of movement in improving education in South Carolina. I had become active in the chamber of commerce. I had friends and neighbors who felt I should run for office," Harrell recalled. "I got up enough confidence to do so. My wife, Cathy, and my parents inspired me to go for it. I felt I could make a difference."

That he did.

Harrell won the seat and was elected as chairman of the freshman caucus. He was appointed to the Ways and Means Committee in 1994—a powerful committee for which he would serve as chair from 1999 to 2005. He was later elected as House Speaker in 2005, replacing the Honorable David Wilkins, who was appointed ambassador to Canada by President George W. Bush. Harrell has been reelected as House Speaker in 2006, 2008 and 2010, the last time by a vote of 112 to 5. He may be there as long as he is willing to accept the many challenges it entails.

Harrell's wife, Cathy, is an optimistic and insightful partner to the cause. She is slender, pretty and confident—and serves as Harrell's last best defense.

"Cathy has another sense that I don't have," Harrell intimated. "She can see the underlying motivations that some people have. She gives me my best advice and reads people better than anyone I know."

Their thirty-one-year marriage has produced son Trey Harrell, a student at the Charleston School of Law, and daughter Charlotte, a junior at the University of South Carolina Honors College. Trey also graduated from the state's charter university—where Bobby and Cathy Harrell graduated in 1978 and 1979, respectively. Bobby Harrell received his degree in business with an emphasis in insurance.

Aside from wife Cathy, Harrell turned to an old family friend, Tommy Hartnett, for early political advice. Hartnett had served as a South Carolina state senator and the First District United States congressman from Charleston for over six years, from 1981 to 1987. Hartnett narrowly lost races for two other major roles—as lieutenant governor and as United States senator. He had been known as a savvy political mind.

"Tommy Hartnett got me to his campaign people, helped me to develop strategies and became incredibly supportive," Harrell recalled. "I owe him much. I got to know Tommy Hartnett working as his page in the state senate while I was getting my degree at USC."

Hartnett saw much in Harrell, even during his days as a page.

"Bobby Harrell studied politics from the statehouse," Hartnett recalled. "I knew his father and saw some similarities in Bobby, but also some differences. Bobby was genuinely excited to work inside the system and to see how things got done at the state level. He showed an early interest, and I am not at all surprised at his hard work and success."

Harrell's career took him to the operation's center of state tax, law and management. He had seen much change across the South Carolina landscape in those twenty years, but nothing like he's seen happen in his own beloved Charleston.

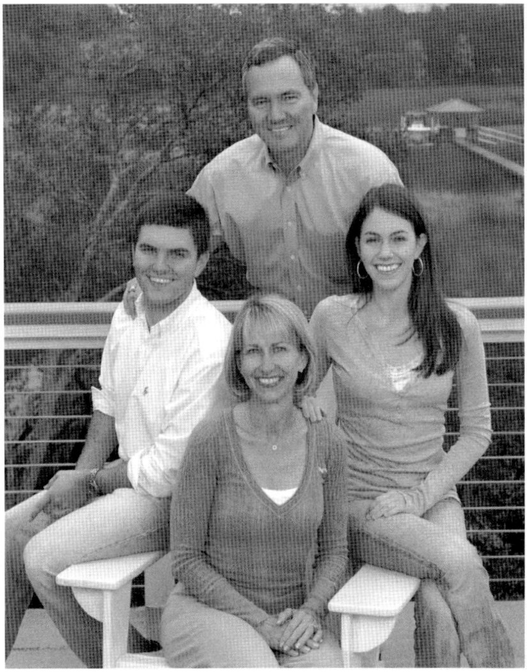

Clockwise: South Carolina House Speaker Bobby Harrell, daughter Charlotte, wife Cathy and son Trey. The Harrell back deck is where they enjoy the closeness of family. *(Photo by Charlotte Harrell, mother of the Speaker.)*

"In my time in the statehouse, much has transpired across the state, but the biggest change has occurred in Charleston," Harrell related. "When I was at St. Andrews Junior High School, my parents told me that nice people should not go downtown. Now everybody flocks to downtown Charleston."

Charleston of 1974—Harrell's Middleton High School graduation year—did not, as yet, have Mayor Joe Riley in place.

"Downtown was considered dirty and unsafe. We had dinner before our senior prom at a Market Street restaurant and then we got back to the safety of West Ashley," Harrell recalled. "But in time, Joe Riley changed all of that.

"Everything changed for the better, except traffic. Charleston was rediscovered by the tourist industry. Exciting things happened. Charleston became the place to be," Harrell continued. "The opinions of people around the state began to change. I see our state's rivalry every day, but even people who are jealous of what we have in Charleston love our city for what it has become."

Indeed, nationally and internationally, the charm of South Carolina is best defined by Charleston. Though it may be like defining England by a visit to London or France by a trip to Paris, Charleston has become the face of South Carolina.

Yet, the statehouse is in a mode of modulation. The support and benefit of government had to be curtailed, and it took the leadership of this most admirable Charlestonian to gauge levels.

"The last few years have been difficult for government as well as our citizens. We have a responsibility to prioritize. When balancing the budget with cuts, it's much like the Hippocratic oath that doctors take—first, do no harm," Harrell explained. "With the cut in general appropriations, we had to look at the least important things. The deepness of the cuts is more bothersome than the cuts themselves. We've tried to prioritize education and economic development. Those are the engines that build our economy. And then there's health care for people who cannot afford it—poor children especially."

The pundits sometimes criticize what they do not really understand. For instance, in the fight ahead that should solidify the Boeing Corporation in the Charleston area, Harrell is less than amused by the level of understanding of business tax incentives. Harrell was at the table to bring Boeing to Charleston. The tax incentive package allows a reduction in future taxes for the benefit of four thousand jobs that will likely grow to as many as twenty thousand more support-industry jobs in the times of a deep recession.

"Most of the business tax incentives that we offer are simply allowing the company to keep a portion of the taxes that the company would have paid to the state or county. When we do it this way, we do not give up actual money the state has, and besides, if the company didn't locate here, we wouldn't receive the taxes anyway," Harrell explained. "We get the jobs for our people, and the taxes that are paid by the company are just a smaller amount. Of course, if the company did not locate here, the taxes we would collect are zero percent of nothing."

Pragmatism is a blessing that runs deep in the Harrell genealogical bloodline.

A current suit by union interests through the National Labor Relations Board is now the talk of national radio and television news. It seems the unions are trying to affect decisions in boardrooms that corporations can decide to pursue plants in right-to-work states. South Carolina is one of twenty-three such states. There will be a full and final report coming soon on this historic suit. Speaker Harrell will be a major player. Don't bet against him.

Typically, Harrell's duties as the Speaker of the House begin in preparation on Monday morning. All of the legislative seats—House and Senate—are considered part-time. The legislature meets from early January to early June each year, with committee work performed during the rest of the year. The weekly meetings to consider law, budget and a plethora of other items that the statehouse must review take place from Tuesday to Thursday. Harrell will work extra hard to deflect the claims against Charleston's Boeing plant. He will perform all other duties admirably at the same time. And then he just might fly home.

Harrell received his pilot's license a decade ago and has the option of flying back and forth to his West Ashley home even during sessions. He comes home as often as he can, but sometimes the responsibility and time commitments dictate otherwise. Cathy Harrell understands.

Cathy said, "Bobby feels called to do the work he does, but in reality it is a family calling. We have to understand the time it takes and realize that he is doing what he believes he is supposed to do. Over the years, it has been a great lesson for the children and me to learn the true definition of a public servant."

Yet Harrell has a personal life that he both protects and enjoys. He spends it with his family.

"Family is so important in the whole picture. I have my children to enjoy, and Cathy is thankfully the perfect balance for me. The two of us enjoy the simplest of life's moments. We like to get a glass of wine before dinner and sit and chat on the back porch," Harrell shared.

"A perfect day in Charleston would be a Saturday with a little extra sleep, a ride down to the farmer's market and a stroll with Cathy. In the afternoon we'd put the boat in and casually ride through the waterways and find a nice restaurant on the way back. We'd get back, and Cathy and I would have our glass of wine on the back deck. Now, that's a perfect day in Charleston!" Harrell exclaimed.

Who could argue with that?

Harrell followed his father's advice in 1979 and became a State Farm Insurance agent at the age of twenty-four. His agency on North Rivers Avenue served a market area between Charleston and Goose Creek, but he gained other business by his good works. He served as president of the Exchange Club of Charleston, the largest Exchange Club in the country, and stayed involved with the Charleston Metro Chamber of Commerce. That chamber of commerce happens to be the oldest in America, established in 1773. It comprises more than twenty-one hundred businesses. Harrell furthered his influence by volunteering to serve his neighborhood in many capacities, including homeowners' association president. Being active in so many interests spurred on his pursuit of politics.

Upon his father's passing, it became evident that Harrell would assume other roles as well. His father's role as a property manager for Harrell Square, a beautiful corner-lot shopping and business center, had to be filled. His widowed mother, Charlotte Harrell, looked to her children for not only care, but emotional support as well. As close as he was to his parents, the loss of his father had to be shouldered on many other fronts. Harrell moved the agency he had built in North Charleston for thirty years to this West Ashley center that his father built. In so many ways, it was like starting over. He hardly had time to mourn the passing of his father, a man largely responsible for his direction and success in later life.

"Daddy was inspirational. He gave great and timely advice, and he made me want to succeed. He was a man who always served others," Harrell reflected.

His father, Bob Harrell, served as a South Carolina highway commissioner who played a major role in the construction of the Arthur Ravenel Jr.

Bridge, the building of Interstate 526 and the widening of Highway 17 between Charleston and Savannah. He once ran for the U.S. House of Representatives, a seat eventually won by Mark Sanford.

Ironically, it was in later years that Governor Sanford (2003–11) pursued a strict ideology, while House Speaker Harrell maintained a stance of pragmatism. Those normally docile views clashed often, with Harrell usually the victor. But it was not easy. The extreme ideology espoused by Sanford reached the bully pulpit and led to many confrontations, most notably with Sanford carrying piglets into the House chamber when David Wilkins was still the House Speaker in 2004. Sanford wanted a photo opportunity of pork-barrel spending, but instead, he ended up with a swine-defecated suit of clothes. The House overturned many of the Sanford budget demands. The Senate overturned them as well. And thus began the rattling of cages in Columbia, South Carolina.

The five principal players—the governor, the House Speaker, the House Ways and Means Committee chairman, the Senate Finance Committee chairman and the president pro tempore of the Senate—play the major roles in shaping policy, spending and appropriations. The state operates best when these five centers of responsibility work well together. Thus the inherent and natural pragmatism of Bobby Harrell becomes the glue to South Carolina's governance. He is most respectful of others, listens first, looks for across-the-aisle input and consults with his friends in the state senate along with all other pertinent factions. He then acts according to what he deems is in the best interests of the citizens of the state. He defines pragmatism.

And, as he says, "It is important that first we do no harm."

The coy smile exemplifies the sentiment. It says, "Let's be diligent, let's be smart and let's be responsible." He is all of these.

It was just after he was elected as House Speaker in 2005 that Harrell afforded me the privilege of lunch with him in the Sol Blatt building cafeteria. Afterwards, he showed me a photograph in the Speaker's conference room. It was a photo of Sol Blatt Sr. He told me about the man whom many considered among the most influential politicians in the history of South Carolina. Blatt had served two terms as House Speaker, for a total of thirty-two years, and was accorded the title of Speaker Emeritus in 1973. Blatt had represented Barnwell County for fifty-four consecutive years. He was said to have benefitted from the so-called "Barnwell Ring." This group of high-achieving legislators was so named as if there were a clandestine conspiracy surrounding them. It never likely happened.

We further discussed the historically disputed impact of having had four (of the five previously mentioned) state power positions filled from Barnwell County, a small, sparsely populated area of South Carolina that borders Georgia. While Blatt was the House Speaker, Senator Edgar A. Brown served in consecutive roles as Senate pro tempore and Senate finance chairman. The one hundredth governor of South Carolina, Joseph Emile Harley, hailed from Barnwell during World War II. At the apex of the controversial Barnwell Ring in 1941, Winchester Smith Jr. filled the fourth position as House Ways and Means chairman. All four of these gentlemen disputed that there was any inside workings of government. Historians now believe that all was proper.

It was a great history lesson. It has a postscript.

For five years (2005–10) the House Speaker, Senate pro tempore and governor all hailed from Charleston. We will not need historians to make a disclaimer for these three gentlemen. While Harrell and Senate pro tempore Glenn McConnell have a wonderful working relationship, and both are beyond reproach, they had another thing in common: the governor rarely worked with either!

So it is that Bobby Harrell has earned the respect of the people of South Carolina, the General Assembly of state legislators and most importantly, those who have known him for a lifetime. It would be fitting that a second Speaker of the South Carolina House gains the moniker some day of "Speaker Emeritus."

On that day, Cathy Harrell will have a special bottle of wine ready for the back porch.

Postscript: Not only did Governor Mark Sanford finish his term amid odd circumstances and marital difficulties, but Bobby Harrell also stepped down after twenty-two years of serving South Carolinians in 2014. The third "power broker," Senator Glenn McConnell, left his key post as lieutenant governor to become the twentieth president of the College of Charleston in 2014. The Charleston base of resurgent political power had vanished in the space of four years (2010–14). The newer highways may grace the handsome Upstate area and in the rolling Midlands. The Lowcountry will need a new champion.

In what many considered a political "witch hunt"—and others a fiasco—Harrell was charged with six misdemeanors related to the use of campaign funds spent on trips utilizing his private airplane. His popularity did not diminish. In fact, the race to replace Harrell in the South Carolina House was highlighted by more than four thousand write-in votes for Harrell, who was not a candidate and missing on the ballot! He had served admirably as Speaker of the South Carolina House of Representatives for nine years. People knew that he was an effective and smart legislator.

"I don't know of an elected public official that I worked with that worked harder than Bobby Harrell," former mayor Joe Riley said. "Bobby Harrell wasn't about talking, he was about doing." That tribute may define the Harrell career. Despite the seemingly endless political infighting that has plagued South Carolina politics, many pundits assume that Bobby Harrell will reemerge. Never ever count him out!

The Children of Dr. Charlie Darby

There is an understated brilliance in many areas of medical care accompanied by a myriad of experiences unimaginable. There is a deep, humanitarian sense of propriety in a higher calling to benefit an entire community. There is a chronicle of accomplishment that bridges generations of youth who have lived to enjoy the fullness of life in its result. There is a legacy developed, red brick by red brick, to the zenith of need. In these and other endeavors, reticence should not be allowed. Humility should be denied any quarter. It is temerity that defines Dr. Charles P. Darby Jr., a boldness that can only be quantified by the evidence of his life's work and what it has meant in enormous benefit to Charleston and the entire coastal region.

Dr. Darby is among the paragons of the medical complex that comprise a full quadrant of Charleston's economic activity. Within an eight-block area near the Ashley River, four major hospitals dominate the skyline. These hospitals tentacle to the entire coastal region of South Carolina. The largest, the Medical University Hospital, is one of only three university hospitals in the state, MUSC being the oldest and largest. MUSC was chartered in 1824[10] and now features expansions including a department of psychiatry, the Storm Eye Institute and a seven-story Children's Hospital. Dr. Darby has served as chairman of pediatrics and director of the MUSC Children's Hospital for two decades. He is the progenitor. The MUSC Children's Hospital is there because of Dr. Darby.

Darby is an articulate and energetic man built solidly by the benefit of his passion—tennis. He is in shape. His knowing blue eyes and more-than-courteous smile seem to invite and inform. It is what he does every day. His personable demeanor of confidence and friendship decidedly eases him and those he encounters. He is singularly impressive in his accomplishment, but more so in his pensive and insightful presence.

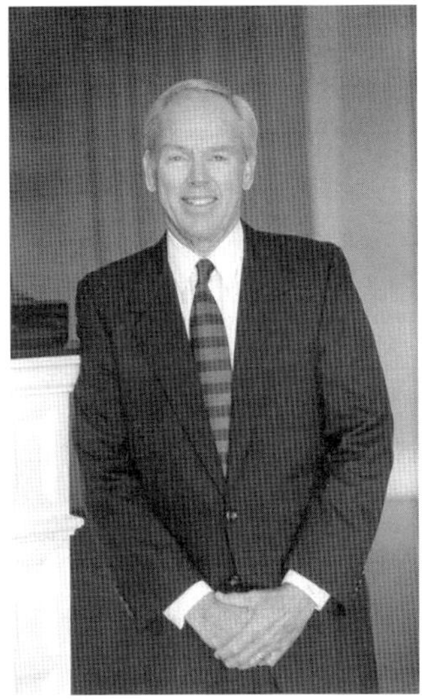

Dr. Charlie Darby has little reason to work every day in what should be his retirement years, except that he knows he is further helping the children of the community. *(Anne Darby Parker)*

The Children's Hospital was built in 1987 and is the state's most comprehensive—and largest—pediatric care and research facility. It is ranked among the finest in the nation by the *U.S. News and World Report* 2011 edition.

"We perform an array of transplants not available elsewhere in the state," Darby related. "We do pediatric transplants for the liver, pancreas, kidneys and heart. In the way of transplants, we are the only statewide pediatric hospital to perform these very delicate operations."

The hospital also boasts a large sixth-floor atrium that has become a gathering place for children in all of the difficult health circumstances. The atrium has stuffed animals, board games and an assortment of safe toys. It is also a fine indoor "park" for parents to enjoy with their hospitalized children. The children come with many storylines—cancer patients, infectious diseases, burn victims and traffic accidents. There is even an intensive care unit for everything aforementioned in addition to neonatal care. In this area, one might find as many as forty premature birth-weight infants, some of which are less than two pounds. The Children's Hospital is not for the weak of heart. Every room tells of another sadness in the hopeful transition to a happy conclusion and release.

Darby has spent his adult life in delivering care to others. He grew up in Mount Pleasant when the town was essentially a sleepy village across the Cooper River via a narrow, two-lane bridge. There were only about two thousand residents. Darby recalled catching the Mount Pleasant-to-downtown bus for ten cents.

"My mother would give us fifty cents," Darby related. "It was ten cents to get downtown, ten cents for the movie, ten cents for a malted shake and ten cents to get back home. I used the other dime to buy something for my mother at Woolworth's. Life was pretty simple then.

"The bus dropped us at Marion Square, and we walked everywhere from that point. The only large retail and movie houses in the county were on King Street. We often walked to the old museum at Rutledge and Calhoun," Darby continued. "There was a whale skeleton hanging from the ceiling. My great grandfather, Captain Robert Magwood, helped to catch that whale in Charleston Harbor. He was a boat captain and delivered provisions to the barrier islands—mostly the Isle of Palms and Sullivan's Island. There was no bridge to Mount Pleasant then. Captain Magwood joined in the chase for that big whale. He fashioned some type of harpoon. His great-great grandfather, Simon Magwood, was president of the Hibernian Society for over thirty years. The whale story was spoken about as a Charleston legend and rated as a great conquest by my family. Today, everyone would be vilified for such an episode."

That account in the *Charleston News* of January 8, 1880, described a daylong conquest of a "fifty-foot right whale" that finally "died at sunset near Shem Creek." The newspaper estimated a "$600 to $800" benefit of whale oil. The skeleton was donated to the Charleston Museum. That right whale took a wrong turn and now hangs from the museum's rafters to the great awe of visiting schoolchildren.

There wasn't much in Charleston beyond the aforementioned museum, itself a vestige edifice from a Confederate veterans' convention in 1893.[11] The columns to that building remain, though the empty structure burned down in October of 1981.

From whale stories to the sleepy summers of Mount Pleasant, the Darby family made an impression for generations. Charlie Darby seems to be the next whale story—and more—for the coming generations.

Darby's scholastic days were proficient. He excelled in his endeavors nicely. Darby became a fine athlete in addition to his academic abilities. As he was finishing Moultrie High School, his parents had no particular advice or insight for a college choice. The Korean War was being waged, and the military draft was active. It was important to make a timely decision. A proposal was made from Citadel football coach Quinn Decker that Darby continue his athletic and academic career at The Citadel. That sounded fine with Darby, as he thought it to be a good fit for his future. He entered The Citadel in 1951.

"I played a few games during my freshman season 'both ways' as a linebacker and a guard," Darby recalled. "I continued through the next two years and enjoyed football at The Citadel. They made me join the wrestling team to stay in shape during the offseason."

Wrestling is perhaps the toughest nine minutes in all of sport.

"I really didn't know how to wrestle until I joined the wrestling team. I had never wrestled before," Darby related. "But I did it to appease the coaches and found it to be another great challenge."

It was Darby's takedown of the academic challenge that exceeded even Darby's athletic prowess at The Citadel. At the end of his junior year in 1954, Darby applied to the Medical College of Virginia dental school. Without the benefit of his diploma, he was accepted. This caused unforeseen results.

"I had no idea I would get accepted into the Richmond dental school," Darby said. "I had been slotted by the ROTC department to fly jets. When I broke the news, an ROTC colonel got up on his desk in arguing my decision. But my mind was made up. I never looked back."

Other consequences were a decades-long delay in receiving both his diploma and his Citadel ring due to, in essence, his meteoric success. In time, a Citadel policy change was in place to accommodate the super successful. He also received an honorary degree from The Citadel.

"I have never missed a reunion of the class of 1955 to this day," Darby said. "I have so many friends from those days, like Al Hutchinson and Ned Montgomery. Al went to Moultrie and The Citadel with me and played football as well. He was the other guard."

After a year at dental school, he returned to the Medical University of South Carolina and completed his degree in medicine in 1959. He continued his training at Duke University. There he saw a modern division of the subspecialties that did not exist in Charleston at the time.

"At Duke, within their department of pediatrics, they had subspecialties in pediatrics to include radiology, surgery, ENT, oncology, cardiology, endocrinology, etc. Specialization was the key to comprehensive pediatric care," Darby recalled. "While at MUSC, we only had two professors in general pediatrics. I had decided to devote my career to this area of community need and, eventually, opened my practice back in my home of Mount Pleasant. I wanted to take that sophistication back to Charleston. By 1962, I had come up with the idea of a specialized regional children's hospital."

"Charlie Darby was always one with great foresight, ambition and capabilities," old friend and mentor Jim Edwards said. "I knew him since I was a young man working in his daddy's boatyard. When he was in dental school, he had come home, and we talked about what he wanted to do. He wanted to pursue medicine. I suggested he finish his first year of dental school, because many of the same courses would apply to medicine."

James B. Edwards was an ideal friend and mentor for Darby's career. Edwards, a practicing oral surgeon, served in the state senate, as South Carolina's governor (1975–79) and as President Ronald Reagan's secretary of energy. He later served the Medical University of South Carolina as president from 1982 to 1999. Darby and Edwards became united in the cause of the MUSC Children's Hospital.

"Charlie's another 'Hungrynecker,'" Edwards recalled, referring to the name locals call residents of Mount Pleasant. "Mount Pleasant was a much smaller community, and everybody seemed to know everybody, including those in the minority population. We all got along very well. Charlie and I have known each other for a lifetime. When Charlie's career came full circle to cross paths with mine again, I was happy to be of any help I could. He has always been driven. When Governor Dick Riley turned down the Children's Hospital funding the first time, Charlie didn't let that stop him. We got it through the second time, thanks to Charlie Darby."

Darby had found the impetus to chair the effort for the much-needed Children's Hospital through personal forbearance and career focus. He eventually opened a pediatric practice in Mount Pleasant. His practice was augmented by teaching at MUSC and other tangential hospital work on tuberculosis and meningitis. He was quite busy when the opportunity came along to conduct research at the largest children's hospital in the world.

"My career path took me to London for a year to work in the Great Ormond Street Hospital (sometimes called GOSH or the Sick Children's Hospital) in 1969–1970," Darby noted. "It was a great experience career-wise and gave me much more insight into the need for subspecialist doctors for a variety of children's conditions and diseases. We had no subspecialists in Charleston at that time."

Thinking outside of the box, Darby's mind was now settled on the great need for not only specialization, but also a dedicated regional pediatric hospital. He never lost focus.

Fortunately, two senior, nationally respected pediatricians became his friends and mentors.

"I had two of the finest mentors imaginable," Darby related. "Dr. Mitchell Rubin was the chief of pediatrics previously at Buffalo [New York] Hospital. He was my senior advisor and a brilliant man. We also had a visiting professor, Dr. Albert Sabin," Darby continued. "He was the inventor of the famous Sabin vaccine."

The Sabin vaccine was invented in 1957 and approved in 1962.[12] The simpler, oral version of the previous Dr. Jonas Salk injection (1952) has been credited with eradicating polio across the world.

"Dr. Sabin was a visiting professor at MUSC and suggested the timing was right to approach MUSC president Bill Knisely and apply for the Children's Hospital project through the board of trustees," Darby related. "I did so. The state had a large bond issue. It was vetoed by Governor Dick Riley the first year and then approved in the second year with a compromise down to a sixty-million-dollar cost."

Darby was serving as the assistant dean to the school of pediatrics at the time. The dean and the president supported his plan for a children's hospital.

"We moved some offices and clinics to the Rutledge Tower. It took four years to build the hospital. In the meantime, I was appointed to chair pediatrics for MUSC on an interim basis at first," Darby continued. "By 1982, I received the permanent role. The hospital did not open until 1987. I can remember recruiting some of the doctors we needed by walking them through the project with hardhats. We now have applicants from all fifty states and hire as many as eighteen interns per year for a three-year residency. The new facility was so nice it became easy to attract doctors and nurses from some of the nation's best children's hospitals."

Drs. Edwards and Darby grew up together in Mount Pleasant and had been boyhood friends.

"Jim Edwards is a few years my senior and has always been a role model and inspiration for me," Darby declared. "Dr. Jim Edwards was a catalyst for MUSC during his seventeen years as president to accomplish great things. We opened the Children's Hospital, and he was the driving force behind many other positive community health initiatives."

The symbiosis for these two models of community benefit will not end for many generations well past their own lifetimes. The James B. Edwards School of Dental Medicine is a 120,000-square-foot, state-of the-art facility that stands next to the Dr. Charles P. Darby Jr. Children's Research Institute. The Darby Institute boasts 121,000 square feet. Symbolically, an enclosed crosswalk joins the two buildings. Edwards and Darby are exemplary connections for MUSC going forward—the buildings as well as the gentlemen themselves.

Dr. Edwards and Dr. Darby worked well together. Darby kept his role as the chairman of the MUSC Children's Hospital for twenty years, retiring in 2001. Well, he almost retired.

"I still work in several aspects of the Children's Hospital, even in retirement," Darby noted. "I assist the hospital with fundraising and even political lobbying to a certain extent."

He is usually immersed in the dilemma of state budget considerations. Some of the very sick children are supported by Medicaid payments. The Medicaid costs are paid by a three-to-one ratio of federal to state dollars. But the State of South Carolina had a situation develop from low revenue that would entail some very difficult cuts in 2011–12. Medicaid sometimes becomes the target. That development would be devastating to the MUSC Children's Hospital.

"I have been working the decision makers in Columbia for their support. This is not about me. This is about the children," Darby declared.

Darby and his wife, Joyce, have five children and sixteen grandchildren. The "Darby Effect" in Charleston is wide and deep. Oldest son Buddy (Charles P. Darby III) has remained active in higher education and manages several high-profile golfing venues under Kiawah Resort Associates, Inc. They own several local courses in addition to the somewhat newer Doonbeg Golf Club and Spa in the southwest of Ireland. Daughter Anne is an established artist and produces a painting daily! Many are given for charity. She also started a unique children's museum on John Street. It has become a popular destination for local children and visitors alike. It is situated next to the City of Charleston's Visitor Center. Son John serves as president of the Beach Company, Inc., a local real estate developer with a stellar record of project design and enhancement. The beauty and quality of Beach Company productions have enhanced the entire area. Daughter Beth lives in Jacksonville, and daughter Joya lives in Denver.

The Darby family has contributed generously to the MUSC Children's Hospital, and they were leading contributors to the Charles P. Darby Children's Research Institute, which was named to honor Dr. Darby.

Darby's life's work has been about children. He lends insight to the cause.

"Everything they need is smaller, from beds to syringes to toothbrushes," he points out. "And we need to get into their world to make them well again by our professionalism, our research and our devotion to their care."

Dr. Darby has thousands of children. Some are now adults. Some have moved away. Some are in that hospital today. But they are all his children.

Dr. Charles P. Darby Jr. feels strongly in stating, "It is the community's responsibility to assure the health and welfare of its children." He has committed his professional life to see that our community provides the best health care possible for our children.

Buoyed by a $25 million lead gift, the Medical University of South Carolina broke ground on a $385 million children's hospital. It will be named for the lead donor, Benefitfocus CEO Shawn Jenkins. The major purpose as a children's hospital is supplemented by a women's pavilion dedicated to women's services. The added facility furthers the life-changing vision of Dr. Charlie Darby.

Alicia Rhett at Home

She said Clark Gable was charming and Leslie Howard was delightful. Olivia de Havilland stayed in touch for years, and Vivien Leigh was just as pretty off the set as she was on. It's mid-March, and Alicia Rhett is talking about her fellow cast members from *Gone With the Wind*, considered one of the greatest movies of all time. She is the oldest living cast member of that epic film.

It was not my intention to bring up the movie—and I didn't. One of her nurses did. I had gone to see this legendary actress and artist to talk about a series of paintings that adorn the offices of The Citadel's president. These paintings depict the times prior to 1922, when The Citadel campus was located on Marion Square in the heart of downtown Charleston. Alicia Rhett was born in 1915. She guessed that she had completed the series in the mid-1970s as a commissioned enterprise from then Citadel president George M. Seignious, a retired lieutenant general. The exact time of these superb productions escaped her. She said there was much she couldn't remember, but much that she could. An examination of the paintings gave dates of 1974, 1975 and 1976. She confirmed this in my second visit when I showed her photocopies of the paintings.

Alicia Rhett has a walker and sits comfortably—well dressed and dignified. She seems to love visitors. I had called to make an appointment. Her room has some career mementos, a few photos and a warm feeling of home. There is an heirloom painting of a formal Rhett ancestor from the sixteenth century, an exquisite rendering of a curly white spaniel from 1987 and a still life she had completed early in her artistic career. She painted them all. She is at home with her work staring inward to her very comfortable surroundings. She is in one of the finest assisted-living facilities on the globe, the Bishop Gadsden Home. She has a daily routine and the spirited attention of the staff. They love her. She is a living legend.

Upon entering, she greeted me in her strong, southern drawl.

"Well, how d'ya do? And how is your dear mother?" she asked.

I assumed that the nurses gave her my name, and she placed it properly as the son of her old friend, Charlotte McQueeney, whom I still call "Mom." They knew each other for years.

"Miss Rhett, it is my extreme pleasure. Thank you for seeing me. I just left my mother after we met at church and had breakfast together," I answered in my best Rhett Butler manners, complete with a slight bow of reverence. "I will be sure to tell her that you asked."

I announced to her the reason for my visit. I remarked about the quality and beauty that she has affixed to the traditions of The Citadel's campus in that seminal series of cadet life paintings I had marveled at for many years.

"Each painting is exactly thirty inches by twenty-four inches. And each frame was the same style and type," Rhett recalled. "I did them from photographs they gave me. I don't remember how many I painted exactly."

Excusing the lapse of specific memory over some forty years is a given, I considered, even though I was fully impressed that she recalled the exact size and the conformity of the framing.

My interest in these paintings had been piqued since I started spending much of my time on the campus over the past few years. The Citadel became a passion to me, and her incredible paintings told a wonderful story of its history. I remembered this venerable lady as a friend of my mother's. But I wasn't sure she would remember my mom. They were two of the dozen or so Charleston artists that founded the Charleston Artist Guild in 1953. They became friends long ago.

Alicia Rhett had been known in the blue-blooded Charleston circles as the finest portrait artist of a generation. She painted the debutantes and the society presidents. She painted prep school children, nannies and some lucky commoners along the way. By her estimate, she painted hundreds of formal family portraits. It was the real love of her life.

Concurrent with my visit, her nurse showed me a short article published within the prior week in a Charleston magazine. It focused upon her only

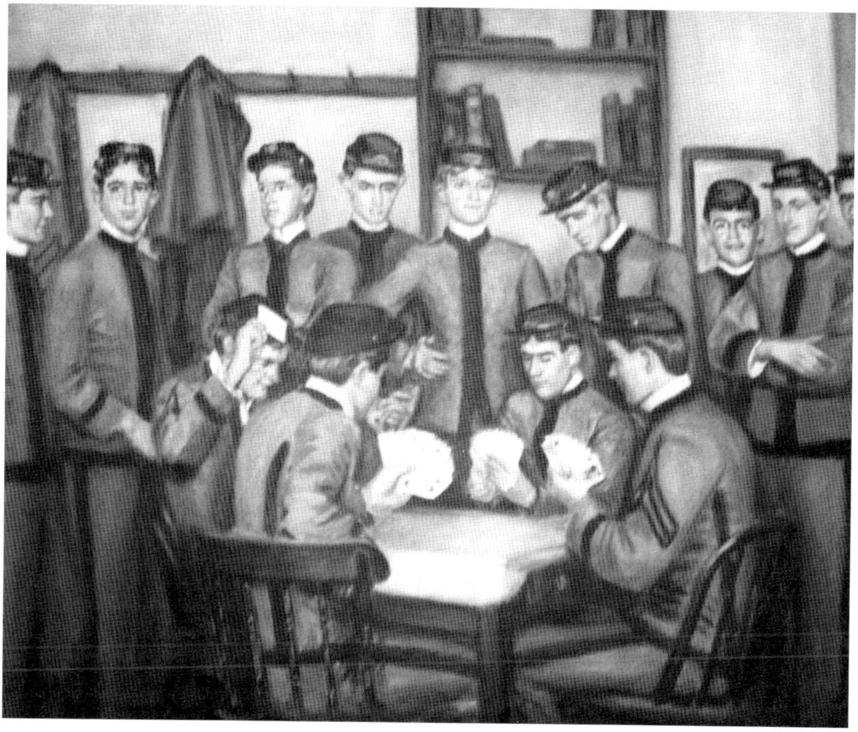

Alicia Rhett, famed as both an actress and a portrait artist, completed a series of paintings that hang at The Citadel's executive offices. *(W. Thomas McQueeney)*

film role ever. The David O. Selznick production started and ended her career—with rave reviews of what became the iconic film of the century. Any century.

She played the role of the sister of Ashley Wilkes. She was India Wilkes, a southern belle with the unfortunate relationships that were doomed to be impaired by the main character, Scarlett O'Hara. Her Charleston upbringing made her character much easier to adopt. She was a de facto genteel southern miss.

She did not become enamored with stardom. It's not that she did not like films. She said she spent nearly a year in California shooting the film.

"Well, didn't you enjoy California?" I asked.

"I enjoyed it immensely. I had the time of my life there," she recalled. "But when the filming ended, I was so happy to come back home."

It was not her comfort zone. She was a stage actress at the Dock Street Theatre, where she was discovered by Hollywood director George Cukor.

She loved the theater. But she was an artist first. She had painted since she was a teenager. She had moved from her Savannah birthplace to her lifelong home, Charleston, after her father's passing. He died during World War I. She hardly knew him.

The artist culture in the Holy City was ingrained and inspirational. She found great solace within her palette.

Only an artist of her caliber could have placed those true-to-life expressions on the faces of those bright-eyed Citadel cadets. One can well see the determination of the cadets in something as simple as a turn-of-the-century card game or a classroom lecture. The paintings show formality, camaraderie, sincerity and joy. Her detail of the scenes included polished shoes and wrinkled dress blouses. It is a view of life not-too-far removed from the South's period of Reconstruction.

Though she could not remember the number of paintings that General Seignious commissioned, she estimated that she had done at least six. In fact, that's all that I could find on campus. Three adorn the facing walls of the president's office waiting area. Another three enhance the Bond Hall expanse that serves as the executive offices. All are inviting views of yesteryear that give the college the ageless rights of tradition.

Alicia Rhett was lauded for her talent as both an actress and artist. Photos of her from the article the nurse gave me showed her to be a stunning beauty. The stated description with it noted her height at five feet, ten inches, and her dark auburn hair. Seeing that her well-coiffed style had changed to a light and curly blonde, she smiled demurely when I mentioned it.

"My hair was always dark and straight," she said as if dismayed by this minor insight. "I could never get the curls I wanted until now. I go to the beauty parlor every other Tuesday and keep my curls fresh."

Her engaging laugh seemed to tell me that she had not been a blonde very long. That laugh accompanies her personal revelations as well as the biographical details she was able to remember. Indeed, she has gorgeous hair that matches her dazzling disposition. She exudes happiness. Her gregarious manner and lofty southern charm came naturally.

She changed the conversation from her hair to her art.

"I liked to paint. It is what made me most happy. I really wasn't interested in making more movies. I was interested in my art," she stated.

When I asked if she remembered what she was paid by The Citadel for the painting series, she could not recall.

"Whatever General Seignious paid you was not enough," I asserted to save her from having to think deeply about something relatively unimportant.

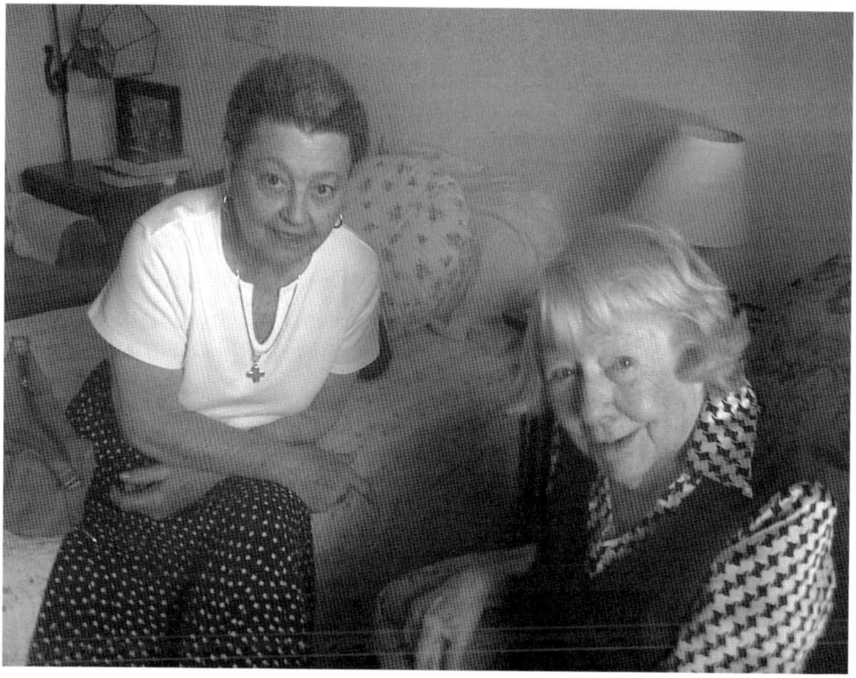

During a visit of fellow charter members of the Charleston Artist Guild, Charlotte McQueeney and Alicia Rhett exchange memories. *(W. Thomas McQueeney)*

"Those paintings are heirlooms. There is no price that is too much."

She let me hear that endearing laugh over and over. No wonder people enjoy seeing her, I thought. She is exquisite.

"Miss Rhett, I see in this article that your birthday was in February," I said with a smile.

"Yes, that's right," she said confidently.

"Well, I have to candidly ask you if you mind telling me how old you are now?" I said, aware that had she been twenty years younger, she would not likely answer at all.

"I have no idea," she answered quickly.

"She's ninety-six," the nurse stated with expected pride.

"Really?" Miss Rhett interjected in a rising voice, as if it just occurred to her. She turned to the nurse.

"That great!" she concluded triumphantly.

That is great. She is a celebrated and stately treasure of the art world, the film industry and our great city of Charleston.

to the emergency situation that now faced me. I needed to have the most unusual of circumstances—Veeck available on the other end of a charged cell phone taking a call from someone he vaguely knew on the evening that might have his Charleston RiverDogs team playing a home game. If the team was away, then I would need to beg him away from his family. That would be the tallest of all tall orders.

You see, Veeck's family is his greatest achievement, his highest high and the most precious of all of his fantastic relationships. There is his wife, Libby, whom he considers the smartest person on the planet. Then there's the son he nicknamed "Night Train," and it stuck. He does not like to be called by his birth-certificate name, William. And then there is his lovely daughter, Rebecca. Rebecca has a degenerative eye disease and is the focus of her proud father's everyday life. He would give up his own vision for Rebecca.

So I am not exactly sure why I had the idiot notion to call Mike Veeck in any circumstance. But I did.

I'm sure he read the panic of my fast and disjointed words from the airport. He had every right to kindly thank me for the "opportunity" to speak unprepared in an hour's time and then go on doing what he had planned to do that evening after hanging up. He didn't do that.

Instead, Veeck showed up at the Hibernian Society that evening fresh and poised. He had no notes. He had the place rolling for a good ten minutes with his witticisms, natural mannerisms and even comic self-deprecation. You could not find that much humor in ten minutes in the best comedy clubs of Los Angeles—and they do it in the desperation of making a living. Veeck did it for a favor.

He then took just a few minutes to reflect upon the value of friendship.

"You guys have something here that you may not fully appreciate," Veeck stated in somber tones. "Friendship is something often taken for granted, understated and underacknowledged. You belong. You have common interests and common goals. You laugh together and depend upon each other for many reasons other than business. I leave you with this thought: 'Cherish your friends, and be a friend to those you cherish.'"

You could have heard the proverbial pin drop. He had struck a chord. There was a short hesitation and then a standing ovation.

The night, in which I was to have been responsible for the embarrassment and accompanying disaster of a speaker no-show, turned into my finest hour. It was all because of Mike Veeck.

I had been veecked.

I'm betting I was not the very first person on earth to benefit from Mike Veeck. There had to be legions before me. These unsuspecting beneficiaries lived in Cleveland and Chicago, Detroit and Charleston—with many addresses in between. Now that electronic information is internationally accessible, it will just be a matter of time before the verb "veeck" makes the Merriam-Webster dictionary. There is probably a website already somewhere in cyberspace.

After all, the gene pool is terrific. Mike Veeck is one of the nine little Veecks that were imbued with the brilliant humor and genius creativity of the "Prime Veeck," their father. Bill Veeck is featured in a display in Cooperstown, New York.[13] He was on display for many years before that glassed-in exhibit was deservedly accorded. The National Baseball Hall of Fame only has the official information. Son Mike can give you an exponential biography on this legendary man whom he held in the highest admiration as a father. The other stuff was gravy. As a father, Bill Veeck batted one thousand and hit as many home runs. There's a bigger and better hall of fame for that.

When Mike Veeck selflessly showed up at the Hibernian that evening, he told me something about himself. He cares.

Within months, one of his staff marketers asked me to consider partnering with the RiverDogs for a baseball off-season fundraiser. The "Hot Stove Banquet" was a fledgling enterprise. They would bring in a baseball speaker and use the proceeds to benefit both MUSC's Storm Eye Institute and The Citadel. That combination interested me, since my Citadel affiliation was more than passive and I saw great value in assisting the Storm Eye Institute. I signed up.

That package included several personal benefits I was not aware of at the signing. Veeck and his marketing manager, Melissa McCants Acevedo, had no way of knowing that they had mined a baseball junkie. I had grown up with a voracious appetite for everything baseball. Veeck was feeding me even more.

The first year, I was able to play golf with RiverDogs general manager Dave Echols (a fine gentleman in his own right) and then Atlanta Braves right fielder Jeff Francoeur. I would have paid the asking price for this wonderful January afternoon on the Ocean Course at Kiawah alone. It was too much fun to describe, lest the reader drool upon this book. The next year could not go even better, could it?

Baseball Hall of Famer and two-time Cy Young Award–winner Gaylord Perry was the featured Hot Stove speaker. We had lunch. The weather was poor. Yet we got to know one another that day at the ballpark. He spoke that night. What happened next is inexplicable. He left, and I never thought I'd have the honor of meeting him again.

In March of that year, Gaylord Perry called me to talk about fishing. I invited him to come to a lodge house on a lake in Gaston, South Carolina, owned by my brother and myself. I had no idea that he would want to come. Besides, I was fifty-seven and had never been fishing in my life. He came anyway. We took my brother and his wife to dinner and started fishing at 6:30 the next morning. I caught fourteen bass and a crappie. He caught thirty-two bass. I never considered he might be a show-off.

Perry was genuine and a tremendous storyteller. I will never forget the unique experience of fishing with Gaylord Perry. In time, he mailed me a box full of North Carolina apples. I figured the postage on the box cost more than the market value of the apples. But that's not the point. He sent them out of friendship. We have been in touch several times since. This association would not have happened without Mike Veeck.

The next two years included lifetime highlights as well.

Former Atlanta Braves great Dale Murphy proved to be every bit the person everyone in the press lauded him to be. He was particularly funny as well. When I can find time to relax, I paint scenery with both oils and acrylics. Had I spent many more years trying to be an artist, I would, no doubt, reach the level of "amateur of little note." But I do it because I enjoy it. Murphy has one of my downtown Charleston scenes in his Utah home.

In January of 2011, Veeck brought in recently retired Atlanta Braves manager Bobby Cox. Nearly seven hundred people showed up to the Hot Stove Banquet. I had lunch with the venerable skipper and even visited the mayor for an hour of baseball stories. Joe Riley was a Brooklyn Dodgers fan and still owns much of the Dodgers paraphernalia. He and Cox traded wonderful stories—along with Veeck's close personal friend, comedian Bill Murray. I need not mention to Veeck that the entry-level sponsorship Melissa sold to me a few years back is now dated and too low for the benefits. He already knows that.

Veeck is old school. A friend is a friend. I had signed on at a level he suggested, and he could have sold that sponsorship many times over for much more money since then. I had been waiting on the call for a price increase. It never came. The best marketing genius I had ever met would not up the price to the new market level because, well, he says I was there for him when he needed a sponsor. Yes, I finally asked him. Amazing. In major league baseball today, a player will arbitrate a $100 million contract because the market moved and he can now get $150 million. Mike Veeck is an owner. He respects friendship well above and beyond any amount of money.

In this way, you could again assume that I have been veecked.

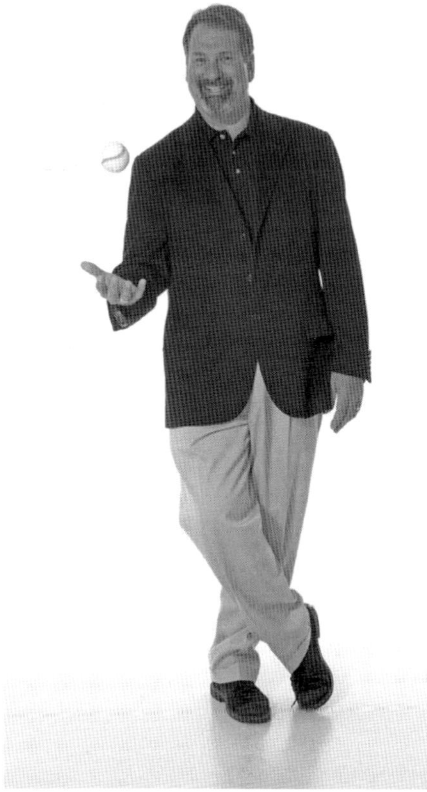

An entrepreneur in every sense, Mike Veeck has been the major innovator of minor league baseball promotion. *(Courtesy of the Charleston RiverDogs)*

Veeck came to Charleston as a duty. It was part of his makeup to travel from city to city to reinvigorate some degree of dormancy in the confines of a ballpark. Charleston was different. Though Marvin Goldklang, a franchisee who owned six ball clubs, wanted Veeck to do his magic in Charleston, Libby Veeck was trying to find the solace of a permanent home. It was 1996, and Joseph P. Riley Jr. Park was being built as one of the finest minor league baseball venues in America. Veeck would have much input. There would be indoor-outdoor luxury suites to enjoy the prevalent southeasterly breezes from the Ashley River. There would be a picnic pavilion, comfortable chair-back seats, updated vending and one of the most dramatic ballpark views anywhere. In baseball parlance, Charleston was being anointed.

It was Veeck's initial entry into Charleston that sold him on wife Libby's position. They had packed boxes every few years since their marriage. They drove downtown to look around. They saw the fine preserved buildings, the nice restaurants and even a few horse-drawn carriages carrying tourists. It was near the College of Charleston that they noticed the hand-in-hand stroll of a mixed-race couple. They could see the comfort this young couple had and immediately decided that if ever there were a place where everyone is welcome, it must be Charleston.

Their initial impression never changed.

"You can talk about the history or the buildings or the beaches, but what Charleston has above all others is its people," Veeck said. "You can find no place friendlier. They grow great smiles and attitudes here. This is home, and I'm proud to be a part of Charleston. It fits me.

"I once said they could scatter my ashes at the old Pitt Street Bridge (in the Old Village of Mount Pleasant)," Veeck continued. "I can think of no place more beautiful."

Ironically, it was not initially what Veeck had expected.

"Some had warned me that I wouldn't be accepted here," Veeck added. "Are you kidding me? I have never once felt like an outsider. Yet, Charleston is still a well-kept secret."

It is no small circumstance that his great friend, Bill Murray, followed.

Murray is in high demand but will work his schedule to spend time with the Veecks whenever possible. It's all about friendship. He must have been veecked, too.

It is in Charleston that Veeck gained national headlines for his one-of-a-kind promotional ventures. The Charleston RiverDogs hosted events like "Vasectomy Night," "Nobody Night" and "Nuns Giving Backrubs Night." His wildly successful promotions are now the rule and not the exception. He has merited the Holy Grail of the sporting world—ESPN SportsCenter. There is a growing generation that may not have yet studied the great Bill Veeck. But they know of Mike Veeck.

Bill Veeck is a daily inspiration to Mike Veeck.

"My mother and father were both joyous people. My father died broke. Nobody remembers that, because he never showed any sadness. He was happy every day of his life," Veeck recalled. "Do you know how special that is? He made everyone around him happy, too."

Could it be that the first Veeck veecked the second Veeck?

Mike Veeck is about fun. His book, *Fun Is Good*, tells it all. I wear a "Fun Is Good" hat to play golf now, thanks to Mike Veeck.

The Veeckian philosophy is exposed—as if you didn't grasp it upon first meeting its naturally gregarious promoter. Veeck penned this delightful book, infusing the rollicking experiences of his upbeat life along with insights into corporate enhancement principles—and all becomes relative to the endearing title. Indeed, fun is good. The book zoomed to bookshelves well beyond Charleston. In it, Veeck brings the reader inside the mind of effective marketing by the hiring and motivation of fun people. He even teaches this buoyant philosophy as an adjunct professor of sports science at The Citadel. His classes stay full.

The book has become a syllabus outside of Veeck's sphere. It is used by teachers and librarians as well as physicians and nurses. Corporations you would recognize on stock tickers have applied its basic tenets of making the workplace productive by making work, well, fun!

Veeck tells of the letter he received from the Oak Park, Illinois, police department.

"They sent a T-shirt to me with a picture of a house with hundreds of bullet holes. The caption underneath said, 'Our day begins when your day ends,'" Veeck said with a laugh. "The other T-shirt had an even funnier caption with the same picture—'We don't drive by—we stay!'"

By invitation, I had the privilege to attend a RiverDogs marketing meeting at Riley Park a couple of years ago. It was different than any marketing meeting I've ever seen. You were expected to come with ideas and applaud or ridicule others, all in a sense of fun. It was a most productive experience of cooperation. I offered an attendance booster idea—"Good Neighbor Night"—which would be on four Monday night home games. The premise offered was to get a neighbor couple in free with the match of proximity addresses on a driver's license. They actually used the idea. There is no telling how much money I have cost Mike Veeck.

Veeck is trying to boost attendance over three consecutive years by one thousand fans so that Charleston can attract the next logical step—AA baseball. This next rung of the ladder is close. At opening night on April 15, 2011, I was a guest of Dave Echols and witnessed a packed house of 7,011 fans as the RiverDogs beat the Rome Braves in extra innings. The game featured a Mayor Riley first pitch caught by the ever-accompanying Bill Murray. There were sumo wrestlers and "midget races" between innings. A trained yellow Labrador retriever served as home-team batboy. That dog won over the entire crowd.

With all of his experiences, Veeck has been most impressed by those people who are genuine and loyal and who exhibit a like sense of humor—much as his father did. I could not help but think about my own father when Veeck tenderly reflected what his father had meant to him. My father—my best friend—had passed away a week earlier. Veeck's had died fifteen years earlier. Yet you could well see that Bill Veeck was a part of everyday Mike Veeck. We honor our fathers by living out their expectations of us. My dad, an old Boston Braves fan, would have been quite honored to have met Bill Veeck. Dad imbued me with a love of baseball.

Mike Veeck has lofty precepts for his circle of close friends. They have to be real people with a real zest for life. He's met many along the way.

Southern Gentleman

Judge Sol Blatt Jr.

Growing up in Barnwell County during the Great Depression and World War II left an impression. Sol Blatt Jr. was the son of arguably the most powerful elected official in South Carolina. His father ran the state as the Speaker of the South Carolina House. Sol Blatt Sr. served that position as Speaker for more than thirty years over two terms (1937–46 and 1951–73).[15]

South Carolina remains an anomaly among the fifty states as the one with perhaps the weakest executive powers. The governor has limited authority. Instead, the House Speaker and Senate president pro tempore wield the most power and influence over state law, spending and capital projects.

The senior Blatt was the son of Jewish Russian immigrants who settled in Blackville, South Carolina, a small town in Barnwell County. Over time, with the rise of other personalities from this small and charming county, Barnwell became the center of South Carolina Democratic politics.

"My father mentored me to become a public servant and to be a good lawyer," Blatt recalled in humility. "His aim for me was not necessarily the result."

Ostensibly, it may be that the plans his father had for him were well exceeded. Sol Blatt Jr. is the senior acting United States District Court judge in South Carolina. The main courtroom is named in his honor. To say that he is active would be an understatement. Normally, a federal judge would retire from the bench around the age of seventy. Judge Blatt nears ninety at the time of this writing. His daily habits, along with his routine of exercise and healthy diet, would predict his retirement to be at about age 145. He is an amazing man from every conceivable viewpoint.

Senior status for federal court judges allows a reduced role should the age and years of service add to eighty. For instance, a judge with fifteen years on the bench who has attained the age of sixty-five would be eligible to move to senior status. It is notable that senior-status judges try 15 percent of all federal court cases. Judge Solomon Blatt Jr. prides himself in his syncopation of work activity, regardless of senior status.

"Trying criminal cases takes a lot of study and energy. Some of these cases would make you cry, but I do my best to pursue justice and the protection of society," Blatt explained. "The victims you never hear about are the families of the criminals. You do have to feel more for them than you do for the criminal; in so many cases, the criminal doesn't care, but their family is devastated."

He stays quite active in trying cases. It is his life's work. But it is not his life. He separates it.

Indeed, another senior-status judge tries to keep up with him. Judge Michael Duffy has been on the federal bench working next to this paragon of social justice for nearly sixteen years.

"Judge Blatt is an example to all judges, because he is the embodiment of the most important attributes a judge should have. He is a gentleman in the truest sense of the word—so he has a great judicial temperament. He is bright, industrious and energetic—so that he is always prepared. He is kind and open—so that every person is given a full hearing. He grew up on the knee of power—so he knows the best use of unquestioned power is not to exercise it. He is the reason that federal judges in South Carolina are among the most collegial in the nation," Judge Duffy asserted. "I love him, and I am grateful to be his friend."

President Richard M. Nixon appointed Blatt to the United States District Court in Charleston in 1971. He is celebrating his fortieth year on the bench. Accepting the role in Charleston meant leaving his beloved Barnwell home. He was fifty years old when he left.

"We always thought the world of Charleston. Carolyn and I felt that we had really found the perfect place to live, though leaving Barnwell and so many friends there was most difficult. The people of Charleston stepped forward and took in a country couple," Blatt recalled in a jovial sense. "As we became more established here, our friendships grew. There is no better place than Charleston."

Blatt married the former Carolyn Gayden in 1942. Carolyn Blatt passed away in 2004. She was the love of his life. They met when she was at the

University of South Carolina in Columbia. Their three children, Greg, Sherry and Brian, are all productive in their respective communities. Their closeness of family life remains evident. Even so, it is apparent that the judge misses Carolyn deeply.

"She was a great influence on my life, but I really didn't realize how much bigger her role was until after she passed," Blatt reflected. "She did all of the little things. She was a tremendous mother, and she was my friend when I came home. Our children benefitted from her more than I realized. None of them ever gave us problems like you see today—alcohol and drugs."

His touching tribute to his late wife brought on a pause of silence. He was resolute in his feelings and admitted his difficult adjustment in making it on his own after her death.

The silence was broken by a call into his office from the tall and imposing bailiff I met upon entering his chamber. Jason, the bailiff, had gone downtown to a grocer and wanted to know if the judge wanted him to pick up something for his supper.

"Can you get me a small piece of salmon with the skin on one side?" Blatt asked on the phone.

The conversation returned to influences he extolled as guiding forces in his younger life.

"Frankie DeMars was the boxing coach at the University of South Carolina. He preached that everything gained in life that was worthwhile came from work ethic. I never forgot the lesson. He was a character builder, a motivator and a man that fostered growth in each individual person," Blatt stated. "He taught me much more than boxing."

He must have taught him boxing pretty well, too. Sol Blatt became the 135-pound champion boxer of the old Southern Conference of the late 1930s. That foundation conference included the University of North Carolina, LSU, Florida, Clemson, Duke, Maryland, North Carolina State and The Citadel, among others.

Blatt had learned boxing from a former USC boxer, Red Watts, who coached a youth team in Barnwell. Blatt also played football, baseball and basketball in high school. But his first love was boxing. He was also fortunate to have come to the University of South Carolina under the tutelage of Coach Frankie DeMars.

"I was young and confident of what Coach DeMars taught me. I felt I could compete with anyone," Blatt recalled.

"There was a time that I found that I was a little too confident as well. We had a fine boxing team, and we were scheduled to box against Presbyterian

College. They were not at our level but had maybe the best boxer in the country, Frank Sutton, in the 145-pound welterweight class. My good friend, T. Allen Legare, was our welterweight. Sutton had a record of 88-0, all by knockouts. Unfortunately, Allen Legare could not go that week to Presbyterian due to law exams. Stupidly, I told Coach DeMars that I was willing to move up and fight the great Frank Sutton," Blatt remembered. "So we went to the match, me confident that I could dance a little, attack him early and confuse him with a very aggressive strategy.

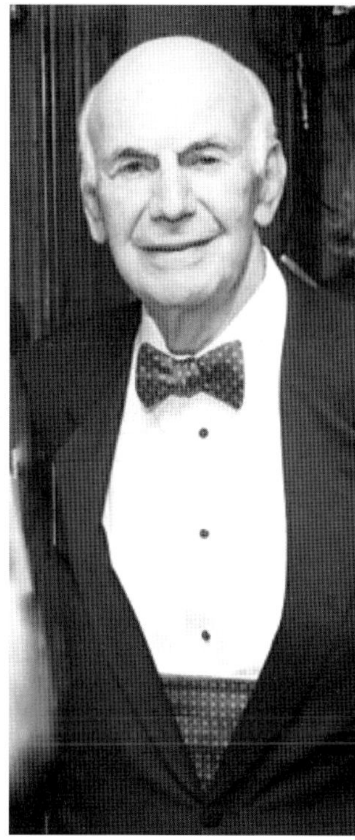

Ever dapper, Judge Sol Blatt Jr. has served the federal bench in Charleston since 1970. *(F. Ritchie McQueeney)*

"Well, Sutton was a much better fighter than I imagined. I got a few punches in, and just as I thought I was doing well, he flattened me. I wobbled and got up, but my corner could see I was dazed. They threw in the towel. It only took Sutton fifty-eight seconds to go to 89-0!" Blatt continued. "I became friends later with Frank Sutton. I suppose his fighting career ended like everyone else's—because of the war."

The story lingered on for decades, but Blatt was unaware of the residual effect. By happenstance, Blatt's boxing teammate and dear friend, T. Allen Legare, became a fine Charleston attorney.

"Allen had a case that came to my court in the late 1970s, as I recall. It was a dispute about a right-of-way or an easement of some sort that made it to a federal hearing. After considering all of the facts and evidence, I ruled against Allen's client," Blatt resumed. "And I didn't think anything of it until a mutual friend, John West (former South Carolina governor John C. West) called and told me that Allen was upset with me. As John related, Allen had blamed the case loss on him not showing up to fight Frank Sutton forty years earlier! I laughed, because I had forgotten all about that.

"But John went on to describe what Allen said. He berated me for holding a forty-year grudge. So I called Allen to set the record straight and to let him know that I had volunteered to Coach DeMars to fight Sutton back then because my ego at that time was to become the first guy to beat Sutton. Allen thought Coach DeMars ordered me to fight Sutton and that I was angry with Allen for not showing. After a few laughs and the explanation of what happened, all was right again."

Indeed, T. Allen Legare was one of Blatt's very best lifelong friends. Legare, a Charlestonian, had served as a state senator performing a pivotal role in the growth of the State Ports Authority and the Medical University of South Carolina. He had played football and boxed at the University of South Carolina before becoming a World War II hero by parachuting behind enemy lines twenty-nine times. He was well decorated and well admired. Legare died in 2010.

"Allen was a dear friend and a man I always respected. He could get things done in Columbia as a legislator, and he was a fine lawyer," Blatt reminisced.

That generation that produced former governor John C. West, T. Allen Legare and Sol Blatt Jr. is passing from history all too fast. Judge Blatt emerges from the era in great physical and mental form. He is witty, affable and perceptive. He has a wide circle of friends and a deep reverence within the hallways of the 1896 federal court building that accentuates the Four Corners of Law. He hears the bells of St. Michael's Episcopal Church on the quarter hour. He busies himself in his reading and his daily routines. There has to be a secret to his life that permits his exceptional demeanor, physique and acuity.

"The good Lord blessed me. I work out. I eat properly and—this is important—I have friends. Close friends," he counseled. "You cannot make it without friends. I really don't dislike anybody. You just can't carry hatred. Getting upset damages you more than you know. It is just as tough sentencing now as it was forty years ago. You have to separate it from your real life outside of the chambers."

Blatt explained that the federal sentencing guidelines had cycled over the forty years. There was ample room for consideration, then no flexibility, and now a little more leeway in the guidelines.

"It went from total discretion to no discretion to some discretion. There is so much to consider in every case. I have not seen any two the same," he noted. "But all of them have things in common. A sentence is given because a law is broken and there is injury to a victim or to society as a whole. It is a mighty serious situation."

Judge Blatt still has an affinity for outdoor activities. He has been an avid golfer and a fine fisherman. He would sometimes drive up to the Columbia area and meet son Brian at his Gaston fishing lodge on a weekday afternoon. The judge loves to fish for bass and bream.

"That's a fine spot. Great fishing and a comfortable setting," Blatt pointed out. "There's another spot I discovered a few years ago up near McClellanville. The fish are a little bigger. I hesitate to tell anyone where it is, because the owner lets me on as a favor, and I wouldn't want to betray his trust.

"I find that everybody wants fish brought to them if they are already cleaned. So, I fish for a few and clean a few and give away a few," the judge revealed. "I never take more than I'm prepared to eat or give to friends fully cleaned. I've fished on that basis for decades."

It seems he's done much more than fishing over the decades. He has watched much that has been static and much that has changed.

"Charleston has changed over my forty years here. As good as it was, it is even better now. What has changed Charleston the most are the visitors. If you drive down Meeting Street, you might see a hundred people waiting outside of Hyman's Seafood. There are other restaurants and businesses that have a great visitor following as well. The economic climate has improved immeasurably. I ascribe Charleston's rise mostly to the mayor, Joe Riley. He's done a great job. What he starts, he finishes. Give him the credit," Blatt recounted. "And many of those visitors come back to live here. The new move-in Charlestonians have added so much. They have expanded our culture, improved our education and built our businesses. We often overlook those who have come here and made us an even better place."

One is likely to champion the life of Solomon Blatt Jr. in that same sentiment.

Sol Blatt Jr. died at his home in Charleston at the age of ninety-four in April 2016. He had diligently appeared at his office daily and made his "rounds" visiting friends and associates within his routine up until his last brief illness. The visitation at the Charleston Federal Building was truly a celebration of this well-meaning adjudicator's lifetime. The funeral service was held at the Church of the Holy Apostles in his hometown of Barnwell.

Among his considerable accomplishments, Blatt navigated the complicated bankruptcy hearings of Hilton Head Island in the 1970s. His forthright and decisive action saved the island from what would have been a catastrophic outcome.

Blatt's forty-five years at the bench guaranteed him status as the longest-serving federal judge in the history of South Carolina.

By Any Other Name

JAMES B. EDWARDS

If he is anyone to be defined down to his basic principles, it is quite evident that he is a gentleman. He's a gentleman's gentleman at that. He is bold, but tempered; academic, but grounded; deeply convicted, but considerate of others. He does not command the spotlight, yet he is most engaging and personable. It is no wonder that this fine man is one of the most respected personas to ever grace the community. Very few of those in his periphery even know how to address this gentle man of many experiences. A simple "mister" does not fit.

Jim Edwards has made a footprint in Charleston, in South Carolina and in the South. In time, he became a nationally recognized figure. All of these places changed because of Jim Edwards. His impact is like his personality—broad, meaningful and profound. It is why people line up to shake his hand in public places. He is the man you want to know and about whom you will tell your grandchildren.

No one Charlestonian may have evoked more confusion over the properness of the title that heralds his formal name than James B. Edwards. His profession as an accomplished oral surgeon has earned him the title of "doctor," the name I called him these many years. He was the dentist I regarded with great disdain as a child—as much as any child may have experienced the fear of drills and needles and dentistry. His political rise started as the chairman of the Charleston County Republican Party. He was "Mr. Chairman" to a fledgling organization that many thought had no prospects in 1960s Charleston. His prowess as chairman gave him an avenue for other formal salutations. He became "Senator Edwards" to the state legislature in Columbia, South Carolina. He was an upset winner for the first time over the presumption of another in a succession of Democratic wins. He had more in store. His second upset win was when he became "Governor Edwards," the first Republican governor of South Carolina in one hundred years. That news made regional and national headlines. The Democrats had the inside track in the Deep South—especially just after President Richard Nixon's Watergate fiasco. After serving as governor, he was selected by President Ronald Reagan to fill the cabinet position of secretary of energy. Washington staffers and others addressed him as "Mr. Secretary," whilst the folks back home were still dithering over "governor," "doctor," and even "chairman." Yet his longest titled position was as "President Edwards," a seventeen-year stint that led the largest teaching hospital in South Carolina. MUSC president James B. Edwards was the steward who brought that hospital to the twenty-first century. He still has an office there.

The emeritus status he earned at the Medical University of South Carolina could have been for other merit than his guidance of this major regional health institution. He helped to grow the Health Sciences Foundation into the new MUSC Foundation. His personal office is in that foundation suite on Calhoun Street. It was here that he and I met and chatted for an hour. Upon leaving, this paragon of deep southern sensibilities insisted that I use a completely different moniker than the surplus of those that he had earned in a lifetime of unparalleled Charleston-based success.

"I prefer that my friends use the name my mother gave me Jim."

It may take me quite a while to get used to calling this great man by his mother's favorite name. I secretly hope that I get to do so in front of someone I want to impress. Jim Edwards is a living legend.

I may think of him from now on as "Gentleman Jim Edwards." It certainly describes him. He is confident and secure in his judgments. He is wise but modest in his sense of self. In June of 2011, he turned eighty-four years of age. Yet he has a routine of MUSC Foundation duties and a modicum of work he performs on his farm near Huger, South Carolina, that keeps the "R" word at bay. He is not retired.

His wife, Ann, is his constant. She has been there for him during his highly successful career over the past fifty-nine years. She is the computer address for his emails. She is the cute girl he first met when they were preteens in Mount Pleasant, South Carolina. They are together, it seems, even when they are apart. Upon seeing Ann the following evening at a formal function, she dazzled by his side. She is petite, spirited and charming. The first part of her email address introduces her personality—"objoyful!"

Jim Edwards is the trailblazer of South Carolina politics. He doesn't call attention to the sense of his early convictions other than noting that it happened in a reasonable progression.

"There were others that were a part of it, including my good friend Arthur Ravenel," Edwards deferred. "And a few more, but there weren't many of us."

Together they edified the flagging Charleston Republican Party, a group that routinely finished second in every election cycle. Their prospects were dim, but their leadership was changing and their fortunes, in time, rose. They took their cue from an unlikely source who had no plans to even enter politics.

Edwards had recently negotiated a deal to add onto a newly constructed dental office belonging to his good friends Dr. Bernard Ray and Dr. Charlie Fabian. The office was a half block down Gadsden Street from MUSC. With his outstanding educational background as an oral surgeon, he was sure to grow a large and productive practice. Edwards had received his dental degree from the University of Louisville and an advanced degree from the University of Pennsylvania Dental School.

He was a young family man, comfortable in his lifestyle and building a meaningful professional career. It was 1964. So why did he risk it all?

"I know it sounds corny, but it was what it was. We had young children, and I had started my dental practice in the early 1960s," he explained. "I was concerned about world events—especially the rise of Communism in Europe and even in Cuba. I read books on the subject to understand why we should fear the Communists infecting America. It was a truly serious threat."

Indeed, Edwards cited books by Vladimir Lenin and Karl Marx that got his attention. He found it startling. It was during this time that someone recommended that he read another book, *The Conscience of a Conservative*. The 1964 Republican presidential candidate, Senator Barry Goldwater, wrote the book. Senator Goldwater was—politically—ahead of his time. The retrospective insights of that book placed this failed candidate into the arena of this country's finest political thinkers.

"I couldn't put the book down. He had all of the practical answers for society. Yet he lost the election to Lyndon Johnson," Edwards continued. "It was then that I started weighing whether I wanted to become a success as a dentist to protect my family's financial future or become active in the Republican Party to—in my mind—turn this country away from Communism. There were many other concerns that bothered me beyond Communism, to be sure."

He chose the latter course.

"I had a friend that asked me to go to a precinct meeting. I said I'd go, but I had to ask him, 'What's a precinct?'" Edwards remembered laughingly. "I attended during the Goldwater campaign, and it was announced that every precinct would have to raise $1,500 to support Senator Goldwater—$1,500 was a tall order for a small group of hopeful Republicans in a heavily Democratic precinct."

It was in the discussion of how to raise the money that the hesitant Edwards raised his hand. It could be said that his raised hand changed his life.

"I asked them to consider having a barbeque cookout at Alhambra Hall at ten dollars a head and donations. Since no one had a better suggestion, we planned a barbeque. More people showed up than we had food. We had to make several trips to the store to keep feeding the crowd. We sold water in bottles labeled 'AU-H20' for 'Goldwater' for as much as ten dollars!" Edwards recalled. "We stayed up at my house until two in the morning counting the money. We had raised nearly $15,000 in our effort to raise $1,500! We were amazed at the support for a conservative candidate in the Charleston area. It was not expected back during those times."

Owing to this success, even though the election did not produce Senator Goldwater as the new president, Edwards became a known commodity. In time, he was approached for something bigger than a barbeque.

"A few of the fellas from that barbeque experience asked if they could meet with me. It was a number of months later. I met seven gentlemen after finishing with my final dental patient at my office on Gadsden Street. It was at about 6:30 p.m. They came in and sat down. They asked me to serve as the Charleston County Republican chairman. I was caught completely off guard. I had not expected such a big role so quickly and was not prepared to answer them. I thought that accepting that role would divide my patients and ruin my young dental career. I told them that I would discuss it with Ann and get back with them," Edwards stated. "It was time to make the biggest decision of my career.

"After talking with my wife and thinking about what was more important—my dental practice or defending my children from

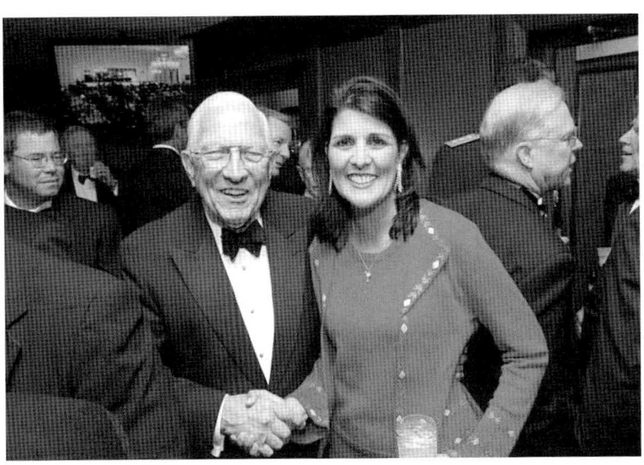

James B. Edwards, the first Republican governor of South Carolina since Reconstruction, and Governor Nikki Haley, the current governor, also a Republican. *(Courtesy of the Hibernian Society of Charleston)*

Communism, the slow progress of socialism and the other political evils I had come to be so concerned with—I consented to accepting the role," Edwards said confidently. "My worries about my practice were never realized. I was not aware that I ever lost a patient. I took the chairman role seriously and tried to build a strong base of others that had the same political views I espoused."

In time, those views were to be heard publicly. In late December of 1970, the very popular Democratic First District congressman from South Carolina, L. Mendel Rivers, died. He had been in office for thirty years. Rivers was the current chairman of the powerful House Armed Services Committee and, as such, was responsible for many federal benefits finding their way to Charleston from Washington, D.C. A special election would replace him. In a heated battle, Rivers's nephew and staffer, Mendel J. Davis, narrowly won the seat over the political newcomer, James B. Edwards. Eyebrows were raised. The Republican had almost won. In the process, Edwards appealed to many crossover voters. His common-sense approach, calm demeanor and academic insights made their mark. He was more than viable. He was a force.

Two years later, Edwards placed his name into a contest for the South Carolina Senate. The voters remembered the eloquent gentleman with the mindset of practicality. Edwards won a seat held by Democrats for decades, and he quietly had his first political victory. Many thought it to be just an aberration. Jim and Ann Edwards did not feel that way. In two years, Jim felt strong enough in his convictions to challenge in the statewide gubernatorial race. Few took his challenge seriously, because he was still a relative unknown, and the well-worn names in print of those times were also "in the hat." Though—as was previously mentioned—there had not been a Republican governor in South Carolina since the control of a Union Army selected one in 1874, Edwards saw the opportunity to express his ideology to others. The crowds grew. He would have to upset an accomplished military man, General William C. Westmoreland, just to win the primary. Westmoreland's name recognition was not only statewide but national. Undaunted, Edwards persevered and won the earnest following of the Republican Party statewide. He had—to the surprise of many—vaulted ahead of the Vietnam-era general. But Republicans were, by far, the minority party of 1974 South Carolina politics.

"So many thought that I would be the next footnote to a Democratic landslide, but Ann and I never felt that way. We spoke to enthusiastic crowds. We were able to raise money well. We stayed strong on the issues, and we kept our energy up. My team worked hard and never considered finishing second," Edwards asserted. "Our opponent was expected to win, but they had some problems in their own primary. There was every opportunity to win over the voters—and we did."

Jim Edwards would have to take a leave of absence from his dental practice to run the State of South Carolina. He once famously stated that "getting consensus out of the state legislature was like pulling teeth—and I know something about pulling teeth!"

His term of office began in January of 1975. During the next four years, Edwards was successful in several initiatives, some minor but controversial law changes and the establishment of a number of state benefits to tourism and industry. His practical know-how and ability to build coalitions made for considerable progress. He was a much-loved governor. He had given the state the new experience of a pragmatic conservative who had gained tremendous respect from across the aisle. It would be that legacy that benefitted the new Republicans in years to come.

He served with youthful energy and meticulous care. He had the patience and pragmatism to work diligently in winning over the confidence of a Democratic House and Senate. They had a deep respect for Edwards.

That respect rolled forward throughout his career.

Indeed, at the celebration of the formal St. Patrick's Day Banquet at the Hibernian Society Hall in Charleston on March 17, 2011, the venerable governor received a standing ovation. More than eight hundred tuxedoed well-wishers from across the community heard his prepared toast to the United States of America:

> *There is but one guiding light on the shore and it shines the brightest of all.*
> *It is the light of opportunity and justice where people live free.*
> *It is brighter when we inure it with our values, our principles and*
> *Our common national will to provide, protect, educate and prosper.*
> *That light has guided us for 235 years.*
> *It is God's Blessing and it is our Country.*
> *To the United States of America!*

United States Senator Jim DeMint sat near the former governor. He immediately rose to applaud. The other eight hundred attendees joined him in vehement support of everything Edwards had represented to so many for so long. It may not have mattered what the toast said as much as who was saying it. It was the unity and spirit of those joyous souls celebrating this unique gift to our community. The world was right and the future bright because of Jim Edwards. They all knew that.

"I had a warm feeling about things when I experienced the jubilation of the Hibernian Society that night. The audience was very respectful of our first female governor. They gave a standing ovation to Tim Scott, a fine young man just elected as the First District congressman," Edwards revealed. "The people of Charleston should be very proud of where we have arrived. The world is a much better place."

Scott is a minority congressman who was elected in a landslide as a Republican candidate. He is one of only two African American Republicans currently serving in the United States House of Representatives. His rise would not have been even fathomed without the energetic work of Jim Edwards some forty years ago.

"Tim Scott will be a star in Washington," Edwards predicted. "He has the right stuff. He can lead, and he can make great decisions. I like him. Years ago he asked me to send a recommendation letter to his prospective employer. I'm sure it may have helped, but his interview would have clinched that job. He is very impressive."

The approval of Edwards means everything. He proctored other young candidates in local, state and national elections, serving on top-level election committees. Those would include Tim Scott, Jim DeMint, Senator Lindsey Graham, Governor Nikki Haley and even President George W. Bush. Edwards was a part of his national election committee.

When Edwards spent time in Washington as President Reagan's secretary of energy, he crafted several initiatives. Much of our multi-tentacled development of future energy can be traced to Edwards. But Edwards was aware of a chance to follow a dream path and move back to his beloved Charleston. He was offered the role as MUSC president. That role does not open often. After much deliberation, he accepted the role, and that position did not open again until his formal retirement in 1999.

Getting back to Charleston meant getting back to his old friends—people like Arthur Ravenel, Dr. Biemann Othersen and Bernie Puckhaber. With Edwards, these three men were all members of the College of Charleston's class of 1950, a class of less than one hundred students. It still stands as the college's most impressive class.

Ravenel's political life took him to Washington, Columbia and even into local county school board meetings. The highest cable-stayed bridge in the Western Hemisphere is named for him. This eighty-four-year-old Charleston icon has a farm just three miles from the Edwards tract. This jovial statesman is the other bookend in the Edwards-Ravenel matched set.

Dr. Biemann Othersen is one of the most respected pediatric surgeons in the region. He was the first medical director of the MUSC Children's Hospital. Dr. Othersen is every bit the prime mover that seeded the growth of pediatric care in the Charleston area. That eight-story, red brick hospital is his monument. It has been his life.

Bernie Puckhaber was the college's first star athlete as a basketball player. "Pucky" is a stockbroker who still works daily. His community deeds include serving as president of several civic organizations, most notably the Coastal

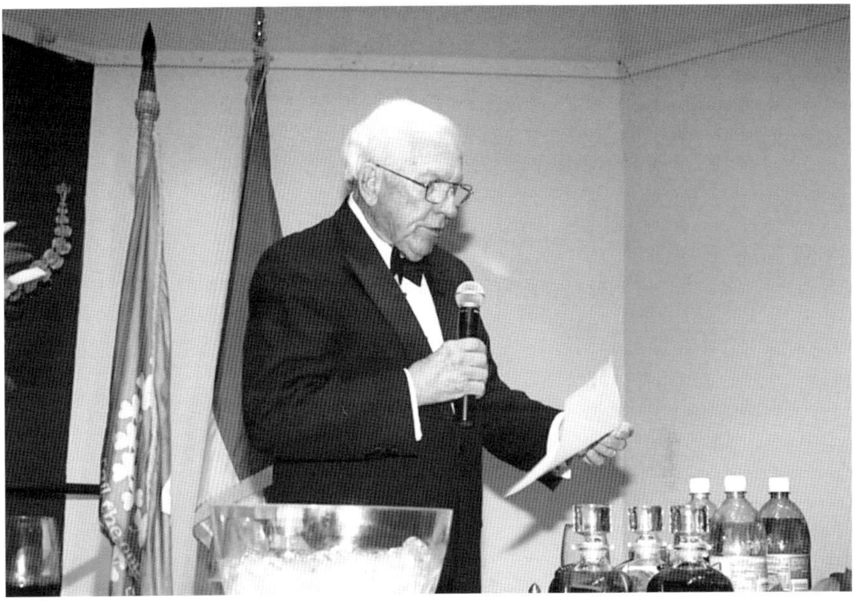

Former South Carolina governor James B. Edwards gives the traditional Hibernian Society of Charleston's St. Patrick's Day Banquet toast to the United States of America. *(Courtesy of the Hibernian Society of Charleston)*

Carolina Fair, an enterprise that now channels more than a half million dollars back into Charleston-area charities every year. Puckhaber is well known for his unique sense of humor and ingenious pranks.

To be sure, the College of Charleston was founded in 1770, when Charleston was under British rule. It was chartered in 1785 as the first municipal college in the new United States of America. Its founders included three signers of the Declaration of Independence. In over two centuries of educating young men and women, there has yet to be any dynamic to equal the level of the graduates of 1950.

Edwards is justly proud of his fellow graduates, not because of their common class year, but because of their long and meaningful friendships.

"We just had our sixtieth reunion. We had a grand time, and it's always great to see Arthur and Bernie exchanging their special humor," Edwards recalled with a knowing smile.

Edwards had many opportunities to assume roles elsewhere but loathed the idea of leaving Charleston.

"I've had real, honest-to-goodness friends here. They are irreplaceable. Charleston has always been in my heart. If home is where the heart is, then my heart is Charleston," Edwards pronounced.

When former South Carolina governor James B. Edwards died the day after Christmas 2014, the Charleston community lost one of its very finest citizens. Thousands lined up at the historic MUSC Chapel of St. Luke's for the ensuing visitation. The 1825 chapel had little room for a crowd of such numbers. The line meandered for blocks, so many within it who had known the former MUSC president and Reagan cabinet appointee personally. It was a rare circumstance to see a solemn multitude gather out of such widespread respect for a man considered universally as a "good friend." Edwards had gained tremendous admiration from diverse people of every background across both the state and the country. Through it all, his wife, Ann Edwards, persevered to thank those who came. She had to be exhausted within the demands of the experience, although she was profoundly wrought with emotion. Jim Edwards was a unique person in every regard.

The funeral services at St. Philip's Church included the attendance of the sitting governor, Nikki Haley, and three former governors—Mark Sanford, Richard Riley and David Beasley. Other dignitaries arrived from across the country. As a seventeen-year president of the Medical University of South Carolina, the medical profession was fully represented as well. Edwards, the affable and confident public servant, had made the difficult post-career transition to trusted friend, philanthropist and confidant. He enjoyed his life, and those around him enjoyed his unassuming yet captivating company.

His sixty-seven-year marriage to wife Ann was storybook. His selfless career was based on his energetic performance in navigating to the goal of whatever institution he led to realize its potential.

Edwards's passing was, in many ways, a microcosm of Charleston's re-inspection of its value system. Here was an iconic hero of the Lowcountry—a dentist, a farmer and a woodcraftsman who stood up against long odds to lead with honor. He had completed many tasks by faith in others, especially those not necessarily politically aligned with him. He reached out.

There will be many Charleston legacies that had origins in the "age of the rise," but few will grow in stature over time like that of James B. Edwards. Like Charleston, he began in meager circumstances and reached a stratum above most. They will know his name in the centuries beyond.

Cliff Poole and Charleston's Last Bombardment

It was on another temperate April morning that a defense was planned. The troops were aligned, and a battle cry was invoked. The attackers were likely to arrive from the North at first and then from every compass point. It would turn out to be the greatest battle of our times.

There was animosity, for sure. Great orators and established authors pondered the visions of mankind. Lawyers shrieked on both sides. Large sums of money intended for other purposes were dispensed upon the emergency. And it was only April.

There are timeless irritations of social norms. The biblical Cain started it all. There were armies we know of now that had fallen from the pages of history like the Saracens, the Picts and even the feared Mongols of Genghis Khan. The world was born of conflict. We have progressed woefully to the wars between bordered nations and theocratic ideologies. Conflict evolved to modernity. Our world now enhances the specter of civil revolts and jihads. It may be because we built trebuchets before we built silos.

In the mid-1990s, Charleston staged the largest conflict of all time. There were three billion combatants on each side. Well, almost…

It was in Charleston that the simple tradition of single-gender education that had accented formal academia for centuries well outside of The Citadel's gates was pitted as an epic confrontation: man versus woman. This public referendum split households.

In the aftermath of the result, it was a man that came forward at the focal institution, The Citadel, to lead the defeated troops to other battles—with the added role of female inclusion, of course.

Brigadier General Roger C. "Cliff" Poole was not your average college president. He did not want to be a college president. He took the job in stilted hesitancy on the basis of a shortened tenure promised to direct a transition. After all, he wanted to get back to his comfort zone—academics administration and the classroom.

The classroom was where this 1959 Citadel graduate and English major taught dollar signs, quantitative decision-making and bottom lines instead of spliced commas and dangling participles.

"I had an affinity for numbers. I was always a numbers guy," Poole divulged. "The English department was a perfect background for the business world. I preach that to my students today. The world is about communication, concepts and the media. All are related to a foundation of the written word. I moved into finance in my postgraduate years and found it to be fast-moving and an everyday challenge."

Poole's impressive background in the academic world is—in the written word—spectacular. He followed his Citadel degree with a master's in business administration in management from the University of South Carolina. His doctorate in finance was attained from the same university in 1974. Poole was commissioned in the Army Reserves and, over a career, rose to his current moniker as General Poole. He even notched another degree from the Army War College in Carlisle, Pennsylvania. He received a postdoctoral certification in international commercial policy finance at the London School of Economics. Wait, there's more! He was certified in the London Business School for the international teachers program. The honors, awards and work experience were every bit as extraordinary.

Poole instructed students at Voorhees College, the University of South Carolina, Virginia Commonwealth University and the University of Richmond before returning home to The Citadel. He served on both business and college trustee boards in multiples. He was invited to join the great national academic societies and to speak at the finer international institutions. He received medals and awards at every step along the way. You would never know it.

His humility is exceeded only by his humor.

Brigadier General Cliff Poole, a logistician, was assigned to the U.S. Army's Operation Center during Desert Shield/Desert Storm in 1991–92. Dr. Cliff Poole lectured and participated in the Oxford Round Table in Cambridge, England, in 1999. It was the same year The Citadel named him the Alumnus of the Year—just after they held a cadet parade to present the

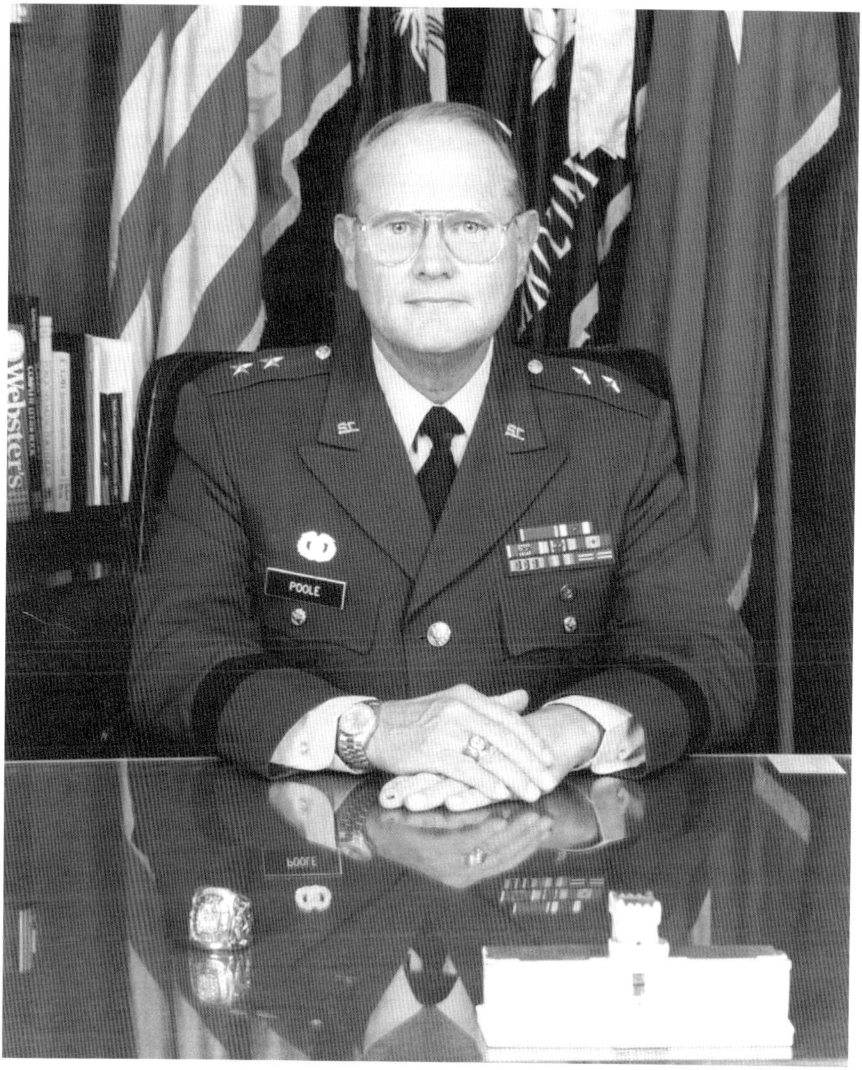

Major General R. Clifton Poole served as both the nineteenth and the twenty-first president of The Citadel on an interim basis. *(Courtesy of The Citadel Archives)*

prestigious Palmetto Medal to Poole, the highest award bestowed upon an individual by The Citadel Board of Visitors.

There is an international award Poole brushes aside. It is officially the Officer's Cross of the Sovereign Order of St. Stanislaus. This distinct honor was bestowed upon Poole for his work in academia and for charitable contributions.

The ever-present conflict of man versus woman will always be. It cannot be resolved at The Citadel, in the justice department or at a bridge tournament. It can only be forestalled by wisdom, meaningful progress and pragmatism.

Should any institution be led professionally by one of humble spirit for an agreed-upon short stint, there exists a great man who will not want to do it. A cagey veteran of the wars, Cliff Poole is in the comfort of his nearby classroom. Indeed, he was called upon again between permanent presidents in 2005 for the fall semester. This time, the next president appeared in a timely manner.

If the life of a man is ennobled by his toil, the forgotten selflessness in the care of others and the magnitude of his resolve in the face of challenge, then the life of General Cliff Poole exceeds the reason of duty. It defines the pursuit of honor.

He is the man that saved The Citadel.

Charleston's Great Hope

Congressman Tim Scott

When Tim Scott met me for lunch perhaps a dozen years ago, we had already known each other. When we met for lunch yesterday, he was still the same sincere and deeply spiritual man I knew before, but now the forecasted "rock star" of Washington politics. We were both older, but nothing else had really changed.

The hint of spring rushed through this windy day in a West Ashley retail center. Scott took what little time he had to devour a salad between a full slate of appointments at his Charleston congressional office on the second floor. He had just been briefed by a Coast Guard admiral on the importance of dredging Charleston's natural harbor—one of the major shipping ports on the East Coast. He had other visitors scheduled and likely waiting for his return from the brief respite of lunch with an old friend. Tim Scott is a very busy man.

Scott has a physical—as well as spiritual—presence. He is built much like a weightlifter, with powerful biceps and forearms. He is solid. Yet the presence and warmth of his friendship exudes. He has care in his stare and the safe domicile of a sheltered smile. This is precisely why he has become Charleston's Great Hope.

In so many ways, one would surmise that Scott is an exception, an aberration or a counterculture public figure. It is very apparent to me—and anyone who is around Scott—that those assessments are bogus. He is the rule, the norm and the reality. This could not be clearer than when he stops to take the time and position his view on a variety of subjects. The sentiments he expresses are pensive theorems collected from a lifetime of doing what is right, leading by example and taking personal responsibility. It is not like he had a choice.

Scott was born on the other side of the tracks—literally. He grew up near the train yards of North Charleston in a single-parent household. His closely proctored upbringing included Sunday church services, healthy team sports and academic pursuit. It helped that Scott was also a formidable athlete in his teen years at R.B. Stall High School. A powerful running back, he received scholarship inquiries from several fine colleges. The timing for a serious ankle injury from a car accident prior to his senior season could not have been worse. He had dreamed of playing at The Citadel under Coach Art Baker so that his mother could easily come to the games. After surgery, returning to his pre-injury status was in question—even though Scott worked out in earnest. College sports being more a business than a purist opportunity for aspiring scholar-athletes, coaches always prefer the safe choice of noninjured prep stars. Scott settled on the best offer he had, from Presbyterian College in Clinton, South Carolina.

It was in his growth to adulthood at Presbyterian College that Scott found great solace in his spirituality. He was always a Christian, but not committed to his beliefs in his everyday life. That changed. He was born again.

Within months, Scott decided to resume his collegiate career at Baptist College of Charleston (now Charleston Southern University). There, he could partake in the humble daily experiences of Christian teachings while completing his academic pursuits. It is there that he decided upon a life of service.

His service is a kaleidoscope. It is overflowing with volumes of brilliant colors in accord with its own patterned motion.

Scott busied himself in his personal service to his faith. He found that all things were possible through his deep and sincere trust in the blessings of his Creator and the sacrifices of God's holy Son, Jesus. His value foundation was well edified. Scott then became active in charitable endeavors to the extent of what his time, talent and limited income could remit. It is in these services to his neighbors, friends and his church congregation that he further developed his interpersonal skills. He took on significant small projects—a homeless family, a medical need for an elderly person and even a high school senior victimized by a tragic auto accident leading to a disability. It was touching to see Scott operate behind the scenes by calling friends and like-minded individuals who cared. He found peace in helping others.

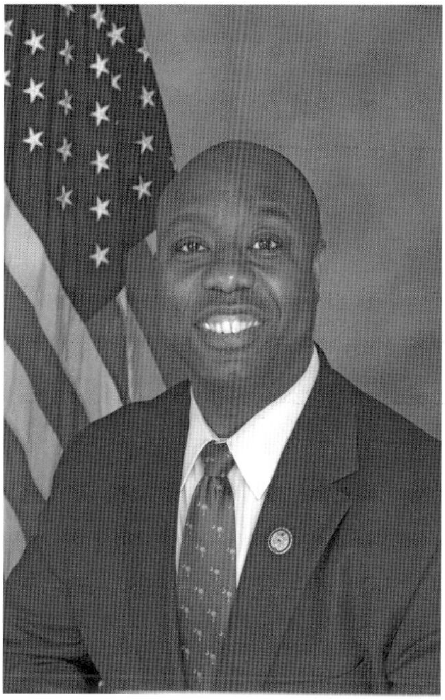

The Honorable Tim Scott serves the people of Charleston as one of only two minority Republicans in the 112th United States Congress. *(Courtesy of the United States Congress)*

Scott gained an affinity for the insurance business and started working in an independent agency environment. During this time, his sense that there were things he could do to improve his community came to the forefront. He was elected to county council in 1995. In doing so, Scott became the first black Republican elected to a countywide seat in South Carolina since Reconstruction.

Scott was later recommended for another fine opportunity in the business world in 1998—ostensibly because of his abilities combined with an established reputation of selflessness within the community. He interviewed after a few friends had sent letters on his behalf. He succeeded in landing his own agency with Allstate Insurance Company. He built a fine small business.

"I sent a letter recommending him, but I think Tim Scott got the agency because of his interview. He's quite impressive," recalled former South Carolina governor Jim Edwards. "I could tell he was a good man. He is one of the great political leaders of the next generation."

His diligence in this career built his business quickly and built his associations with others in the same expeditious manner. This gave him even more opportunities to serve. He served Charleston County in an exemplary manner and was honored by being elected as Charleston County Council chairman in 2003–04. He was again elected to the chairmanship in 2007–08. His ability to work with the public, incoming industry and especially the other council members was essential to his continuing rise on the local, state and national stage.

His groundbreaking political headlines continued. He became the first African American Republican elected to the South Carolina House in over a hundred years in 2008.[17] That minute statistic never fazed him as much as it may have excited the press or the political party wonks. He became a Republican based upon his values and beliefs—and not on any other forecasted label, suggestion or prerogative. Instead, he may have become one of the most unifying voices of our times on the subject of race.

"It's in Acts 16. 'One blood.' That's all you ever need to know about race. My blood and your blood is the same," Scott related. "Good people have good intentions. We should all have knee-jerk reactions to helping our fellow man—black or white, male or female. 'One blood.'"

Scott has been served an overdose of pragmatism. He is scary smart and has a reservoir of savvy.

"In the same way, I work with respect to all. I don't assume that a Democrat is wrong or that a Republican is right. I don't assume that Democrats want to hurt our country," Scott continued. "To the contrary, I respect all points of view. In many cases, I find that everyone has a right to be wrong, but I should not criticize. I should always argue with respect and use my mother's value system. She always believed that the best win in an argument is a 'win-win.' That means to find common ground and build a strong solution together."

His pragmatism brought him a landslide victory in 2010. This time, he assumed a bigger role on an even bigger stage. He is the First District congressman from South Carolina in the United States House of Representatives. One would presently infer that it will not be mentioned again that he was the first whatever from wherever in how many ever. He does not really concern himself with that trivia. He is busy working on bigger and better things.

Scott has a team. It's called Team South Carolina—a moniker the four freshmen congressmen from this youth-movement state call themselves. They are Scott from the First District, Jeff Duncan from the Third District, Trey Gowdy from the Fourth and Mick Mulvaney from the Fifth. They are in constant contact with one another. They hope to make a difference in Washington. Team South Carolina is building a future and promises to be a bigger voice.

"Ninety-five percent of the time we are on the same page. We freely share information and viewpoints. We all feel it is essential to stay united as much as possible to best assist our state going forward," Scott intimated. "I'm not sure that this type of focused cooperation from these districts has ever occurred before now.

"As individuals, we need to pay back when we can. But there is also the concept of paying forward," Scott explained. "We have a responsibility to the next generation and the next after that to make their world better and safer with more opportunities."

The foundation of Scott's ideology can be attributed to three sources: his mother's values, his mentors' philosophies and his principles of faith. His mother's simple precepts kept Scott focused on building character. His mother experienced times when she worked sixteen-hour days. Her son could not be more proud. She became a living example of "paying forward."

Several professors and coaches were responsible for mentoring the young Scott. He took away much from their tutelage. He found that success was a process of going the extra mile and that true entrepreneurs plan beyond success. Somehow, one could see Scott in the handful of great statesmen that build upon success with the result of significance.

His principles are passed through the millennia. They are rooted in scripture—both the Old and New Testaments. He does not have to carry the written text. He has much of it memorized.

"Read I Peter 4:12–13," Scott advised. "And then read I Corinthians 9:24."

Not being nearly as versed in scripture, I wrote it down and later located these passages.

> *I Peter 4:12–13: Beloved, think it not strange concerning the fiery trial which is to try you, as though some strange thing happened unto you. But rejoice, inasmuch as ye are partakers of Christ's sufferings; that, when his glory shall be revealed, ye may be glad also with exceeding joy.*

I have interpreted this passage as it applies to Tim Scott. I imagine that he will have a fiery trial before him and that—in the end—he will be joyful, for it will be his belief in Christ that will propel him. I certainly hope so.

But the verse from Corinthians is difficult.

> *I Corinthians 9:24: Know ye not that they which run in a race run all, but one receiveth the prize? So run, that ye may obtain.*

Scott has run the race. He will run more races—but they may be well past the political arena. Should the scripture pertain to receiving a prize, my interpretation is that the prize is not of this earth. His strength lies in scripture. It has guided him to persevere, to reflect and to act. In this surly world of special interests and political maneuvering, my hope is that Tim Scott will always be able to speak with the courage of his own convictions, drawing upon his encyclopedic knowledge of the Holy Word.

His healthy attitude in the performance of his new role is refreshing. He represents something one would not usually expect from Washington —directness and truth as opposed to political spin.

"It is crystallizing to me that so much more gets done when there is no expectation of personal credit or other return," Scott pointed out. "Service is an honor and a responsibility. I will not forsake my commitment."

In time we will all monitor events and outcomes, reasons and reactions. The wholesome dedication of one congressman from one community would not likely change much of what we will see in the "fiery trial" ahead. Only time will inform us. That said, any reason for great optimism that I personally harbor for my children's future is being "paid forward" because of the man I believe will earnestly run the race—and ultimately "receiveth the prize"—Tim Scott.

He is Charleston's Great Hope.

Congressman Tim Scott was appointed by South Carolina governor Nikki Haley to fill the unexpired term of U.S. Senator Jim DeMint. DeMint had resigned to lead the Heritage Foundation in Washington in November 2012.

Subsequently, Scott ran for the seat again in November 2016 to fill the final two years of DeMint's term before his reelection for a full six-year term. His articulate insight and passion to serve others have accorded him profound respect among his contemporaries. As the junior senator from South Carolina, Scott has quietly become the major force left from the Lowcountry political clout that dominated South Carolina politics a decade earlier. His charisma and sense of duty will likely make him a Senate mainstay, unless Tim Scott sets his goals on a higher office.

The Character That Is Frank Abagnale

Frank Abagnale moved to Charleston from Tulsa, Oklahoma. It was an arrangement from a promise made to his wife, Kelly. Abagnale didn't come to Charleston in the same timing that his furniture arrived. In fact, he shipped his cars, his boat and the furniture concurrently. Then he changed his mind.

Abagnale couldn't disconnect from his Tulsa home where his three boys had been raised from childhood to adulthood. The empty, six-thousand-square-foot house on several acres enhanced his deep emotion of withdrawal. The Tulsa home was in stark contrast to the quaint, historic downtown Charleston address the Abagnales would assume. But Kelly Abagnale had found the perfect Charleston residence, built in 1784 and restored, complete with a video chronicling the effort of some two hundred carpenters, electricians and others. It was Kelly's dream circumstance. The Abagnales bought it. It took Kelly three days to unpack the kitchen alone. Since the house was smaller, some furniture would need to be stored. The cars had arrived. The boat was delivered. But Frank Abagnale could not get past leaving the Tulsa home. He told Kelly of his reluctance and arranged for everything to be moved back. It was an extraordinary turn of events. A Tulsa neighbor later told him that they thought he had lost his mind. In a good way, he did. He was lost in melancholy.

The Abagnales decided to keep the Charleston home as a second residence. They reinstalled the return-to-Tulsa-bound furniture and reestablished their previous life. It was a deeply emotional reversal. For a matter of months, the episode subsisted. Then Abagnale realized that he had gone back on a promise to the woman he loved. He had promised that, once the youngest of the three boys was emancipated from the household, he would go wherever Kelly wanted him to live "as long as it had great air service." He put the Tulsa home on the market and, with Kelly, came to Charleston. There they bought new furniture and accessories to fill their Church Street home. Incredibly, they performed this mammoth task all in just one day! The Abagnales became instant Charlestonians. Frank Abagnale has often looked back, but he has become an eminent fixture in Charleston because of his ability to look forward.

He has fulfilled community roles as a graduation speaker, through a fundraising effort for a homeless shelter and in a college criminal justice class, among others. There are dozens of appointments, commitments and appearances that fill his electronic calendar.

"I feel an obligation to bring a moral message. I entertain first, then I bring a purposeful insight," Abagnale stated. "My career has been to protect businesses from fraud. I'm personally paying back with a second chance at life. I can never fully pay back until death. Life is not short, but long. I feel that I can save young people from making wrong decisions. Living with the burden of wrong decisions will be for a long time. Life will come back and remind you. Think before you act."

This gentleman with thick, white hair is emboldened by his own experiences. He is much too humble and understated for what he has been able to give back to the world in sensitive parenting messages, ethical guidelines and moralistic stories that inspire. He has saved businesses—big and small—billions upon billions from would-be criminals. Abagnale is contemplative, naturally pleasant and forthright. He is justly proud of his children and steadfast in his reverence of his wife. She changed him. His depth of purpose is the sidelight to his career, though it could certainly be seen that his life's work has not been his career but his self-imposed duty to reassert needed morality in every quarter.

Abagnale gave a poignant example that he had experienced when his three boys were younger. It spoke to his moral cause.

"We had stopped at a Wendy's drive-in and made a small purchase of under ten dollars. The young clerk gave me back change for a twenty even though I had only handed her a ten. I immediately corrected the mistake and gave her back the ten-dollar error," Abagnale explained. "One of my sons noticed it and asked me upon leaving why I did not just keep the money. I asked him if the ten dollars would make any difference whatsoever to my life. Of course, he answered 'no.' I then gave the devastating other side. The young lady that made the ten-dollar mistake would cash out on her register short by that amount. She would likely be accused of stealing and could be fired from her job. So, I asked, 'Would it have made a difference in her life?' My son immediately understood the importance of morality."

Character for Abagnale has been defined is a variety of notions. Character could be a person of distinction or some other detailed positive qualities. Character could be simply a reputation or the enhancement of values like courage, personality or especially morality. There are developed characters—mostly contrived—that are famous in our literature or even in movies. In the sense of partygoers, a character is someone that may attract comment because they are unique and unusual. Someone acting "out of character" would be doing something unexpected given the reputation of his or her previous actions. Frank Abagnale is all of the above and more than this; he may symbolize, more than anyone, the resolution of character over a lifetime. He is a redemption realized.

The character that is Frank Abagnale has heightened the sense of cleverness as it is detailed in his best-selling book (and the later movie and Broadway musical) titled *Catch Me If You Can*. It was written in 1980 upon a suggestion by famed late-night television host Johnny Carson. In fact, it was published by Carson's own publishing source. It has remained in constant print for over thirty years and is available in thirty-five languages.

The persona in that book and movie was a uniquely developed character. Fact is indeed stranger than fiction! The book essentially details the honest and true account of Abagnale's four-year journey from a shattered home to a federal prison. Two of those years had been spent in other prisons in Sweden and France. In between, he had posed as an airline pilot, a schoolteacher, a stockbroker and a doctor—among other characters. Incredibly, owing to his profound academic prowess, Abagnale passed the State of Louisiana bar exam after studying for only two months. The Federal Bureau of Investigation special agent, Joe Shea ("Hanratty" in the movie version), who had pursued the composite character of Frank Abagnale, was certain he was trying to apprehend a seasoned mastermind of extraordinary experience, deception and enterprise. He thought him to be in his midthirties. His intensely pursued suspect was only a teenager.

Abagnale had left his New York home at the age of sixteen. He had been summoned from a high school classroom to a courtroom by a judge to choose which parent he would live with after a divorce was decreed. He would live with neither. He ran away. In the years that followed, though he spoke with his father by phone, he never saw his father again. It was a much-lamented circumstance of a bad decision.

The young runaway's acute abilities and believable sincerity had channeled him to a life of fraud and other crime. He became adept at the

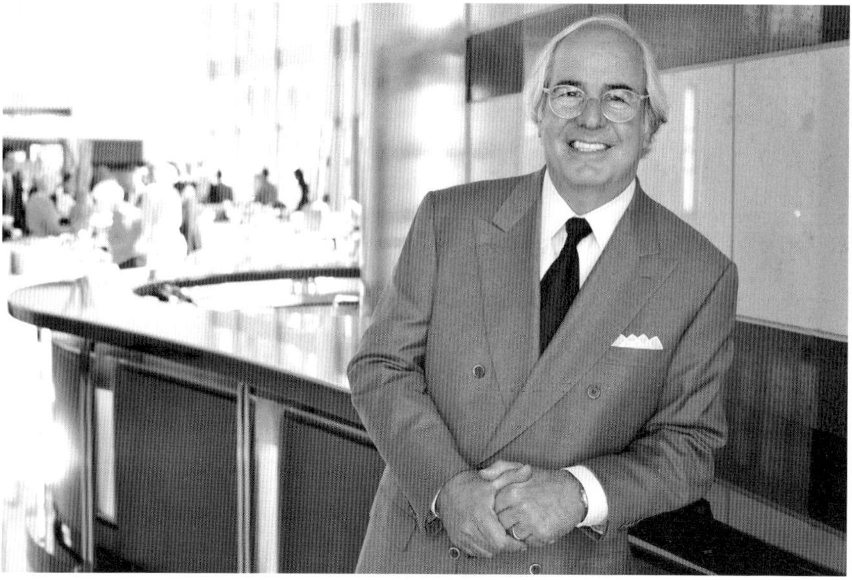

There is no question that Frank Abagnale is a brilliant and successful man. His selfless devotion to the moral principles he espouses has already made an impact upon Charleston's youth. *(Kelly Abagnale)*

art of defrauding large corporations by counterfeiting their payroll checks. He realized there was no turning back. He expected to get caught, and he did. He was extradited from a Swedish prison to the custody of the FBI at the age of twenty-one in 1970.

Abagnale and Special Agent Shea had a common thought. Both knew the eventuality was that Abagnale would be apprehended. His twelve-year sentence for what amounted to nearly $2.5 million of fraudulent corporate checks would have seemed to be the book's last chapter. It was, in the reality that is life, only the beginning. What followed placed Abagnale on a path to become a man of great character and impeccable morality.

"I'd like to say the prison system works and it changed me or that I became born again or that I had grown up and matured and was contrite," Abagnale stated. "But none of that happened."

Something much more meaningful in Abagnale's life changed him. But before that could happen, another event would present itself. Precisely because of his now-catalogued file of ingenuity, Abagnale was not a forgotten inmate number.

The pursuer, Joe Shea, came back to Abagnale to work a deal in 1974. Abagnale was not a violent criminal. He did not defraud individuals. He showed an unusual pattern of honesty throughout the pursuit. Real criminals depend upon dishonesty as a weapon. He was just a child who had reacted to an extreme domestic circumstance by striking out on his own. He did not steal from people or carry a handgun. He only targeted the megafunded entities like banks and airlines for what amounted to survival. Shea pleaded for a deal with the FBI. They refused at first and then consented. The FBI would let him serve his final eight years working directly with their fraud investigation unit. It was a no-brainer for Abagnale. He not only worked the final eight years of his sentence but also continued to work beyond those initial testy years with the FBI. Other career FBI employees did not accept him in the first few years. It took several years to gain their trust. He continues to work with the FBI even today after thirty-six years. Shea, who became a second father to Abagnale, died in 2005 at the age of eighty-eight.

"Joe Shea had two daughters," Abagnale related. "We stay in touch with them and their children even now. One lives in Greenville and the other in Georgia. Joe never had a son. In a way, he adopted me in that role. He saw that I had a value system and, despite the crime, was an honest person. He had a sense of sympathy that I was a runaway. I think he saw that I was a talented person that was on the way to wasting my life. He personally came to see me. He personally worked the release deal. Joe Shea gave me a second chance.

"Joe was a caring and deeply religious man. He was a loving father," Abagnale continued. "He was very persistent in his career and a very tough FBI agent. He was creative and talented."

He was smart enough to recruit Abagnale from prison. And in time, the events led to the Abagnale life-changer.

"I was working undercover in Texas in 1975. I met Kelly as part of this assignment. She was an innocent aside and not a part of the focused criminal operation. I immediately fell in love with her," Abagnale intimated. "I did the unthinkable and blew my cover. She had total faith in me. She believed in me. She trusted me despite everything I told her in honesty about my background. Against the wishes of her parents, we were married in 1976 in the Catholic Church.

"Her parents, once they knew of my federal prison time and lack of formal education, tried everything to dissuade her from marrying me," Abagnale offered. "And you could see their point. They thought it was another con and that my life, once my service to the FBI was over, would revert to crime. It was foolish for me to try to convince them otherwise. They were trying to protect their daughter."

Their daughter was trying to save the life of the man she had consented to marry. Abagnale knew what he felt. It is rare to hear a man speak so lovingly about his wife.

"She made me see that a marriage and a family can be so very positive. She knew that my parents' divorce was the catalyst that started my life of crime. She elevated my belief in people and especially in marriage," Abagnale continued. "In this way, she was the real reason my life changed and I was able to go back to my true core values I had learned in parochial schools. My entire life turned on the love of a woman."

It is character that is illustrated by an incredible restoration of the human spirit. Abagnale's *deus ex machina* wasn't deity or a mechanically produced solution from an unconsidered source. That character change came from extremely human intervention—the caring woman who would become his wife of thirty-five years.

The Abagnale value system is exemplary and refreshing. It is indeed his resolution of his own character and reputation over a lifetime. He benefited from his own upbringing. He was taught by Catholic brothers. His father, in contrast to movie's perceived character, was honest, responsible and diligent.

"He fostered a strong sense of right and wrong. He was wonderful and good-hearted and loved my mother," Abagnale stated.

Abagnale's French-born mother never remarried, as the movie depicts. She is an octogenarian and still lives in New York, near Abagnale's other two living siblings. His youngest brother died of a liver ailment just a few years ago. Frank William Abagnale Sr. died in 1971. Son Frank was denied a bereavement leave to attend his father's funeral.

"I'm one of the very few prisoners ever denied this type of leave," Abagnale somberly reflected. "I suppose they still considered me a flight risk, given my background. The experience of mourning in prison and not being at the funeral was emotionally devastating.

"He was never a con man or dishonest and certainly may have been prone to alcoholism," Abagnale confided. "He was conservative and honest. He had a high school education and ran a stationery store. His younger brother was a CPA who did not pay the taxes and caused the business to fail. Yet, my father, though angered, eventually forgave my uncle. My father was a good man."

The character portrayed in the movie by actor Leonardo DiCaprio would lead one to believe Abagnale was a suave and sophisticated con artist that reveled in the activity for the thrill of it all. That was not quite what Abagnale really experienced. He was always on the run. He could not afford to trust anyone. In part, his activities were based on simple survival. The two years in European jails were not emphasized in the movie, as they were in the book that detailed the misery. The French prison he endured was a hundreds-year-old facility lacking modern conveniences. It took Abagnale great resolve and personal fortitude to tolerate these spartan experiences. It took character.

That foundation of internal character is personified in the fully evolved Abagnale. His core value system grew to embrace the tenets of impeccable ethics and staunch morality. This became his personal triumph. That leap is greater than any book or movie could perceive. It is a lifetime resolved and a commitment to the goodness within.

His post-FBI venture of protecting businesses from fraud has saved billions. His speaking ability, though so very entertaining, arrives at a conclusion of a very special message. He is clear in his point.

"I am so glad that I was raised in a Catholic school. It's not so much about God and religion as much as it is about right and wrong. You may make mistakes, but there is always a rope to pull yourself onto the right path. You can change your life. My wife, Kelly, also went to a Catholic school. My parents saved money to send me. Back then, 99 percent of the students were Catholic. Now it's more like 50 percent. Others see the benefit today. Public schools simply do not teach right and wrong," Abagnale noted.

"When my children were going through Catholic schools, I sat next to a Jewish man. I asked him why his child was there," Abagnale continued. "He said, 'Here you learn respect, you learn to pray, you learn about God.' Others see the importance in learning ethics and morality, which are not taught elsewhere."

Abagnale sees a grave concern that is associated with his career. Last year alone, he estimated that $950 billion was lost to fraud. He sees that as a direct result of our families not disseminating proper values to their children and an education system that does little to teach moral values.

"Nearly 50 percent of all high school–age students consider getting instant answers for a test from 'Googling' on a cell phone to not constitute cheating," Abagnale explained. "There is a dire lack of morality in our society today. It must be addressed."

Abagnale's appearances have been largely gratis and have been to benefit others—so many being in support of local causes. There was an aforementioned address to The Citadel's criminal justice majors, a completely different talk at a fundraiser for the Interfaith Crisis Ministry and the ever-timely graduation speech. There are many others. His message may be the rope he describes to pull someone else back to the right path. After all, he has seen crime from both sides. He is the crusader that has experienced what wrong decisions can cause and warns of such so that the listener's decision is always for what is right.

His route of redemption brought him to the Holy City reluctantly at first. Now he loves it.

"I spent ten years with the FBI in Houston and moved to Tulsa to raise my family in a smaller setting. They each knew my story from an early age. I wanted to give them a loving environment and a place to grow up away from the big-city problems. To them, I'm just 'Dad.' They were each great children and never a problem," Abagnale intimated. "We only had one really strict rule—no physical hitting or fighting, not even in horsing around. As a result, my three boys are very close."

Scott Abagnale is the oldest and works with the FBI in Baltimore. Brother Chris is the middle sibling and lives in Charleston. He's Kelly's partner in running their chic fashion shop on George Street, the House of Sage. Youngest son Sean is teaching in China. The three of them are in constant communication. One month the phone bill from Chris to Sean in China was sixteen hundred dollars.

"I know that's high. But Kelly and I agreed that the significance of their frequent sibling communication was more important than the phone bill," Abagnale related. "That will serve them both for a lifetime."

The Abagnales had considered coming to Charleston before. They had purchased a lot at Kiawah in 1995 and loved the area so much that they contemplated leaving Tulsa then.

"The boys were still in school, and we really feared the drive from Kiawah down River Road, especially at night," Abagnale recalled. "And now we're here and enjoying Charleston permanently. My wife, Kelly, says it best. 'How could you not like it? It's like living in paradise.' We've found the people here are different as well. They are not suspicious of you here. They fully accept you—unconditionally. Where you're from or what you do or where you go to church doesn't seem to matter. It's not like that anywhere else."

In Charleston, Frank William Abagnale Jr. is a character we enjoy with the character of great warmth and sincerity, teaching lessons of moral character to our entire community.

Catch him when you can.

Frank and Kelly Abagnale moved to Daniel Island from Church Street in 2012. Abagnale continued consulting work with the Federal Bureau of Investigation, along with another career in the development of security detection systems for banks. His sincere kindness is highlighted by his public speaking acumen, especially his ability to relate to youth, which he does freely within the community. He is profoundly entertaining. He has continued his commitment to his family, his humanitarian outreach and his support of his church.

Abagnale has paid back "the system" a hundred times over but still laments his youthful years. Yet no person has accomplished what he has in terms of guiding others, exemplary parenting, the teaching of youth and his humble generosity of time and talent. He has turned down multiple presidential pardons, stating that he felt that what he did "as a runaway youth was unpardonable." Abagnale has become an enormous credit where there was once an IOU. A Charlestonian, whether a "beenya" or "cumya," could find no better friend.

Considering Les Robinson

The National Basketball Hall of Fame in Springfield, Massachusetts, does not inform a retired basketball coach that he is not up for consideration. It's just as well. Les Robinson is not waiting to hear from them.

Had he been elected, Les Robinson's acceptance speech would have been about everyone else. He would have extolled the qualities of players he had coached that became engineers, ministers and doctors. He would have talked about having the privilege to coach young men who got degrees and excelled at life. He probably would have spent some time telling stories about coaches and colleagues whom he had either admired or played a practical joke on—or both. He'd get serious for a moment to talk about the love of his life, Barbara, and their four children and eight grandchildren. Then he'd likely end his acceptance speech by talking about the people he had met along the way. They would be people like the late Murray Benoit or the late Keith Hamilton. Both had been very close friends that did not coach or play basketball at the upper levels. They were part of his memory of all things good in college basketball. It would be noted that these men and so many others treasured Robinson's friendship immensely.

There is another side of Les Robinson that the Hall of Fame may have left unexplored. He has served on both the NCAA selection committee and the NIT selection committee. In doing so, he has been able to perform the two things he does the best—make pragmatic decisions concisely and confidently and spread the joy. It is the latter sentiment that defines his life.

There is no question that Les Robinson has uncommon common sense. It is why committees and other coaches call him. It may also be because it is a great pleasure to talk with him.

From the rudiments of a fifth-grade essay, Robinson informed the world of his intentions to be a basketball coach. He was in a St. Albans, West Virginia, grade school. His father was an entrepreneur who brought in talent for an annual weeklong camp and basketball tournament. He and a partner did it all—advertising, ticket sales, lodging, concessions, organization, programs and even officiating. The Charleston Civic Center was abuzz the week of the camp. The cavalcade of players included the likes of Jerry West, Oscar Robertson, Bill Russell, Hot Rod Hundley, Jerry Lucas, John Havlicek, Billy Packer, Lenny Rosenbluth, Billy Cunningham, Bobby Knight, Jim Harrick and others—many already enshrined in the National Basketball Hall of Fame. Seeing this, the young Robinson wished a wish and followed his dream.

Les Robinson learned the game. Basketball was his passion. His skill set took him on full basketball scholarship to one of the legendary coaches in the land at the time—the great Everett Case at North Carolina State University. Coach Case was among the handful of most lauded coaches in the profession with Coach Adolph Rupp, Coach Henry Iba, Coach Joe Lapchick and Coach Phog Allen. Coach Case was the venerable "Gray Fox" that started the tradition of cutting down the nets after a big win. He famously enlisted in the navy after the Pearl Harbor attack. He was forty-one. Case was in poor health at the apex of Les Robinson's playing career. He hired a brilliant assistant that became Robinson's mentor, Press Maravich. Case died in 1965. He was conscientious enough to have listed Robinson—among several others—in his last will and testament. It was a small stipend, but it left a lasting effect on and appreciation in Les Robinson.

Both Case and Maravich saw something in the young Robinson. Coach Maravich took immediate interest in the player with the on-the-floor coaching mentality. He convinced him to take a job training N.C. State's junior varsity in the philosophies of winning basketball. Robinson was able to handle the head junior varsity coaching chores while taking graduate courses. Press Maravich took him in like a son. His actual son, Hall of Fame player "Pistol" Pete, was completing high school in the Raleigh, North Carolina, area. Robinson influenced Pistol Pete as well. He and young Pete took on all comers on the old Reynolds Coliseum practice floor. Several stories of top college prospects that did not sign with N.C. State surfaced in later years. They couldn't beat Les and the Pistol two on two, even when paired with another top Atlantic Coast Conference player. Press Maravich couldn't quite quantify just how good the Pistol was—even in high school.

Les Robinson and Press Maravich remained coach and mentor throughout the remainder of Maravich's career. More than that, they remained close friends. Robinson scouted teams for Maravich and sent him information on promising high school players when Maravich took Pistol Pete Maravich with him to Louisiana State University. Robinson became the family friend that was there for more than just basketball. Maravich, in turn, was diligent in directing the young coach towards a fine career path.

Robinson followed directions well. He gave and earned respect. He recruited players that he felt were outstanding human beings and made them better basketball players. They included players like Chuck Cordell from Marion, North Carolina.

"Coach Rob recruited me, but he really recruited my mother. He saw that she was going to help me make the decision," Chuck Cordell related.

Cordell went on to a Hall of Fame career at The Citadel in both basketball and baseball. He is now a golf course developer who makes his home in Pinehurst, North Carolina.

"Once I got to Charleston, I found that Coach Rob was everything I admired in a person—honest, competitive, wholesome and with a tremendous sense of humor. It's no wonder he is so well known around the country," Cordell stated.

Robinson's career started in another Charleston, in West Virginia, as a high schooler prior to his stint at N.C. State. The West Virginia roots are only mentioned at about the same pace London's Big Ben strikes a new hour. Robinson often cites others in the common purview of a group that may have a West Virginia background. There's Jerry West and Jim Harrick, Hot Rod Hundley and NCAA referee Ted Valentine. Robinson finds a way to make sure every story told pays some tribute to "Almost Heaven." His incredible stories—all true—have long defined his companionable personality and penchant for remembering details.

Robinson's basketball career at N.C. State was workmanlike and injected with team successes. He entered his senior season looking for the career in basketball he had always imagined. It was then that Coach Maravich played one of his greatest player hunches. He called Robinson in and asked him to consider coaching the junior varsity team. Robinson jumped at the chance. After serving as the junior varsity head coach, his academic work was complete. He then pursued his first independent coaching opportunity.

TIMING IS EVERYTHING, PART TWO

In his fifth and final season as N.C. State's brilliant choice to bring academic quality and national esteem back to the program, Robinson suffered through a season of incredibly poor luck. His season ended with a 15-16 record. Yet, ten of the losses were by less than five points—and six of those by a made basket or less. Had his team won half of those, they would have undoubtedly headed to the NCAA tournament. Had it been reversed and they had won all ten, they would have been a number-four seed or higher. Instead, the amiable Robinson felt he wasn't getting enough wins to feed the fan base. The win-loss concerns had put pressure on the athletic director and administration as well. He took the responsibility and resigned. He was only fifty-four. Every player on that N.C. State team graduated. He had brought the program back. Nobody could have done it better with more class, ability and character.

He never again coached a college basketball game.

After twelve years as athletic director at N.C. State and then The Citadel, Robinson retired in 2008. He had served as athletic director while coaching basketball at East Tennessee State as well. The business of college athletics was pursued in earnest to the betterment of each institution. He was able to engage the best of his assets. His influence brought each of the three schools better-than-expected football game contracts, expanded facility initiatives and passionate alumni buy-in. He had served as athletic at the three Division I colleges where he had also coached—the only coach in America to accomplish that level of respect and responsibility.

Robinson's stint as athletic director at The Citadel transcended athletics. The small military school of barely two thousand students was going through a major transition in athletics. The football stadium had to be replaced. In the two-year period during which The Citadel played with only one side of its spectator stands up, Robinson used his Rolodex as well as his marketing know-how to stem the financial shortfall. He scheduled games with every Bowl Championship Series football conference over a period of years, sometimes playing two of the big schools in a single season. In doing so, the Bulldogs took their show on the road and played Florida State, Maryland, Pittsburgh, Wisconsin, Auburn, Texas A&M, Florida, Clemson, LSU, Wyoming and Arizona. The effect was beyond football. The Citadel's reputation grew well outside of the region. Cadet applications began to rise. The year 2011 will mark an unprecedented fifth straight year that The Citadel will accept more than seven hundred freshmen. While there are certainly other salient factors for the college's upturn in popularity, Robinson's inspiration of taking the

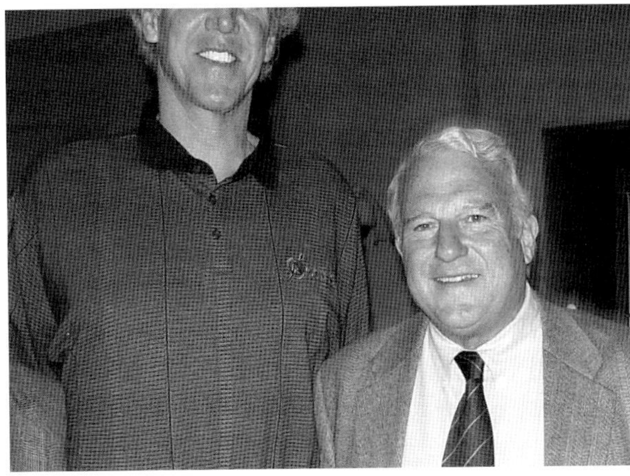

Most of NCAA and NBA Hall of Famer Bill Walton, with NCAA selection committee alumnus Les Robinson (*right*). This serious photograph was taken by my viewfinder-challenged wife, Mandy. *(Mandy McQueeney)*

Bulldogs to the national stage assisted recruiting well outside of sports. The administration benefitted from Robinson's foresight.

The coaches know him. Inside the brotherhood of coaches, he is already accorded hall of fame status. It is because coaching relationships do not have a minimum level of wins or a championship trophy. They have set a bar much higher than that—universal respect and admiration.

"Les Robinson," according to longtime friend Jim Harrick, "is the rarest of rare. He is the only man I've ever met in college athletics who is liked by everyone. He has no enemies."

Other mainstay personalities of the NCAA agreed. University of California basketball coach Mike Montgomery noted, "He's as nice a person as there is in college basketball. And he'll beat you with a smile on his face."

Similar sentiments were noted by Coach Gary Williams of the University of Maryland and Coach Mike Krzyzewski of Duke University. Former University of Virginia head coach Terry Holland counts Robinson among his best friends. There are endless testimonies from the elite of the basketball world that recall a Les Robinson story or retrieve the joy he has brought into the profession.

His best friend in coaching for over thirty years has been Coach Bobby Cremins, former head basketball coach at the College of Charleston.

"Les is what all coaches should be like. He is humble, fair, honest and fun to be around. And he'll kick your butt," Cremins stated. "He's also a great person to go to for advice."

Former Maryland coach Gary Williams offered another insight.

"Who else has ever rebuilt three programs from the ground up, sometimes with the sanctions left over from the previous staffs and always to a point of triumph? With him, it wasn't about wins. It was bigger than that," Williams said.

His respect within the industry is a constant that materializes almost daily.

Indeed, Robinson's phone rings constantly. He carries it with him, and he prides himself on returning every call he receives. His calls range from a reminder of an event from wife, Barbara, to gratis speaking engagement invitations and often to recommendations to fill coaching vacancies—sometimes in college-level sports outside of basketball. With it all, he stays in touch with his wide circle of friends and very tightly knit family.

If there were a family man hall of fame, he would be a first-ballot inductee.

There are other unorganized and unnamed halls of fame. He'd certainly qualify for the sports story hall of fame, owing to his total recall of his favorite five hundred true sports stories, all of which end with a moral or a punch line. He lived each one of them. Some tie into others to make transitions from basketball to politics to football to business. He can recount them seamlessly.

If there were a hall of fame for accommodating the requests of others in a selfless fashion, Robinson would merit top billing. If a hall of fame selection committee started to grade all coaches in all sports by what they have meant to the careers of their players, again "Coach Rob" would be a major focus. And should they ever rank the best in the NCAA by the joy they've given to others, it would be called the "Les List."

His energy and appetite for life and the personalities around him are ever evident. He makes your day when he calls or stops by. His social network includes realtors, electricians and military officers—and even retired basketball referees. He is perhaps the most jovial and welcome persona in all of the behemoth that is called NCAA college basketball.

And yet, he has not prepared an acceptance speech.

Les Robinson remained active in college basketball, specifically dedicated to the NIT and the NCAA men's basketball selection process. In 2016, Robinson accepted an interim athletic director position at Lander University in Greenwood, South Carolina. He did so as a favor to a friend and to assist the university in hiring a permanent director of athletics. Robinson also has much of his life chronicled in a book set for release by the spring of 2017, *Around in Circles*. Be ready to be amused!

Anita Zucker and the Monument

Meeting Charleston's number-one benefactor at any place would be surreal. But meeting the elegant lady who gave our entire generation the pensive memories of the caustic impact of history was so much more meaningful.

She approached in the distance. The April weather had seeped into an identity mindful of July. The breezeless afternoon was humid and overcast. I sat waiting on a bench alongside austere and imposing metal framing. I had come early to get a sense of spirit—to become one with the Charleston Holocaust Memorial.

It was providential that I had become acquainted with Charleston's most significant philanthropist, Anita Zucker, perhaps twenty years earlier. It was even more providential that she would take the time to accede to my silly request. She has a system-overload schedule daily. She is in great demand. Yet her sense of friendship and zeal of purpose overcome everything else.

She had every reason to be everything else than what she clearly is—down-home real. She is well based in her foundations. Her name is at the forefront of every crucial Charleston initiative—and many beyond.

Her agreement to meet me at the Holocaust memorial was made several years ago when we served on a community board together. I did not want to chance the history-tour version from the staid and insensitive monotones of those who may have memorized the statistics from a guide manual. It would mean much more to me hearing it from her. She carried the passion.

Unfortunately, the interim years brought much sadness to the Zucker family. The man that our generation would consider as the very pinnacle of Charleston's business elite, Jerry Zucker, had passed away. He and Anita had been married nearly thirty-eight years. In that time they had changed Charleston forever. It was obvious that the Zucker loss was an enormous Charleston loss as well. I mourned his passing along with countless others.

The Zuckers were at the vanguard of every major initiative to improve education, industry and social programs in the Lowcountry. Nobody did it better, more often or with as much funding. Jerry Zucker was a self-made billionaire who never forgot his roots. The enterprising couple always gave back.

On a personal note, I can remember Jerry Zucker telling me that he had his three young children call into national fundraising programs—like Jerry Lewis's March of Dimes Telethon—ostensibly to practice the exercise of giving back. The young children were even encouraged to call into a local telecast bidding on Christmas gifts for the underprivileged. They learned from the Great One. The tradition continues.

A mutual friend, the late Bill Ackerman, once described Jerry Zucker as "the greatest example of applied genius I've ever known." His term "applied genius" stuck with me. There are legions of smart people. There was but one Jerry Zucker.

Anita Zucker remains as a perfect example of a community institution. She and Jerry were there for everyone. They funded faculty chairs, scholarships and private research grants. Jerry's passing—though a startling and major event that paused so many other lives—only furthered the family resolve. They kept his larger-than-life commitments to a spectrum of beneficiaries. Charleston benefitted from the graciousness of a genius, and the family Zucker bonded to continue his legacy.

Anita Zucker is high energy, high intellect and highly engaged.

Within five hours of our monument meeting, Zucker announced a half-million-dollar donation to the Interfaith Crisis Ministry to effect and initiate a building project that assists the homeless. I happened to be at the event to join in with the collective awe at the munificence of this great Charleston lady. It was another of the frequent and incredible contributions by this most generous of Lowcountry families. Their largesse in the field of philanthropic endeavors is unparalleled.

Things could have been different.

The Zuckers had the knowledge and experience of horribly sordid history in their rearview mirror. Anita Zucker's eighty-seven-year-old mother could personally relate.

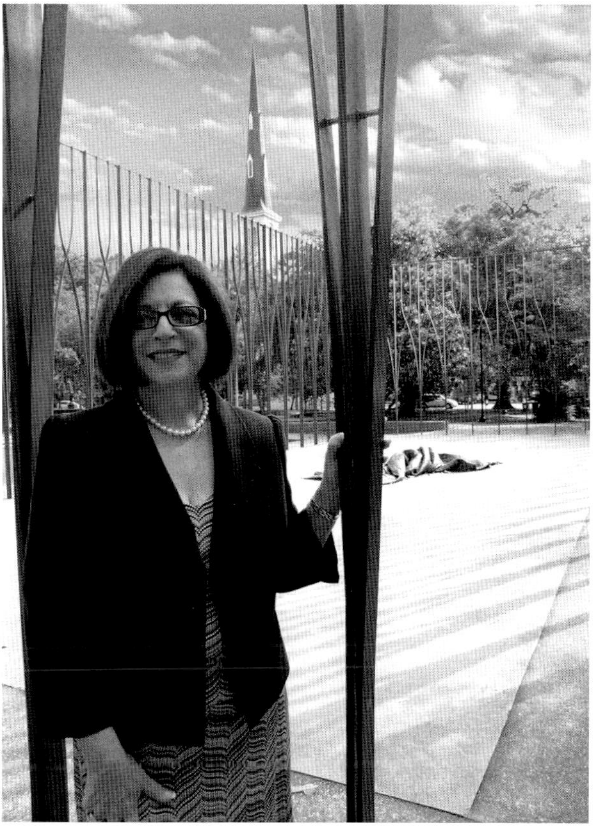

Charleston's most dynamic community patron, Anita Zucker, at the Holocaust Memorial monument, a place of special meaning to her and so many other Charlestonians. *(Torrey Monroe)*

"Both of my parents and both of Jerry's parents were Holocaust survivors," Zucker started. "They were conscripted to work crews in Poland. They were among the very few of the lucky ones, because they had specific jobs.

"Jerry's parents were from Lodz, Poland, and my parents were in Vladimir Volynskiy, then in Poland, now a part of the Ukraine," she explained. "My own sister was born in a D.P. [displaced persons] camp in Eshvega, Germany."

Her mother's family lived in these austere camps after World War II in order to be either located by previously separated family or relocated if no prewar family was found. They were in Eshvega from the end of the war in May of 1945 to 1949. This is a postscript to the dreadful and appalling chapter detailing the Nazi Holocaust. Over six million Jews were murdered by the most horrific means imaginable. The Holocaust memorial in Charleston—a major port of religious freedom that predated the United States—can only begin to ignite the sensibilities of this repugnant misadventure.

It's in Mark Twain's *Adventures of Huckleberry Finn* that the author expounds upon the issue of "man's inhumanity to man." Zucker found that the Holocaust memorial had other intentions than the obvious. She mentioned the historical themes of slavery, apartheid and Russian leader Stalin's mass executions, along with those of China's Chairman Mao.

"Even recently, there was the example of Darfur," she added.

The numbers from the Red countries of Russia and China have been estimated as high as twenty million deaths—from forced starvation, political executions and work camps. The Holocaust cannot ever be overlooked for what it was—the rule of one over another based on bias. Inhumanity still exists. To sit in front of the Holocaust memorial reminds one of these nauseating atrocities and that it must not ever happen again.

Yet building the landmark memorial was not as easy as one would assume.

"We had certain expectations from the City of Charleston that had to be fulfilled. Then there was the Board of Architectural Review, funding needs, approval from the Washington Light Infantry (they own Marion Square, where the memorial is located) and others. There were architectural concerns and a selection made from five submittals. There had to be a plan for deferred maintenance," Zucker continued. "And we needed to have a message beyond the Holocaust itself and the reporting of history. The Holocaust memorial speaks to tolerance. We study what happened so that we can better understand how to avoid it happening again."

So much community input is evident. The names of the contributors belong to other largely significant community patrons.

"The metal frame is rectangular and is open-spaced. The view is to the sky in the profound symbolism of looking to heaven. The side configuration is remindful of the windows of a sanctuary," Zucker noted.

There is a central focus. It is a tarp-like sculpture in representation of a tallit.

"It is symbolic of the mourning of death—specifically of a male," Zucker explained.

Her expression was solemn and respectful. One could easily surmise the deeper and more compelling meaning to her. She took the lead role in the establishment of the memorial. She personally raised much of the funds. She tapped into a community and championed the significance. The effort became nothing less than a groundswell of enthusiasm because of her. She proctored the project from beginning to end. It was when I had—in my Gentile awkwardness—mispronounced the word "tallit" that she interjected the reason for the missing tassel-like fringe from the corner of the representational sculpture. It was indicative that a Jewish man had died. She remained composed. I didn't. I thought of the relevance that she must have internalized for my sake. The man she most admired and was the other half of her life had passed just three years prior.

Yet Anita Zucker was true to the spirit of the Holocaust memorial. She took her precious and valuable time to meet me and assist me in a quest, because she cared enough about the memorial and about friends like me. She has met thousands like me along the way. But to her, people matter. People always matter, and the advocacy of tolerance, acceptance and devotion is paramount.

What other family in what other sizeable municipality approaches the significance of the family Zucker in Charleston, South Carolina? There had to also be a "regrets" response to many of their invitations. She and husband Jerry had done so much for so long that they likely had to plan meaningful family time, decline hundreds of events and perhaps even a few award presentations. Yes, every significant Charleston-area award rendered has had their name associated with it. It seems that nearly every major charity, every local college and every Charleston event has a Zucker signature. It is not by accident. They have properly given back and then heaped multiples more upon the less fortunate, the medically needy and the educationally unfunded. It is unlikely that anyone has ever done more in the Holy City. Ever.

"My two primary passions are family and education. Family always comes first," Zucker related. "And providing access to education is so very important."

Indeed, she has funded one of the few college initiatives on Jewish studies in America at the venerable College of Charleston. She had just returned from a guest lecture. Poignantly, she was the lecturer.

"Jews date to the late 1600s in Charleston. They became a viable part of the community where others came to seek religious freedom. They were accepted. They chose to be good citizens and cared deeply about the community. They had lots to give in talent and resources. They were themselves tolerant and respectful of others," Zucker explained. "Charleston became a great example of cultures meshing for the benefit of all."

The Zucker dynamic is and has been on the world stage. Among their many holdings is the oldest established continuing business in North America, the Hudson's Bay Company. Anita Zucker is its first female governess. The company is the pride of Canada. There are other businesses, hundreds of Jerry Zucker patents and devoted charities that the three Zucker children earnestly administer. Some are in Europe, the Middle East and other global sites. Jonathan Zucker serves as president of the giant InterTech Group, Inc. The line continues with Andrea Zucker Muzin and youngest son, Jeffrey Zucker. They form the ZGT—Zucker Give Team. This cornerstone family could orchestrate its enormously impressive empire from anywhere they might desire to live. And that's exactly what Anita Zucker has done.

"I live in Charleston, because I love Charleston. My children were raised here. It is a place of comfort and acceptance," Zucker opined. "There is so much warmth here in the town I love."

It's a perfect love story.

Charleston loves Anita Zucker.

In June 2012, Anita Zucker announced a $5 million gift for the Zucker Family Graduate Education Center at Clemson University. Just two years later, Zucker pledged another $2 million to The Citadel for the Zucker Family School of Education. Her generosity, especially in the field of education, continues to benefit students and inspire others to invest in the generations that follow.

The Zucker family generosity remains one of the impressive humanitarian and philanthropic chapters of Charleston's meteoric rise.

The Man Who Would Be Moses

Mayor Joseph Patrick Riley Jr.

When Joe Riley left law school to build a practice in downtown Charleston, he saw the future of a simple life with summer seersucker suits and an after-work toddy at the Hibernian Society back bar. He was ready for what a life in Charleston could bring. But, as instincts are wont to do, they took over. He never looked back.

If ever a man were born to lead, it was Joseph Patrick Riley Jr. Riley had a knack for service, uncommon energy and an impeccable sense of ethics. These qualities have not ever changed. What he didn't necessarily have was what everyone thought he always had, in retrospect.

"I would not have envisioned Charleston 2011 back when I became mayor in 1975," Riley related. "The bones were there. The city had been preserved. We had a very good council, and we knew we could make this a great city. We did have a goal of excellence. But largely, our role had yet to be recognized."

The man we all cited as a true visionary did not really cite his early mayoral role in terms of a vision. Nonetheless, we will not change our minds. The man *is* a visionary.

Despite the rudimentary beginnings of his service in 1975, the city began to move forward. His goal of excellence needed to be shared by council, the many departments and the citizens of Charleston.

"Like any business model, it was important to prioritize. We had to use the resources we had responsibly," Riley said. "We had way too much to do to try and do it all at once. So I sat down with council members and others and put a framework plan in place that could be implemented."

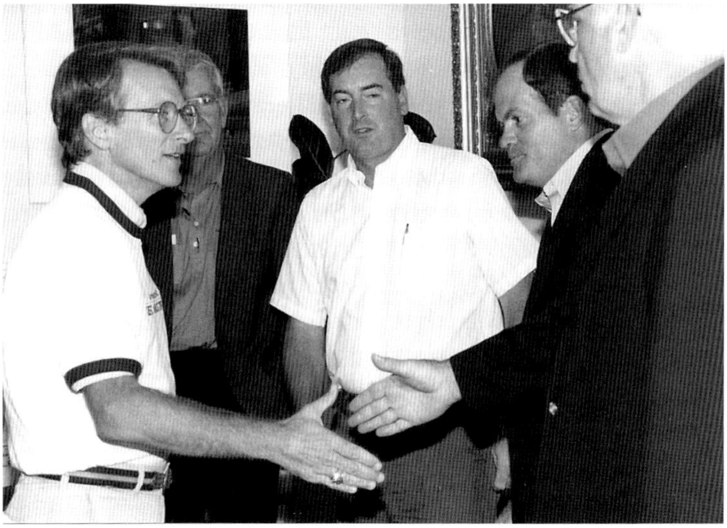

Leadership counts. In the most devastating hurricane ever recorded in Charleston, the category five Hurricane Hugo of 1989, Riley worked seemingly endless hours to best serve the community in its recovery. Here, Riley is pictured with State Farm Insurance Companies president and CEO Ed W. Rust Jr., along with other representatives setting up a recovery fund for those in dire need. *(Bob Webb)*

convention hotel, combined with the energy and vitality of the city in a place where there was mostly vacant buildings and unsightly lots."

Indeed, Charleston Place changed downtown Charleston. King Street had tumbled out of local favor with the advent of suburban malls. It came back mightily with local boutiques, family restaurants and other mercantile establishments. The trail dust of Charleston Place brought other familiar branding names to the discriminate shopper, like Banana Republic, The Gap and Pottery Barn. Meeting Street capitalized with even more unique shops and an upsurge in restaurant activity. The tourists demanded more.

East Bay Street became the golden mile of critically acclaimed restaurants. The former warehouses—many of which were vacant—now gained national merit for culinary quality and choice. One former car dealer, Tom Parsell, sold his dealership and built three classic restaurants within two blocks of each other—Magnolia's, Blossom Café and Cypress. They are all high on the list of elegant and exceptional Charleston eateries. There are dozens more. In the 1960s, one could travel the peninsula and find but one great restaurant, Perdita's. Today's Charleston will challenge the aficionado to dine at a different restaurant every evening for a fortnight and beyond without falling below a four-star rating. Charleston's culinary fare offers in quality and breadth and buttereth what many associate with New York or San Francisco. New Orleans? We passed the Big Easy more than a decade ago.

The City Market came back as well. A just-completed renovation of the vendor spaces, some engineering nuances to divert rainwater (the City Market is low at the East Bay Street end) and a general upgrade of restored buildings has made the market the focal avenue for tourism. You can find anything in the City Market—from local artwork to exquisite, handmade, cultural sweetgrass baskets to candy and ice cream. The market is now a favorite destination for passengers from the cruise ships that have found Charleston on their nautical maps. The cruise business is growing and as such will propel plans to upgrade the cruise terminal.

There is still work to do.

"We review various presentations and plans to see if they are in line with the growth and development of the city," Riley related. "I personally look at plans for this or that and ask myself one question: 'Will this be important five years from now?' We have to be diligent in protecting our city and its charm. For that reason, there are stringent rules we have to adhere to and much scrutiny. We spend an inordinate number of hours to be fair and, at the same time, treat the concerns of our citizens with great care."

Riley is a brilliant man with the uncommon added assets of leadership, judgment and persistence. His passion for the city he loves and has guided is unquestioned. The gene pool dictated much; the environment did the rest.

"My father was everything to me. He was a wonderful man, civic-minded and outgoing. My mother was quiet and shy but was insightful and most knowledgeable. She was the number-two honor graduate in her class at the College of Charleston," Riley shared. "Both were engaged in the community, Daddy more prominently. They were both honest in their dealings, worked hard and went out of their way to be nice to people. Their role was the same as so many others—to make the community a better place."

Riley continued to touch upon influences that helped him to commit his life to service and to the people of Charleston.

"I was fortunate to have an eighth-grade teacher at Cathedral School, Dot Gnann (Sister Mary William), who taught leadership, though I didn't realize what she did for me until years later. She was also the principal. She had high expectations of me," Riley reflected. "Father Sterker and Cardinal Bernadin both influenced me as well. They were wonderful mentors whom I greatly respected."

His later life brought other influences.

"Politically, Fritz Hollings helped me immensely. He instilled in me the importance of hard work and great integrity," Riley added. "And Ted Stern was encouraging. He influenced me as a visionary. He led the College of Charleston to become a wonderful institution."

Indeed, Riley cites Stern and the college for their positive impact upon the peninsular city. But Riley was someone who saw great upside to the college's controlled growth. The impact upon the city over the past forty years cannot be underestimated. The college was its own economic engine. It powered real estate, college-related event activity from the arts to sports and, most importantly, young people who stayed, married, had families and edified a full city renaissance. The college became a major player in every facet of Charleston.

Riley noted his own personal friends for their timely advice, profound friendship and political support.

"There are so many wonderful relationships I have been fortunate to have experienced over these many years," Riley considered. "My best friend from school, Pat Brennan, is a doctor in Texas. Pat built his own winery. We stay in touch. Then there are the other long-term friends from both Bishop England High School and The Citadel—Michael Robinson, Mike Duffy and Jimmy Kerr. You couldn't have better friends than that. I also enjoyed my classmates like Tommy Hartnett and Tommy Lavelle and a rich group of others."

"Joe was always a great friend and was in our wedding," Hartnett reminisced. "I first met Joe when he was seven. We became fine friends in the neighborhood. We played pick-up sandlot sports like basketball and baseball and found so many other things to do in Charleston growing up. We took our bicycles to Colonial Lake and to the little corner stores. Joe was fun but had a serious side, especially as a student. When people asked me what event changed Charleston, I point to the biggest one—Joe Riley's election as mayor in 1975. That changed everything for the better."

The Hartnett-Riley duo also shared time in the South Carolina State House. They have remained steadfast friends for a lifetime.

Riley graduated from Bishop England in 1960 and from The Citadel in 1964. He completed his law degree at the University of South Carolina in 1967.

"I roomed with both Mike Duffy and his brother, Larry, at different times going through Carolina law school," Riley said.

Both Duffy lawyers became judges. Larry Duffy became a magistrate, and Mike Duffy became a federal judge. They both mention Joe Riley as one would mention a person nearly beatified.

"Joe Riley is the greatest visionary of our times," Mike Duffy said. "I ascribe every great thing that has happened in Charleston over the last thirty-five years to the common denominator of one man's passion—Mayor Joseph P. Riley Jr."

"I knew back in law school that Riley was special. He was driven, he was intelligent and he displayed fine judgment and care for his fellow man," Larry Duffy recalled. "It is no wonder that we Charlestonians have received tremendous benefit from his leadership."

At the 2011 Hibernian annual St. Patrick's Day Banquet, Riley was cited as the Hibernian Society's honoree with a formal biographical page and a toast. Mike Duffy performed the toast in which he related to the 826 tuxedoed attendees, "We are living in the 'Age of Riley.'" The full toast brought all to their feet in elongated applause for this humbled, but deserving man.

Politics being politics, there are others always seeking the role of mayor. But it is the contention of this author and throngs of voters that Joe Riley, now age sixty-eight, will be the mayor of Charleston as long as he wants to be. There is probably no mayor that has worked harder and provided more anywhere. His days are scheduled by the half hour, end to end. He has little daily time for anything but lunch with his wife, Charlotte—when even that is not preempted. He has multiple evening events every week. He is careful to weigh events and try not to hurt feelings when he cannot physically attend. This dilemma is constant.

Yet Riley balances it all as well as anyone could possibly expect.

"I work hard at balancing. It takes emotional energy to weigh things," Riley noted. "To be successful, you need to be both creative and energetic. You need to be in shape. I book my schedule weeks at a time. If I'm not away or going for dinner as part of an event, I go home to Charlotte. I go into work early, and when I go home, I do not take my work with me. I close the file."

The file on Joe Riley is not closed. He is running for mayor an unprecedented tenth time. If (read: when) elected, Riley will take Charleston through forty years of progress. Make that incredible and unbelievable progress. He would have taken a city in the yawn of a deep sleep to the top of the world stage. He will have completed forty years—the same number of years it took Moses in the Old Testament to lead the Jews through the desert—with purpose and determination. Like Moses, he would have won over skeptics and instilled a sense of destiny. Unlike Moses, he somehow knew where he was going.

"When you put something on the world stage, you accept the role of what's expected," Riley concluded.

It is expected that Charleston will continue to rise under Riley's leadership and likely beyond because of the foundation he established. He raised our sensibilities as well as our expectations. He enlightened us. He captured our imagination and forged our pride.

He is not a man that can be bracketed within forty years or a hundred. He is a man of the ages. Indeed, he is the defining man of his own age.

He is the man who would be Moses.

It was a sad day when Mayor Joe Riley, who wrote the foreword to this book, stepped down as the four-decade mayor of Charleston. A biography of his life was written by a *Charleston Post and Courier* writer, Brian Hicks. It was titled *The Rise of Charleston*. Yes, that's the name of this book, too! Upon seeing this, I contacted Brian to apprise him of the impending confusion and congratulate him on his production. He was embarrassed about the title oddity since mine was written five years earlier. No worries. If you think you're reading Brian Hicks's *The Rise of Charleston* right now…apologies. It was quite well written, and I highly recommend it.

Joe Riley accepted a position as the first professor in the newly established Joseph P. Riley Jr. Endowed Chair of American Government and Public Policy at The Citadel. As a fan of the mayor's, I attended the announcement. Appropriately, it was made at the return of his class of 1964 for its fiftieth Citadel reunion.

Riley accomplished more for Charleston in his forty years as mayor than perhaps any other Charlestonian ever. He did so by epitomizing the values of perseverance, faith, leadership, assertiveness and creativity.

There will never be another like him.

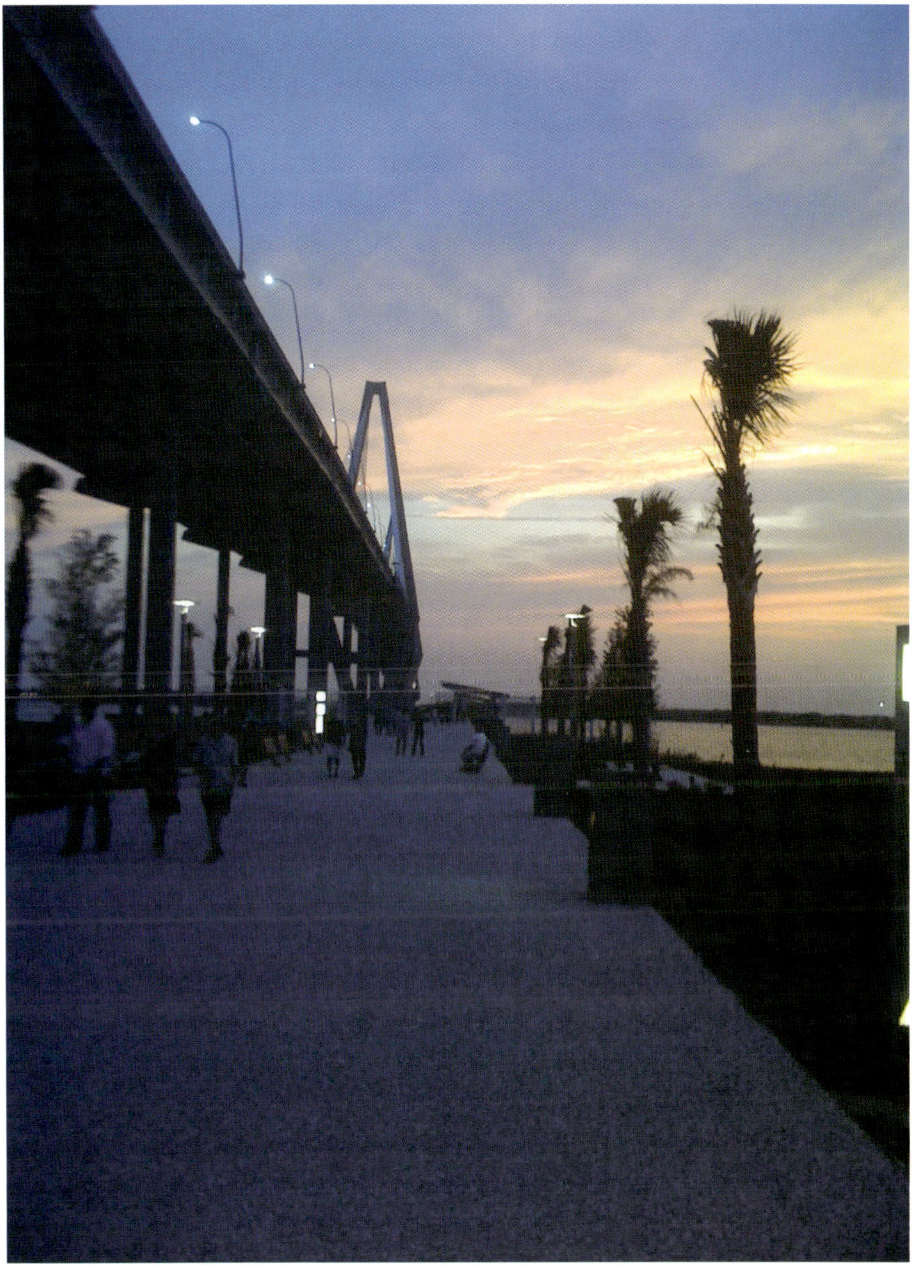

An evening at Mount Pleasant Pier, where fishing, dancing and ice cream augment the best sunset over Charleston across the Cooper River. *(W. Thomas McQueeney)*

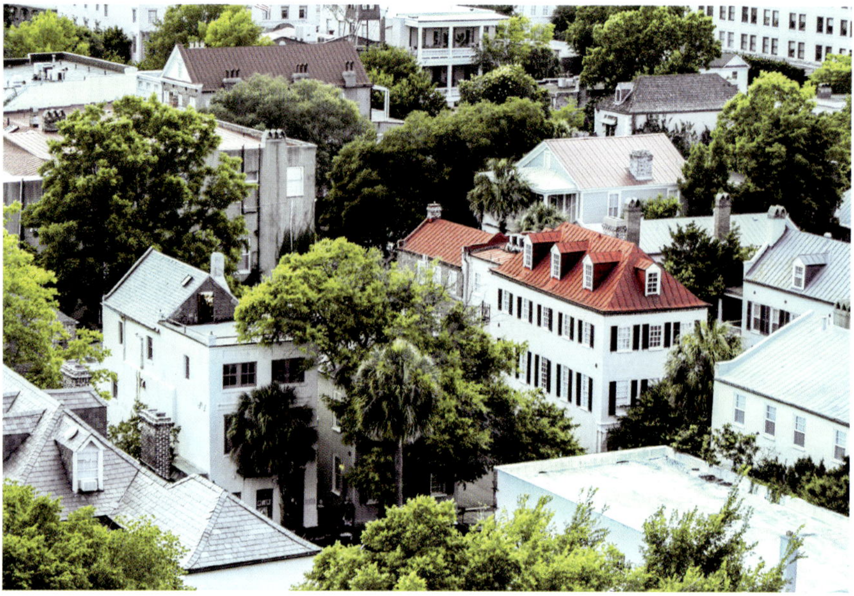

Charleston from the People's Building. The weave of rooftops and foliage stretches from the harbor to the two rivers, the Ashley and the Cooper. *(W. Thomas McQueeney)*

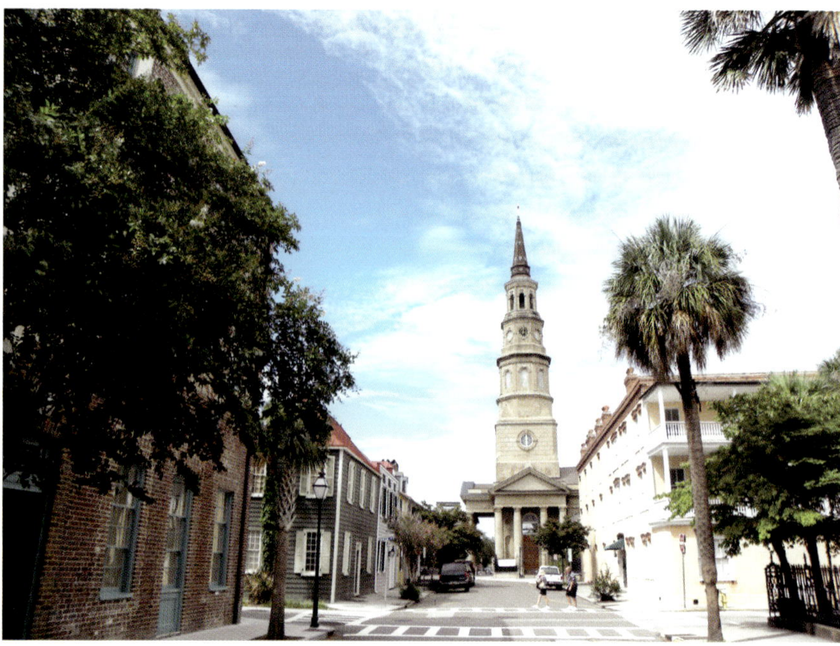

A view of St. Philip's Church. The Holy City is a collage of influences that originate from Europe and Africa, as well as the flourishing of religious freedoms. *(W. Thomas McQueeney)*

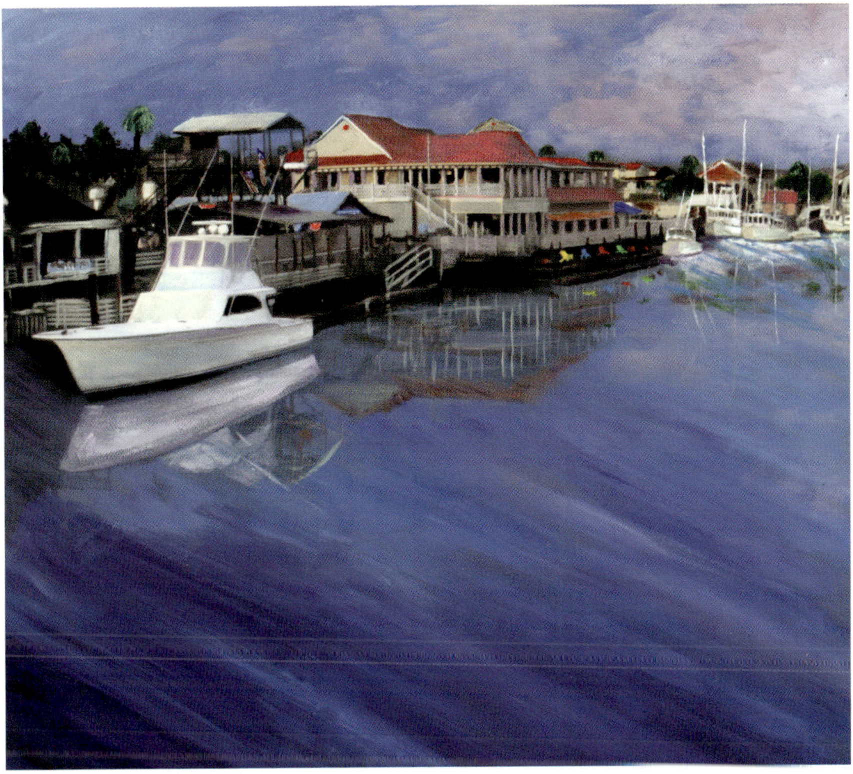

The closeness of the ocean has been beneficial for a commercial fishing industry and the resulting group of fine seafood restaurants along Shem Creek.
(Acrylic on canvas by W. Thomas McQueeney)

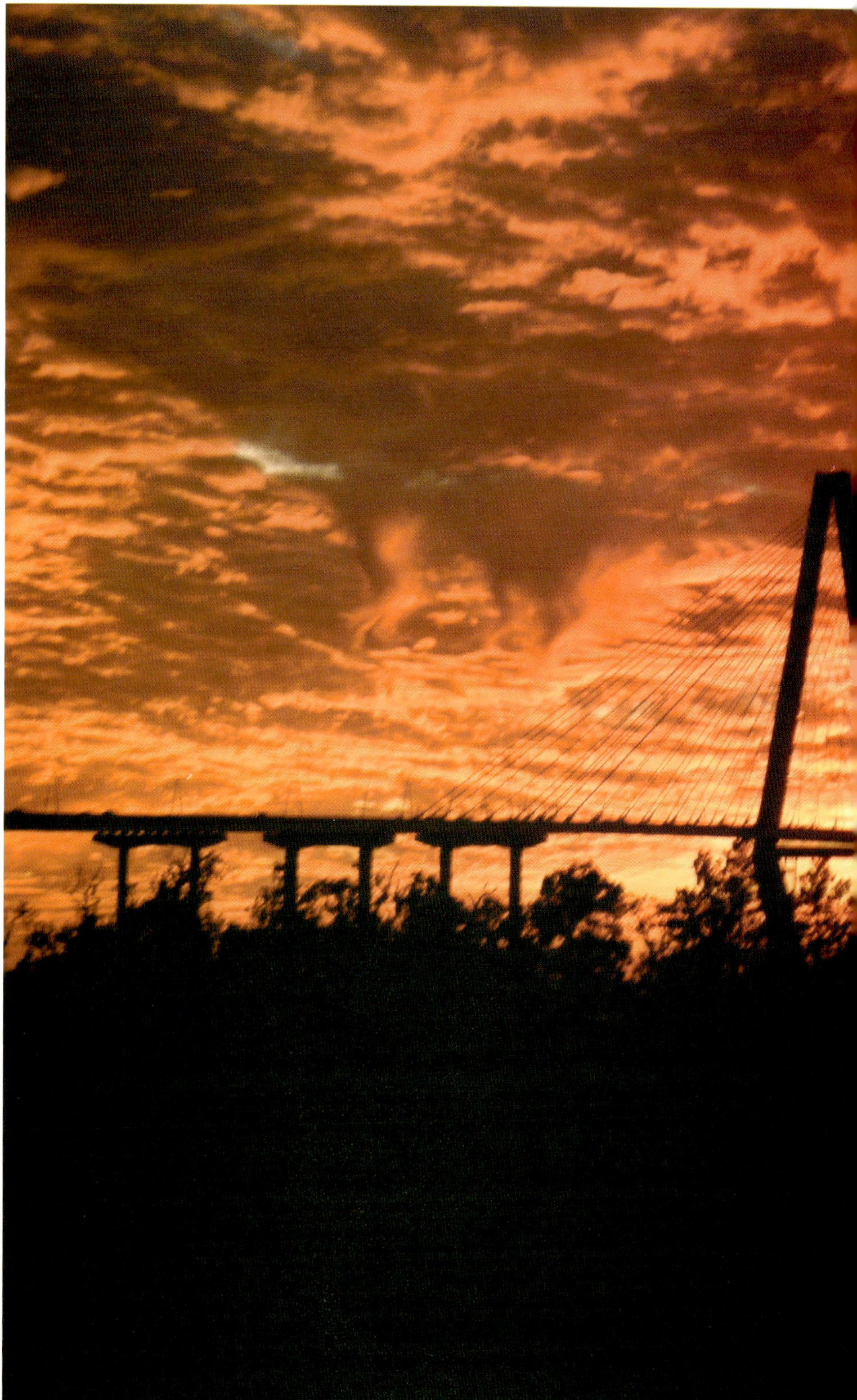

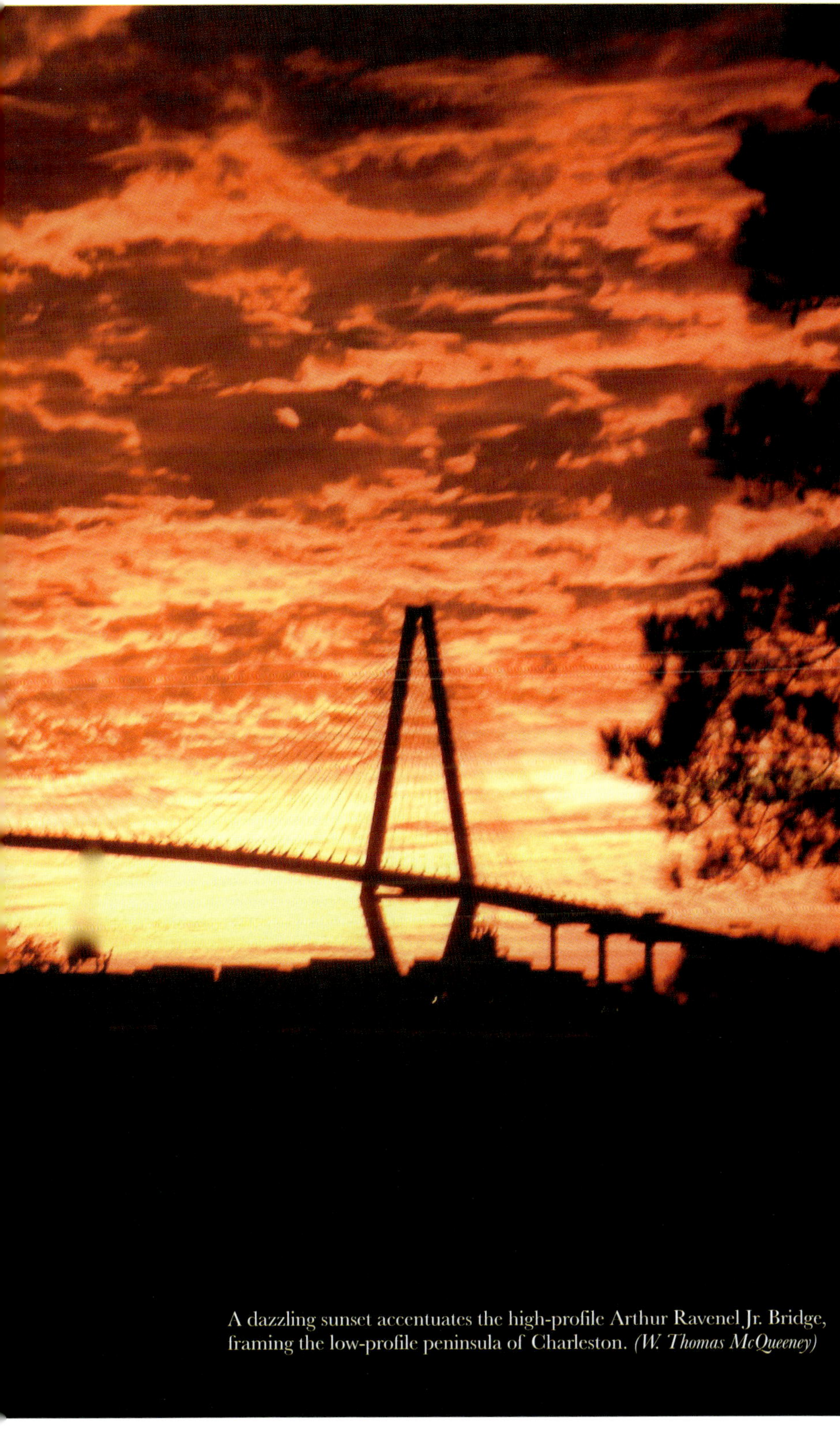

A dazzling sunset accentuates the high-profile Arthur Ravenel Jr. Bridge, framing the low-profile peninsula of Charleston. *(W. Thomas McQueeney)*

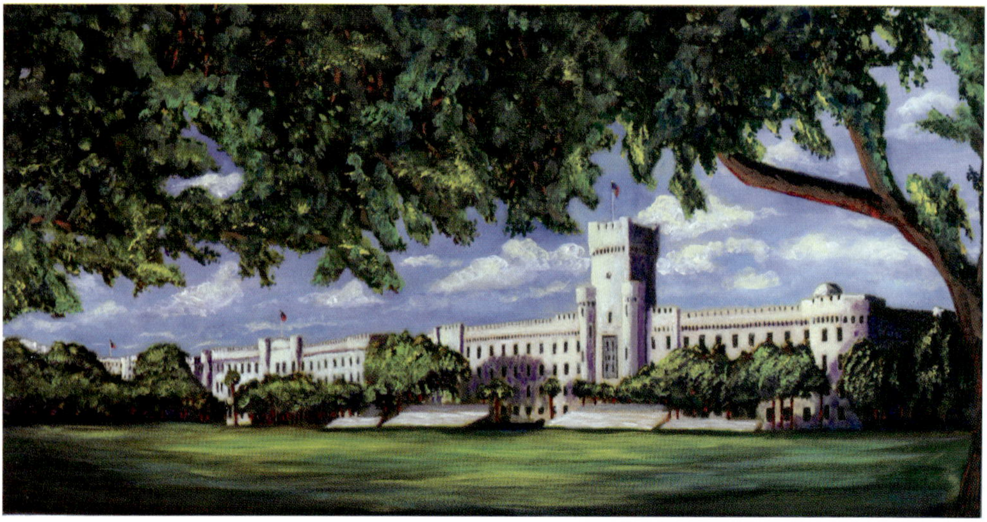

The Citadel, founded in 1842, became coeducational in 1996. The institution espouses "duty, honor and respect." *(Oil on canvas by W. Thomas McQueeney)*

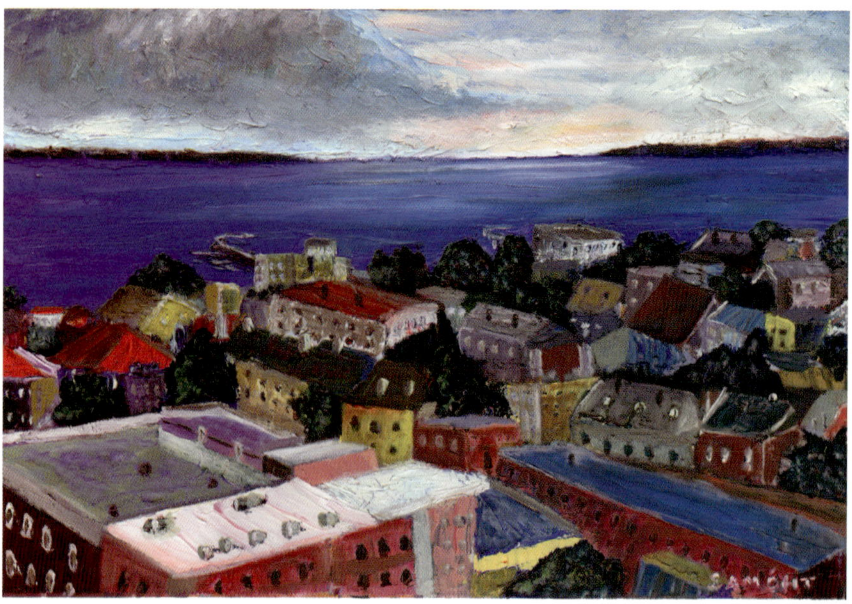

Palette knife painting of Charleston's rooftops. *(Oil on canvas by W. Thomas McQueeney)*

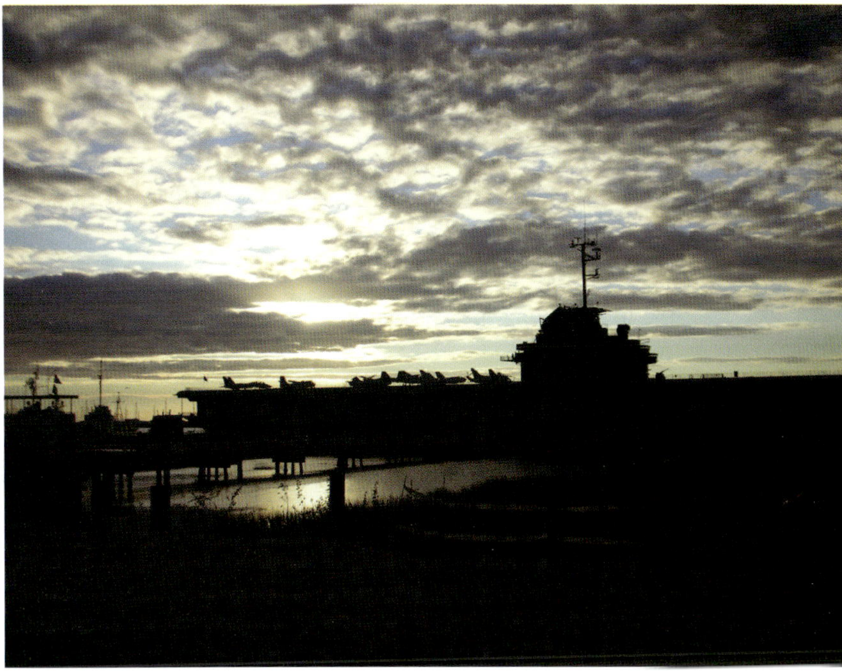

The *Yorktown* at sunset. The "Fighting Lady" has become a fixture of Charleston Harbor, like Fort Sumter, the Morris Island Lighthouse and the High Battery. *(W. Thomas McQueeney)*

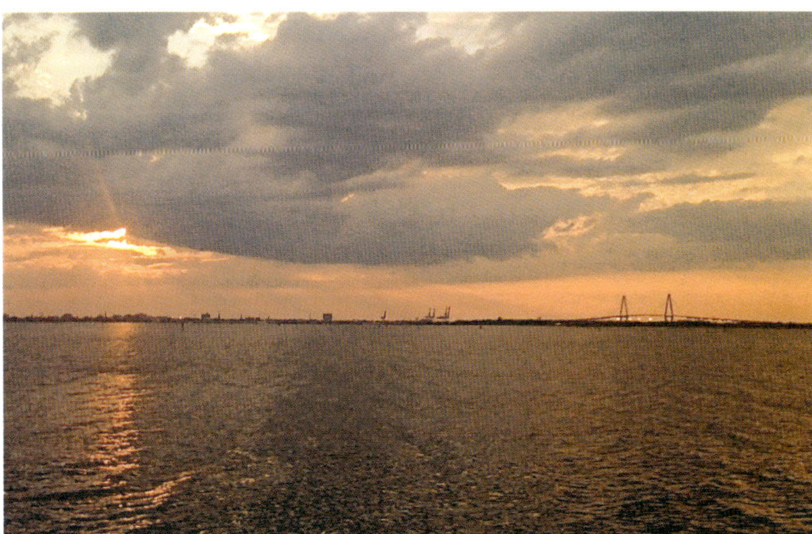

Charleston Harbor from Sullivan's Island at sunset. The wide, deep harbor helped to make Charleston the largest city in the colonial period of the South. Founded in 1670, Charleston still depends upon the economic benefit of its natural harbor. *(W. Thomas McQueeney)*

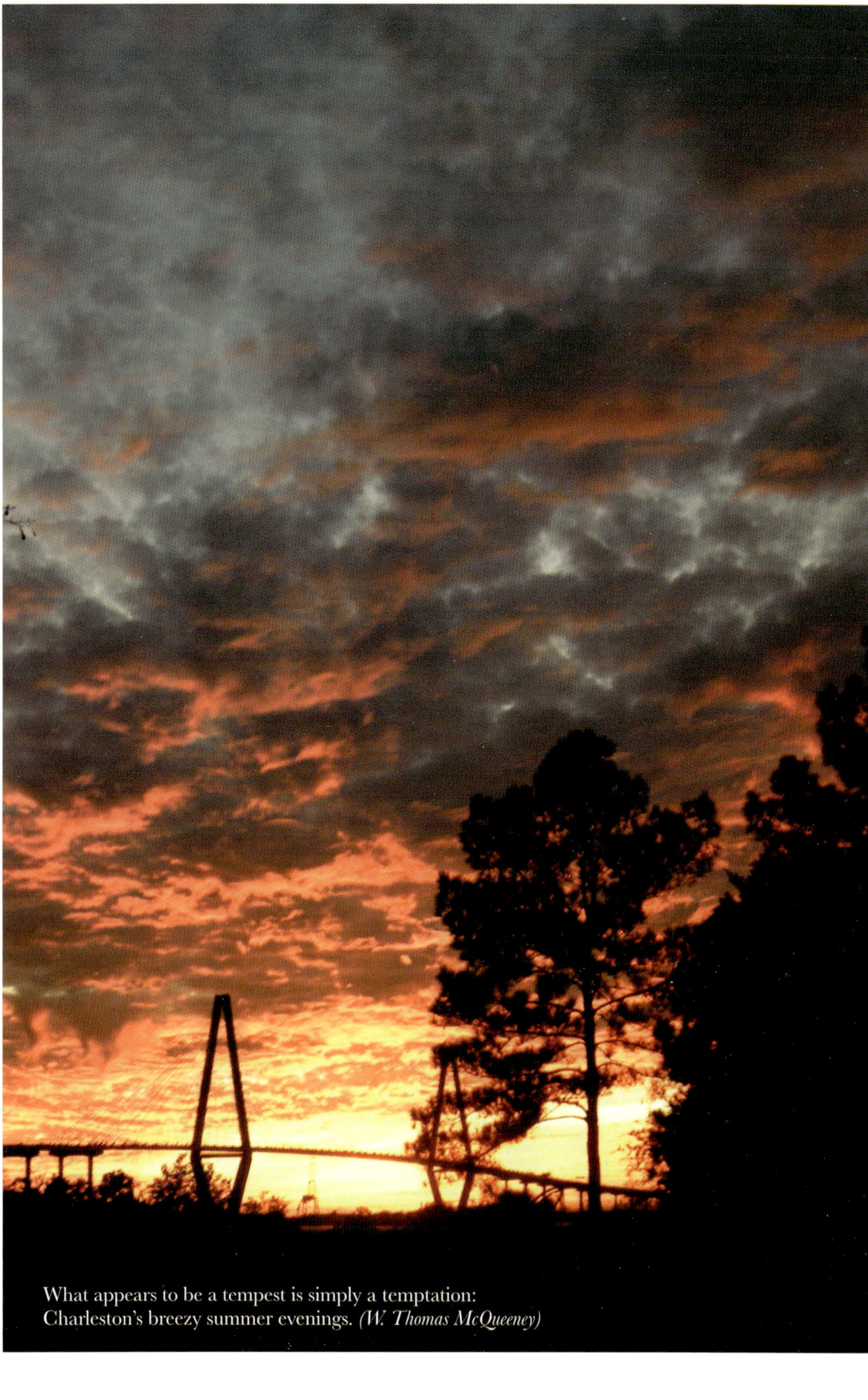

What appears to be a tempest is simply a temptation:
Charleston's breezy summer evenings. *(W. Thomas McQueeney)*

Alex Sanders at Large

There is a Ben Franklin and a Thomas Jefferson wrapped into Judge Alex Sanders. Throw in a Will Rogers as well. His prowess covers a Renaissance man's smorgasbord—and then some. He began his young adulthood in the circus. With all due reverence to the court system he proctored later in life, he's been in the "big top" ever since. He is an army veteran, a lawyer, a passionate chef and a founder of the Charleston School of Law; he has also been an elected legislator, the chief judge of the South Carolina Court of Appeals, a Harvard Fellow and, for nine years, president of the College of Charleston. There is another handful of significant roles, not counting the accidental ones that happened along the way. He's a husband to the beautiful Zoe Sanders and father to a replication also named Zoe. He is a proud grandfather of the younger Zoe's twin boys.

Sanders is also an author and humorist and may be proficient or accomplished at some other distinct passion or discipline next week or next year. The humorist that he cannot help but be has been unpaid, spontaneous and original.

His Wentworth Street office is full of memorabilia from his dozen or so careers. He works every day with coat and tie ready for the unplanned.

"I've never been able to keep a steady job," Sanders noted, tongue in cheek. "I never planned anything. My life just happened."

He happened to life more so.

"For instance, when I lost the race for the United States Senate, Zoe said I needed to leave the state. She didn't mention whether she would leave with me. So I had an opportunity up in Cambridge, Massachusetts, to teach at the Harvard graduate school," Sanders recalled. "I taught there, and in time the folks at Cambridge wanted me to publish something. So I wrote a chapter. I just made something up. They loved it. So I wrote five more and sent it to a publisher. The New York publisher read what I wrote and then asked me to write a book about Southern politics and Strom Thurmond. I was not interested."

Sanders had busied himself writing about a subject he loved—baseball. His feverish research turned up evidence of games staged in many localities during the War Between the States. His own grandfather fought in that war. His report of the rise of the sport and how it had spread through the most unlikely of events earned Sanders an invitation to Cooperstown, New York. He was asked to present this subject—no doubt delivering other tangential remarks that endear an audience with his unique humor—at the Baseball Hall of Fame in the summer of 2011.

Add "orator" to his résumé.

His run for the United States Senate was uphill, but he made it exciting by closing the poll numbers at the end. He lost to another South Carolina lawyer, Lindsey O. Graham, who had made himself popular in South Carolina as a U.S. congressman in the impeachment prosecution of President Bill Clinton. Sanders had to win from the disadvantage of the minority party against a candidate that would have to make egregious errors along the way to lose. Graham stayed the course and nosed out Sanders, although Sanders did gain crossover voters with his inimitable brand of homespun humor.

"Senator Graham painted me as a liberal, which I am surely not. He campaigned by stating that 'He may not be a liberal, but his friends are liberals.' Well, I suppose I have friends of every variety, but that has never made my ideology theirs or theirs mine," Sanders pointed out. "Being elected a senator was the one goal that eluded me. Now I'm too old."

Sanders was raised in the Columbia area and graduated from the University of South Carolina and the University of Virginia law school. Getting to Charleston took no planning. It just happened. He was very familiar with Charleston in his formative years.

"My grandmother lived just off Anson Street. I came here as a boy and spent time with my first cousins. Her house was nothing special. I suppose it may be worth three or four million today," Sanders deadpanned. "Charleston was an awful place then. Sailors threw beer bottles out of third-floor windows, there was raw sewage in places and there wasn't much to the waterfront. Charleston was depressing. Joe Riley changed all of that."

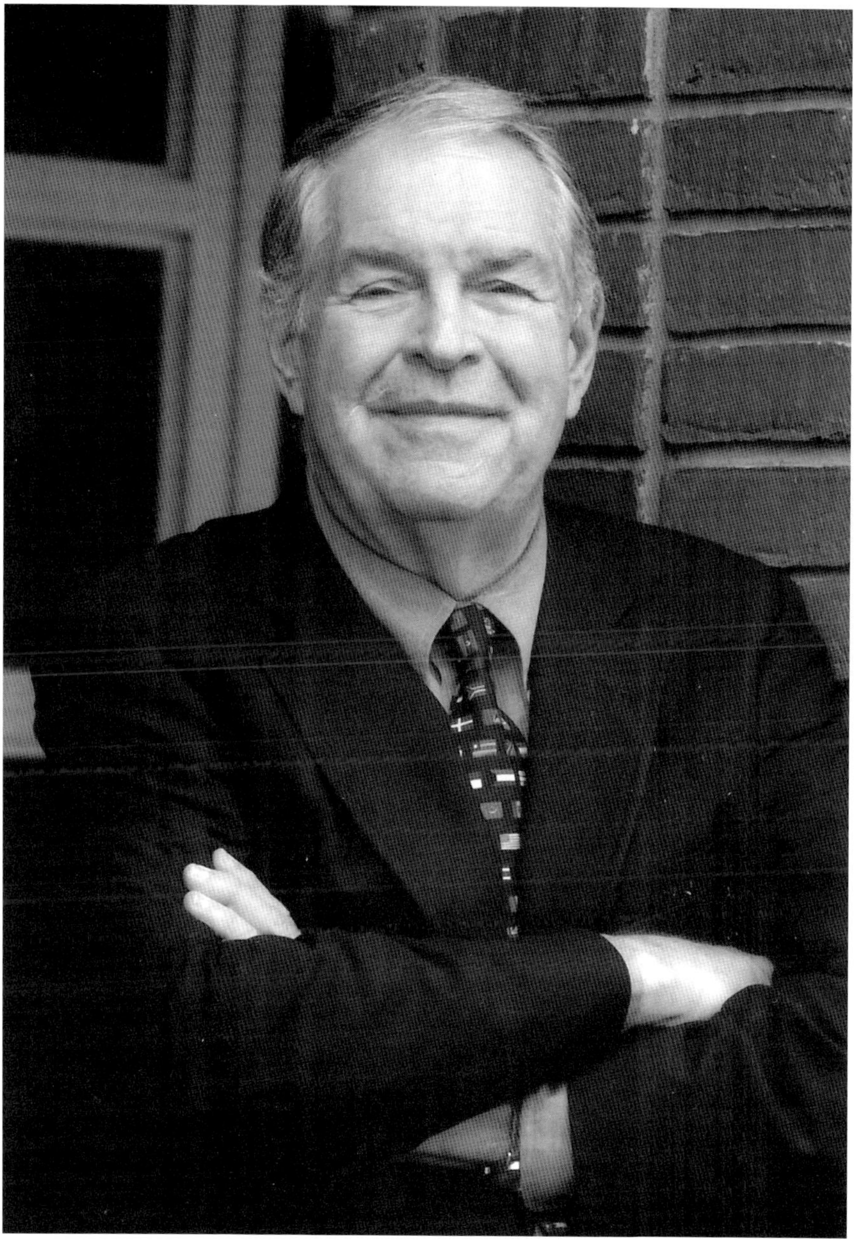

Judge Alex Sanders maintains an active daily routine at the College of Charleston and at the Charleston School of Law. *(Courtesy of College of Charleston)*

Sanders described other ugly scenes on the peninsula that were abominable but now inspire throngs from other lands to visit. His recollections of Charleston at its low ebb were from the late 1940s through the 1950s.

"Broad Street had the drainage problem as well that was obviously a failed sewer. The roads were rough and bumpy, and the sidewalks were as tattered as the houses. The mindset of Charleston was insular still in the 1950s—like the Jews did and the Chinese as well. All three lost conflicts and put up walls so that they could remain unto themselves," Sanders noted. "Charleston withstood the longest siege of bombardment in history—five hundred days of constant shellfire from Union artillery emplacements. It was deeply demoralizing. There developed a siege mentality here well after the war was over. It became a walled city again, without the wall."

The Sanders view was chronicled in yet another paper he wrote. He voiced a story he researched recounting a visit from the celebrated humorist and playwright Oscar Wilde.

"It was in the year 1900 that Wilde visited Charleston. He was hosted by a family that had obviously suffered well past the war and had little to offer and less to show off. The whole city was rather bleak. Wilde was struggling to find something positive to say when they took a walk to the High Battery with his host," Sanders reported. "Wilde stopped at the sight of the rising moon and commented, 'The moon is so beautiful over the water.' His host immediately replied, 'You should have seen it before the war!'"

Sanders perked up to contrast the then-and-now changes of the Holy City. There was much he saw, and, like others from that era, he now finds the transition to a world city almost magical.

"There was but one fine restaurant on the entire peninsula—Perdita's. And the market area was full of drunken sailors and prostitutes," Sanders noted. "Most homes were in some state of disrepair. The infrastructure had failed. And the only decent bar was Henry's at the head of the market. And it was nothing special."

He had mentioned Mayor Joseph P. Riley Jr. as a catalyst for change. The mayor set out to make significant changes from his first day. He recalled the times as well. Sanders had served in the state legislature with Joe Riley.

The mayor had a keen ability to lead, and the city was ready not only to be led, but to leap forward.

"Joe Riley did so much more than anyone to elevate the physical city and to raise the consciousness of its citizens," Sanders continued. "In 1977, he brought in the Spoleto festival of arts. Spoleto brought the world to Charleston and Charleston to the world. The mindset did slowly change.

But even today you read in the paper about someone wanting to block the cruise ships from coming to Charleston. That same attitude is what kept the city in the dark ages not that many years ago."

It was also in that same early transition with the leadership of Joe Riley that the College of Charleston started its expansion from less than five hundred students to more than ten thousand. The college's growth tracked along the same path as Charleston's rise. In doing so, the campus was able to grow in quality with aesthetically appealing buildings lying out casually around the centuries-old oaks and signature palmettos. The economic engine the college created cannot be underestimated. Education is many things to many pundits. But to downtown merchants, it is a business.

Sanders's College of Charleston experience happened because a previous president and classmate from USC, Harry Lightsey, talked him into it. It was another case of not planning, but reacting. The college needed solid leadership after a run that included visionaries Ted Stern and Harry Lightsey. Sanders trusted Lightsey's judgment and guidance. He accepted the presidency of the college in 1992. He left to pursue a seat in the United States Senate in 2001.

Sanders enjoyed his college presidency role immensely. He recounted the experience in the eyes of the student.

"From my Wentworth Street office, you can walk out four or five blocks in any direction and find a viable city of ten thousand citizens under the age of twenty-five. It makes this a city of great interest and sometimes of great conflict," Sanders intimated. "There exist all types of the lifestyles with all their varying values to a community living together amongst us. It is truly an amazing place."

Tommy Eiserhardt, a local businessman with a retail establishment near the college, recalled the enjoyment of having lunch at the College of Charleston cafeteria with Sanders.

"The college's former athletic director and my good friend, Jerry Baker, used to take me to lunch on George Street frequently. Judge Sanders would sometimes join us. He was so incredibly entertaining," Eiserhardt noted. "The professors and students would come by to pay homage, and he'd stop to cordially reply or remark with something either brilliant or hilarious—and usually both. If you didn't pay attention, you might miss it. He was the best emissary the college ever had."

"When I served as the president of the college, I lived at 6 Glebe Street. John Rutledge, one of the signers of the Declaration of Independence, died in that house," Sanders pointed out. "There were Greek fraternity parties across the street on Wentworth, services at Grace Episcopal Church next to us and more services at Mount Zion AME Church next to that. There is no place like that anywhere else in the world.

"There is so much opportunity here that wasn't here before," Sanders continued. "You can go out to Kiawah and find a large community that came here during the same time that the college was ramping up. It's a fabulous community with a perfect plan for controlled growth. They're right there behind a security gate. Occasionally they let the Democrats in to cut the grass."

With all of the humor and rhetoric, it is apparent that Sanders is in his element in Charleston. His hound dog eyes light up when the subject of his favorite career is mentioned.

"It's no secret what I liked to do the best. I liked being a lawyer. Being a lawyer always gave me a higher sense of accomplishment at helping one single human being," Sanders intoned. "Being a lawyer is my life's most satisfying career achievement."

He had so many careers from which to choose. He almost had another one, had he not humored his way out of it.

"Pug Ravenel, a well-known Charlestonian and Harvard graduate, had placed my name into consideration for the vacant job as college president at Harvard University," Sanders related. "It was a preposterous nomination, and I was loath to ever leave Charleston again. Before I gave it too much consideration, my name was among those that leaked out to the *New York Times*. A reporter called and asked me what abilities I could bring to Harvard. I simply answered 'Well, I was able to put the College of Charleston on the map, and I think I can do the same for Harvard.' That ended that process for me."

He has remained here as a gift to our youth, our law school students and our newspaper writers looking for a great quote. He also participates in a number of productions that promote the arts, fund charities and benefit young minds. He was recently asked to join a panel discussion on the subject "Trial of the Century." There are erstwhile trials of the century like the Lindbergh kidnapping, the Rosenberg spy trial and, of course, the O.J. Simpson event near Hollywood. This real trial of the century was before television and radio. It happened in Dayton, Tennessee, in 1925.[25] Sanders agreed to be a part of the lofty discussion that essentially pitted science against the Bible in the Deep South. The world called it the Scopes Monkey Trial then, ostensibly because schoolteacher John T. Scopes taught Darwinian science that conjectured that we all came from apes. Sanders's ability to condense the issues for this interfaith panel was related in summary.

"First of all, it was an unfair appraisal of the great William Jennings Bryan [the famed lawyer who defended the biblical story]. Bryan was not an effective advocate late in his life. He had diminished mental acuity and was not as articulate as he was in his prior years," Sanders reported.

In fact, Bryan passed away just two weeks past the trial's conclusion, having been exhausted but judged the winner, upholding the biblical theorists and ministers.

"Regardless of the result of the verdict, the world of public opinion proved for Clarence Darrow [the other famous lawyer defending the teacher, Scopes]," Sanders continued. "The only place that Darrow did not win was in that Tennessee courtroom."

Add "community panelist" to the Sanders résumé. You may as well add "philosopher," "statesman" and "legal analyst." Sanders is all of these and more.

His role as president of the college from 1992 to 2001 was marked by the college's resurgence and expansion. New athletic fields were developed just over the bridge in Mount Pleasant, and several academic departments were enhanced. Plans for new low-profile dormitories took shape, and the college bought the property that was formerly Bishop England High School. A state-of-the-art university library was built on the site, to include Wi-Fi, a courtyard and a media center. Under Sanders's guidance, this oldest municipal college in the United States would hit its stride. But he is humble in the recollection of his impact.

"I give all the credit to Ted Stern, a wonderful man with a creative mind. He was the first to see the college in a larger regional and even national role," Sanders reflected. "And then my friend Harry Lightsey built upon the Ted Stern plan. He was the perfect college president. These two and others shepherded the college to become a fine academic institution. I simply followed their lead."

If you believed Sanders, you would think that his personal résumé would be a blank sheet of paper.

Instead, it's a lively volume of adventure, accomplishment and anecdotes that should be leather bound for the world to admire. Judge Alex Sanders has lived his life wide, high and deep in multicolor. His unplanned meanderings made it so.

Teaching Responsibility

Yvette and Hillery Douglas

The standard that society uses to measure success is all too often the gauge of wage, the rash of cash. But money is just one of the trappings of success. It seems that the very successful have a much higher goal than money, and the temporary impact of wealth is, to them, often something to direct to charities. The real success of any person can be related to a more valuable resource—their time.

There is a Charleston-area family that can boast of more success than a lifetime would dare to hold. They have achieved it in subtleties. They have given their time.

Yvette and Hillery Douglas began their life together in 1960. It's true that they were "steady dates" at Bonds Wilson High School in North Charleston by their junior year. It's also true that they both came from buoyant and robust families that underscored the sense of personal responsibility in all things. The Douglases were determined to seek the greatness within while living without. They both persevered by accepting challenge, overcoming adversity and listening to the great mentors that formed their world view.

Hillery Douglas is a name familiar to most Charlestonians. Twice, Douglas served as the chairman of the Charleston County School Board. He served that august body for sixteen years, retiring in 2008. In that role, he brought much stability and direction to kindergarten-through-twelfth-grade education in the state's most populated county.

Hillery Douglas is a chemist. He retired from a position related to his expertise with the Charleston naval shipyard after thirty years of service.

The vast shipyard and cohabitant Charleston naval base closed in 1996. Douglas has since operated an independent testing facility, doing work for a plethora of commercial and governmental concerns. He tests water, soil and even gases in his general-purpose analytical lab. Douglas is now in his early seventies but physically impressive and conversationally astute. He is multifaceted and brilliant. Though his temples are gray and his sight is eyeglass aided, his acumen and insight are refreshingly youthful.

"My dad, John Douglas, was way ahead of his time," Hillery reminisced. "He'd say 'It takes two to argue.' He'd just sit there among all of the noise and absorb. He had a great sense about him. He knew things, and he'd just sit and wait until everything calmed down. Then he'd speak. And you can bet that when he did, it usually resolved the issue."

"His dad was an original," Yvette Douglas added. "To tell you how he was, all I have to do is tell you about the night my own father died in 1966. He took me in his arms with so much care and concern and said, 'I'm your Daddy now.' He cared. He was there for us."

Yvette's father, a Native American Cherokee, lived to be eighty-nine. Toby Armlin Jacobs had little formal education, but he did have the qualities one would most appreciate in fatherhood. Yvette is one of five children who benefitted from his enterprise, toil and resolve.

Hillery and Yvette Douglas have been married for fifty-one years. One would be hard-pressed to find another couple like them. They love each other profoundly. It's their first great success. The other successes grew from this like a profusion of conjunctions and prepositions in a sentence diagram. Everything fell into place underneath this relationship.

Yvette Douglas is a coliseum full of personality. It is bigger than imaginable. She lights up a room. Her appearance belies any indication of a supplemental Social Security check. She is set in her principle of morality and self-reliance as an answer for most of today's burning issues. Her consistency of common sense might knock Dr. Phil off of his time slot. One cannot enter into a conversation with Yvette Douglas saddened and fail to leave happy.

The "CliffsNotes" of parenting is a five-minute course at the Douglas table.

"We had cardinal rules," Yvette indicated. "And we didn't have back-up plans for failure. They were simple. First, you *will* go to college. Second, you *will* graduate on time. Anything beyond that and you're on your own. Next, you *must* have a job before you graduate. And that job *must* be out of town."

The out-of-town job rule was at first puzzling. Oh yeah—self-reliance. That clears it up. Everything dovetails back to the Douglas principle—you are in charge of yourself.

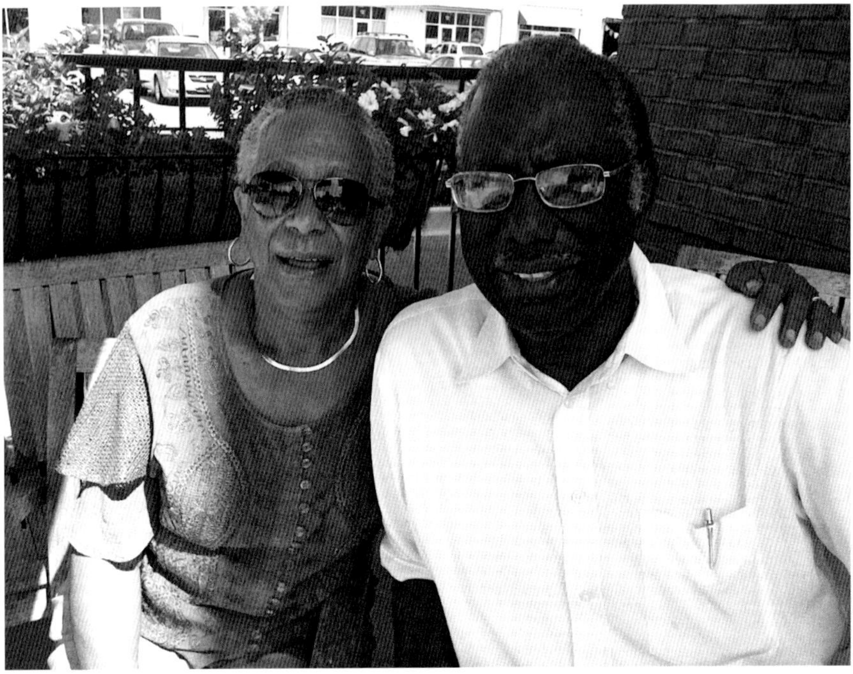

Yvette and Hillery Douglas have raised five highly successful children by their simple precepts of morality, responsibility and academic performance. *(W. Thomas McQueeney)*

"We didn't want any of them to be inhibited by either of us," Hillery added. "It was important to us that each of them became their own person. They could grow their own sense of self-worth without us being an influence to lean upon. In this way, we both felt, they could reach their full potential."

The roll call of their progeny would give a strong indication of the substance of success from formula to result.

Hillery Douglas Jr. and his wife, Cynthia, have five children. They live in Roswell, Georgia. He is owner of Capital Services in Roswell. Hillery Jr. graduated in 1982 from The Citadel, where he was a standout football player. And there is yet another college football player for the Douglases to follow, youngest son J.P. Hillery, a freshman football quarterback at Southern University.

Tony Douglas also played football at The Citadel his freshman year as receiver but decided to devote his time to his studies. He was Company K commander, and he graduated with honors—on time—with the class of 1987. He has achieved the rank of colonel in the United States Air Force.

Tony is the vice wing commander at Eglin Air Force Base near Valparaiso, Florida. Tony and wife Inger have two children.

Maria Douglas Reeve is a politics editor for the *St. Paul Pioneer Press* in St. Paul, Minnesota. She graduated from Davidson College in 1989. Her husband, Tad, is a sportswriter for the same newspaper. Maria and Tad have three children.

Karen Douglas Harris is a schoolteacher at Beck's Academy in Greenville. She graduated from the College of Charleston in 1991. Husband Andre is also a graduate of The Citadel and is a former basketball star. Karen and Andre have four children.

Baby boy Jack Douglas ended his Citadel football career as the number-one all-time rushing quarterback in The Citadel's history with 3,674 yards. He and his wife, Valencia (nicknamed "Vince"), have two children. Jack lives in Columbia, South Carolina, and works in an executive position with Allstate Insurance Companies.

Jack Douglas (named for grandfather John) was the South Carolina Male Athlete of the Year in 1992, the same year he graduated from The Citadel. In the seventy previous years of the Southern Conference, no player had ever rushed for more yardage. He quarterbacked the most successful Citadel football team ever, leading them to a number-one ranking and eleven wins in the 1992 season. His teams beat NCAA Division I-A powerhouses Arkansas and South Carolina. He's in both The Citadel's Athletic Hall of Fame and the statewide South Carolina Athletic Hall of Fame. He also served as vice chairman for The Citadel Board of Visitors.

"Jack was raised by his two original parents and four others," Yvette intoned with humor. "There was not anything that poor child did without the oversight of his four older siblings. He could not ever mess up!"

The self-reliance espoused by their parents proved fruitful for the Douglases' five children. They adhered to the cardinal rules that were set before them without exception. They achieved their individual life identities in other places owing to the precepts their parents established.

Leaving did not preclude visiting. The ever-practical Douglases had another plan. The benefit of sixteen grandchildren lent itself to the development of the next formula. "Camp Douglas" was born.

"As grandparents, it became our privilege to have the grandchildren from time to time," Yvette noted. "And we enjoyed every moment, but the moments could be end-to-end without a plan. So we invented 'Camp Douglas.' It was a way for us to schedule grandchildren visits and have our children and their spouses get time away for themselves. We'd coordinate an agenda and plan events around the grandchildren. We'd take them to the aquarium downtown one day and to the water park another. It was during the summer when school was out. We did this for years until they just got too old to continue. Of the sixteen grandchildren, only one is under the age of nine now."

The camp is over, but the excitement for the Douglases continues. They travel to see their children and grandchildren as often as they can in every season.

"We have a travel schedule, all to do with sports," Yvette pointed out. "We drive to Columbia, to Greenville, to Florida, to Baton Rouge. It's all part of the sports schedule—who's playing what when."

The Douglases are proud members of St. Mark's Episcopal Church on Thomas Street in downtown Charleston.

"It's the largest integrated Episcopal congregation in Charleston," Yvette said. "It is not a church that is exclusive or has difficult political views. It is inclusive. We enjoy going there every Sunday."

The Douglas family has had great input and impact upon the Charleston area when they were only two, then seven and now two again. They recall the road traveled.

"I was born and raised near Lincolnville and Ladson," Hillery stated. "I told everybody I was born in a log cabin and went to a one-room school. I did go to a one-room schoolhouse! That area was mostly farmland then. We had just a handful of acreage but raised a little bit of everything, from okra to squash and tomatoes. We raised corn for the pigs and horses. We raised two acres of cotton to get about three large bales. That could bring in a thousand dollars. That was a fortune. But the cotton was by allotment. If you grew more than your allotment, the county people could come in and plow the extra cotton under. And there would go all of your labor, your time and the expenses.

"I had a natural interest in the education of children," Hillery continued. "On the advice of my father, I pursued my degree at Allen University [class of 1963]. The older folks always said, 'Get your education. Education will carry you where money won't take you.' They said, 'Be a productive citizen.' I took that message to heart.

"When I became involved with the Charleston County School Board, I wanted to provide better opportunities for all children. I wanted to see them develop their interests and their skills. I wanted to see Charleston grow better in the next generation and the one after that," Douglas said. "But in the process, there are politics that get in the way. There are those that run for the school board on a single agenda—and when that agenda is completed or it fails, they have nothing else to do. Unfortunately, the politics sometimes makes for a poor television broadcast report or newspaper article. That sends the wrong message to all concerned—parents, the legislature, the children, business and others.

"There is a school for every child in Charleston. There are magnet schools and those for the arts. The opportunities are endless. What really makes me sad is to see children not take advantage of what we have built here. To see children fail or even drop out is a community failure and a failure of responsibility in other areas, especially parents. Parents are the key. They have to be responsible and teach responsibility to their children. The teacher is the second level. It's the parents that must get involved if we are to have successful education."

One could well see why Hillery Douglas had become a popular mainstay of the Charleston County School Board. His pragmatic wife had another insight.

Yvette gave a more general chronology. "For blacks, education was once illegal. Then it became legal but ineffective, with poor facilities and limited curriculum. And there was also segregation. Eventually, through the toil of so many, integration occurred at a great cost. Expectations rose. And now there are these wonderful opportunities in state-of-the-art environments. To see a young black child not assert his or herself or to drop out after all that those generations before have endured and sacrificed is not only sad, but disturbing.

"We may become a third-world country because of the many opportunities that some in this younger generation, of every race and culture, are wasting. We have to be better parents first. We need to understand the political processes and cooperate in a community spirit. We have to work towards understanding and not be closed minded or extreme. Being extreme in any direction is dangerous. I have great concern for where this country is headed," Yvette explained.

"Sometimes I'd pick up the paper and Hillery would be on the front page trying to move the school board forward in some way. Then I'd turn to the sports section, and there was Jack!" Yvette noted. "So both of them were doing something good I could read about."

Indeed there was much of which to be proud. That sense of accomplishment pervades the Douglas family, where success is the norm. It's because perspective has been properly placed in priority order in the list of life's ideals. They are the fundamentals Yvette and Hillery Douglas demanded during their children's youth—respect, initiative and performance. A remarkable genetic pool amply supported the goal.

The close family relationship exists yet, despite geographic impediments.

"What makes me happy now is to see my grandchildren being raised by my children," Yvette stated in a feigned gush of pride. "The grandchildren are doing some of the same things the children did. And now we see our children as effective and responsible parents."

Hillery added, "To have raised five kids in the Charleston area, who were able to get their education, accepted our guidance and went to church and went on to become successful adults—that makes me personally happy."

Success breeds success. The happiness is in the prepositions.

Those prepositions are five children that sub-bracket those sixteen grandchildren. The thought of each illuminates the Douglases of Charleston.

And that happiness is rooted in the quiet confidence of a generational responsibility fulfilled. It's another element in the careful planning of success—real success that matters, like the constancy in the upbringing of children.

Success for the Douglas family appears in the roll call of connections that are the expected laboratory outcome. They are chains of conjunctions—love and responsibility and oversight and creativity and energy and guidance and faith and, importantly, a sense of humor. There is not a Douglas in Charleston or in the hinterlands who does not employ the warmth of the family smile.

The success that is the Douglas family of Charleston has been exported. Other benefit to other communities has surely followed. Charleston still has the originals.

The Senator from Charleston

Fritz Hollings

At some point in a career, a politician has a chance to deserve an upper-level moniker that goes well beyond being labeled by a party affiliation, a career accomplishment or gaffe or even by longevity to a cause. There is a plane reached when one thinks of a career politician in another light—that of being a statesman. Ernest F. "Fritz" Hollings earned that status earlier in his career than many others.

The venerable six-and-a-half-term United States senator from South Carolina retired from office in 2005. He served the people of South Carolina thirty-eight years in the United States Senate alone. Add in four years in the executive branch of state government and ten more in the state legislature. Oh, and add another three overseas in the United States Army during wartime.

If you're still counting, that amounts to fifty-five years of high-level service to his state and country. He is a resolute and committed statesman.

Hollings grew up on the peninsula of Charleston—on the "shade-tree end" of President Street. He was born of a German family that settled in the Holy City several generations back. Hollings honed his people skills at Charleston High School—just a few blocks away by foot—and at The Citadel. The Citadel was in the opposite direction, also by foot.

He related his childhood memories, especially the youthful working years.

"Our parents were insistent upon culture, manners and ethics. We worked to help the family from early ages. I worked as a night clerk at the Francis Marion Hotel. I was only fifteen," Hollings remembered. "Oliver Riley Strohecker, the principal, got me the job. Everybody worked then."

Growing up in Charleston meant a wide range of things to those of Hollings's generation. He remembered the times, because he remembered his father's mandate to be personally responsible.

"My parents and others in the community grew up with an attitude," Hollings noted. "They demanded, 'We have to work hard, help others, be responsible, and we've got to get better.' Getting better was a mandate."

His reference of betterment was in the context of Southern Reconstruction followed by the Great Depression. A misery index had persisted for nearly one hundred years. Hollings would become a major part of the concept of Charleston's well-overdue betterment. He loved the Holy City and wanted it to benefit from its long road back from the Civil War.

"The Historic Charleston Foundation and the Board of Architectural Review came alive in the 1950s," Hollings noted. "I believe they were trying to protect the community from structures like the People's Building."

The People's Building was completed in 1911 of an ugly, yellow brick.[26] It rose nine stories as Charleston's first brush with modernity. It was like a part of New York or Chicago that nobody wanted in Charleston. It had the city's first elevator. Tour guides repeat the story of when President William Howard Taft came to Charleston shortly after the completion of the People's Building. Taft rode the new elevator to the roof deck. When he strutted out to the parapet wall, Taft is said to have pronounced the view to be the best in all of America. Politicians and sitting presidents were prone to embellishment. Charlestonians retell this tale to add the postscript that it was truly a magnificent view, because it was the only rooftop view of Charleston that did not have the People's Building in it!

"I also recall that Hugh Lane spent the large sum of fifty thousand dollars to preserve the building at 141 East Bay Street, next to the bank at Broad," Hollings recalled. "They had planned to tear it down. There were other people like Hugh Lane that saw great purpose in preserving what had been, rather than building something new.

"It's a good thing these people came forward. When I became governor, Charleston was starting to have more character, and a more robust tourist industry was becoming a reality. I appointed Joe Riley Sr. as the new director of the State Tourism Commission. He did a wonderful job. You could see where young Joe Riley was influenced. His son, Joe, then took Charleston to a new level as mayor. You have to give Mayor Joe Riley so much of the credit. He made the city tourist friendly. Tourists have made Charleston."

Senator Fritz Hollings quietly and humbly changed Charleston as well.

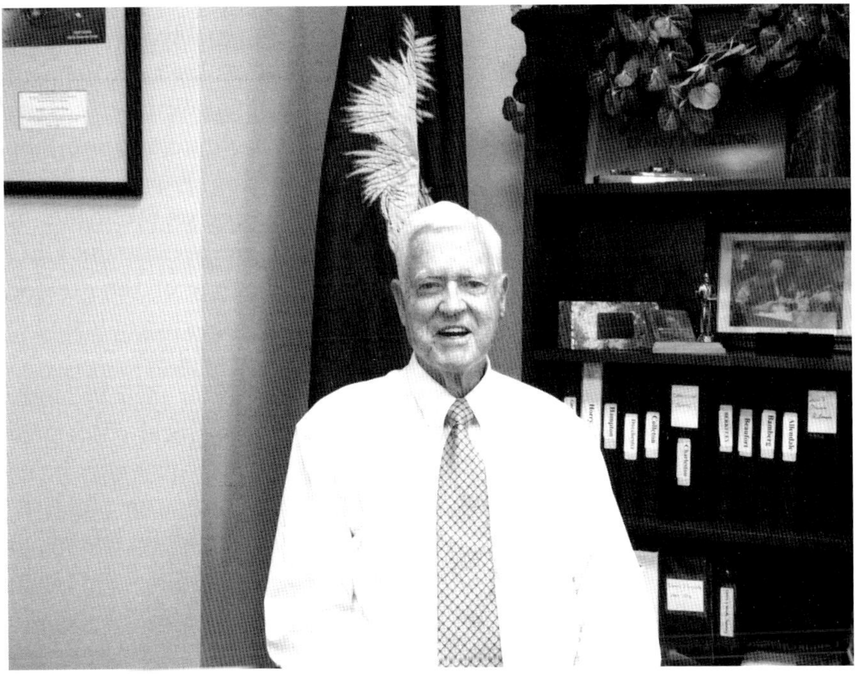

Fifty-five years of formal service to the City of Charleston, the State of South Carolina and the United States of America has not retired Fritz Hollings's concern for the future. He still advises, writes editorials and fundraises for deserving causes. *(W. Thomas McQueeney)*

The senator's career was a vault from a bounce that was part of a catapult. He rose quickly.

He started that career as a Citadel student on his way to shaping history. Hollings neared his last semester at The Citadel when World War II had started.

"I distinctly remember General Summerall addressing the entire cadet corps in the chapel at noon. Summerall had devised much of the military defense of Hawaii and Pearl Harbor several years prior when he served as army chief of staff. He stated that America was at war and that Pearl Harbor's commanding admiral Kimmel would be court-martialed," Hollings recalled. "And, sure enough, he was. He said the commanding army general would be court-martialed, as well." Major General Walter Short was brought up on charges of dereliction of duty but was cleared by war's end.

"We had cancelled drill that Monday after December 7, and everyone was somber but angry. We were ready to retaliate. The entire class signed up for the war," Hollings continued. "And by May, we all went."

"Senator Hollings has let his service to the state and the country get in the way of what would likely have been a spectacular law career," noted Mike Duffy, a former law partner now serving as a federal judge. "His tenacity and brilliance would be no less impressive in the courtroom. There would be no one quite like him practicing in Charleston today."

Hollings was elected to three terms in the South Carolina House of Representatives beginning in 1949.[28] His colleagues in the house elected him as speaker pro tempore twice. He was subsequently elected lieutenant governor in 1954 and, at the age of thirty-six, governor in 1958. During his term, he intensified efforts to support public education. He began the program of technical colleges statewide and ushered in educational television. He was a vibrant and active governor who stayed on theme about making South Carolina a better place.

Hollings began his U.S. Senate career in 1966 in a special election to succeed Olin D. Johnston, who had died in office. He won the seat for the next six elections, making his term of service range from 1966 to 2005. He is the eighth-longest serving member of the Senate and, along with the late Senator Strom Thurmond, comprised the most senior tandem of senators in U.S. history. Though from opposing parties, they worked very well together for thirty-six years.

As the "senior junior" senator in the country, Hollings had his influence on many facets of political reforms and changes. He served as the Senate Budget Committee chairman and helped author fiscal reforms that made it a part of law to balance the budget. The Gramm-Rudman-Hollings Act of 1985[29] (and a 1987 revision) allowed for specific spending-cut measures each year. It was later supplanted by a similar act in 1990.[30]

Hollings entered the 1984 presidential race as one of eight Democrats seeking the party's nomination to face incumbent Republican president Ronald Reagan. Former vice president Walter Mondale emerged from the crowded field that included former astronaut and Ohio senator John Glenn, Reverend Jesse Jackson and Colorado senator Gary Hart. Though he gained valuable experience and insight, the very qualified candidate had little chance to overcome the national attitude of discontent that followed the last Southern president, Jimmy Carter (1977–81). America missed a fine man.

Hollings, at eighty-nine, has a commanding grasp of national politics and international diplomacy. He maintains an office through the Medical University of South Carolina Hollings Cancer Center on Calhoun Street. His voice is distinctive, inflective and toned with his deep, guttural, Geechee accent. He is steely-eyed and committed. He challenges convention on many issues, because he is versed in the idiosyncrasies of beltway politics. He does not blindly follow but rather finds conviction in his own acute judgment. He is the boy on President Street that is now the experienced statesman on Calhoun Street—ever so the same. He is as he always was—a leader.

"The deficit is fourteen trillion. President Bush added five trillion and Obama has added another 4.5 trillion. He may add another trillion to that," Hollings asserted. "And the plan we worked on guaranteed deficit reduction every year. I suppose that's gone by the wayside. But it's got to stop."

Hollings then addressed the expense of campaigns.

"I last ran for office in 1998. The cost was $8.5 million. That is not to be admired. It is to be rejected. Now a senate office seat may cost as much as ten million or more," Hollings noted. "That's over thirty thousand dollars to be raised every day in a six-year senate term. That means that from the day a senator takes office, he begins campaigning for his next election. When does the work get done?

"Getting elected puts you on that fundraising treadmill. It never stops," Hollings continued. "When I first ran, I spent one hundred dollars on cards to give out. It was important to know the county and know who all the magistrates were. I remember going to see John Limehouse on John's Island. He was six feet, five inches and three hundred pounds. I gave him my card and asked if he would consider supporting me. He shook my hand and told me that he'd support me that day and would find me a few more votes. Back then, you got out and saw merchants and farmers and business people wherever they were. Mr. Limehouse and others got behind me. I was the surprise winner, and I did it just by passing out cards. Imagine!

"Now they say President Obama will have one billion dollars for his reelection campaign. One billion dollars!" Hollings said in amazement. "Peddling influence is bigger now throughout politics than supporting your beliefs through a promising candidate. It's all about influence. And that's a crying shame."

In terms of Hollings's eye-opening illustration about daily fundraising, one billion dollars over a four-year election cycle will mean that the Obama team would have to raise just short of seven hundred thousand per day! In a difficult economy, it is very apparent that financial priorities in politics have run amok.

But the politics of politics aside, the government that our forefathers so eloquently established can work. It takes men of moral and ethical vision.

In his insightful book on the matter, *Making Government Work*, the retired senator poses the issues and pragmatically develops the answers. His fourteen-point plan to re-edify the effectiveness of the federal government covers mergers of large federal departments, a proposed withdrawal from the World Trade Organization and a revamping of taxes to include corporate revenue tax in lieu of corporate income tax. Hollings may be well ahead of his time.

"And now they want to get rid of government," Hollings continued, "and replace it with what? Then nothing gets done. We have to reel in the spending and support those who cannot support themselves in some way. We have to protect our freedoms and support our military. Government is necessary. It can work and has worked. But it cannot be abused."

His impromptu stump speech came from the heart to an audience of one. His commitment to this country has never ended. And neither has his mentorship of others.

Joseph P. Griffith Jr. is a Charleston defense attorney who spent time under the tutelage of Hollings, the lawyer and U.S. senator. Griffith also served the United States Attorney's office as assistant to the U.S. Attorney for South Carolina. He further served as legislative counsel to Hollings in Washington from 1982 to 1984.

"Senator Hollings had a favorite saying that 'there is no education in the second kick of a mule,'" Griffith noted. "It was his way of saying we can't continue to make the same mistakes, looking for different results."

It was his same view of the world from his childhood days on President Street. He learned from history's greatest example—experience. Through the experiences of his fifty-five years of service to America, his impact has been influential to all South Carolinians and beyond.

The Hollings influence is not only in Charleston, but in all parts of South Carolina and Washington, D.C., as well. He continues to provide encouragement, direction and energetic service to all concerns.

He is truly a statesman.

The Irish Gavel Banger

Patrick Michael Duffy

The man is vastly overqualified for his career. He knows his profession well, but his cabinet of tools is suited for much, much more.

He is a paragon of living virtue. He is beyond reproach. His ethics are the zenith admired by his contemporaries. His obsession for learning propels him well past the retirement age of other professions. He is more than properly driven by duty. He feels the need to serve indefinitely.

He has tremendous respect in the community and an overflow of friends—good and loyal friends that are the envy of others.

He is a federal judge. He serves the United States District Court for the state of South Carolina. He wields his gavel in the most public of venues in one of the oldest courthouses in America.

His Irish-lineage parents were both from the clan Duffy—unrelated. Well, if you go back to the earliest twig branches, they were of that same Celtic horde that wandered through southern Europe into the Emerald Isle some four thousand years ago. He is apt to say his mother's father kept his "maiden" name, Duffy. That's because he is apt to say many declarations of group interest in his unique style of Irish eloquence.

He is Patrick Michael Duffy. He is proudly Irish. He is a profoundly learned man. He is an off-duty comedy act and yet the final authority on the most serious of capital-crime sentences allowed by our legal system. He knows where bad stuff ends and good stuff starts. There is no confusion.

Duffy is larger than life.

To the legal world, he is "Your Honor." To the periphery he is "Judge." But to those very special people whom he counts as friends—hundreds upon hundreds and counting—he is simply Mike Duffy.

He has a full symphony of passions. They start with his lovely and brilliant wife, Kathy. They include his three children and seven grandchildren. These passions intertwine his busy life with the weave of travel, art, music, sport and the simplest of simple—a dash of vodka on the rocks with a lime twist when the evening hour arrives. It is then that his eyes warm to the notion that the time of his life is now. There is no doubt that this gregarious disposition is his most contagious disease and that bystanders become easily infected. He makes it hard to escape the sentence given—friendship, concern, advice and jubilation. It is the jubilation that pours out the most. It is in this quadrant that he brings his secret gavel.

They say he holds both legal and local court.

The legal one is sometimes difficult and gut wrenching. He has seen too many career criminals to recall. He has sentenced the corporate masterminds that never thought they would be discovered. He has seen the privileged youth of good families stray into the seamy side of violence, drug crimes and even murder. It is a woeful amount of weight to manage in his daily duties. Yet he finds balance by immersing himself in the good things that he consciously anticipates—camaraderie, social events, golf matches, laughter and, most importantly, a close and supportive family.

It's the friendly local court that underscores his vigilance to the precepts of living. Local court is always wherever Mike Duffy is. The invisible gavel is omnipresent. There may be a few ballads sung late into the evening, a round or two bought for the background singers and an assortment of good Irish stories—some that he lived himself. His visits to Ireland include the holy game of golf, the requisite, pub-inspired settlement of debts and the usual melodic foray into the Gaelic nights. These evenings would include a few toasts, some moments of sincerity and the frolic of a prankish fifteen-year-old that lives inside his cunning mind.

You know when Duffy is in the room well before you approach the room. The hallmark sound of hearty and rolling laughter is his and his alone. Nobody laughs quite like Duffy. If prompted, he will go into some of his Billy Crystal act, telling a humorous story complete with the identifiable voices of the most identifiable characters. They range from the two venerable long-term senators from South Carolina—Strom Thurmond and Fritz Hollings—to a troupe of well-known Charleston lawyers, to celebrities and many other public figures. Duffy has a conversation with himself that distinguishes a handful of characters from each other—and none mindful of the vocal source, Mike Duffy. It is an amazing production done without rehearsal. He's a natural.

More than a dozen years ago I suggested, jokingly, that he give up his chosen career and emcee the Academy Awards. There may be no celebrity in Hollywood his equal. Several community event organizers have invoked his considerable abilities as a formal emcee. He even looks dapper in the tuxedo. He is famously good on his feet and has an inherent loud voice boosted by his quick wit and charming Irish sensibilities. It's just another tool in the toolbox. There are many more.

His wife, Kathy, a dynamic consultant with both a master's and a PhD, was first discovered on his homecoming game elbow as Duffy's escort during his senior football season at Bishop England High School. They have been together since.

"She is so beautiful and smart that I feel privileged. Her academic ability caused me to call for an armistice many years ago. I knew full well that I could not compete, so I just got in line," Duffy noted. "She graduated first in her class at St. Francis nursing school, was president of the Student Nurses' Association of South Carolina and in 2008 was recognized by the South Carolina Hospital Association as the most outstanding hospital trustee in South Carolina for her work on the Roper St. Francis Board."

Kathy followed Mike along the stepping-stones of life in South Carolina to law school at the University of South Carolina and then to his three years of service commitment as a military policeman in Germany.

Duffy relates one of the hundreds of humorously interesting stories from his background and experiences. As an M.P. in Germany during a time of student rioting, he saw first-hand how the world is hilariously serious.

"I was an army captain in charge of 185 men when we were called upon to protect the American Embassy in Heidelberg. The rather devious Students for a Democratic Society [SDS] and a group of Communist-bent 'Red Rudies' had assembled—nearly fifteen thousand in all. They were a real threat, and the embassy was on red alert. Our well-trained unit was next to another untrained unit of band members and ceremonial parade soldiers. We had flamethrowers and bayonets drawn. One of the men of the untrained unit botched the process of loading his flamethrower with the riot tear gas. It leaked out everywhere. So now, our entire force had to put on gas masks for our own protection from our own mistake. It wasn't funny then as much as it is now. Anyway, the German police arrived, and they were effective. They had police dogs, water cannons and riot batons. The crowd quickly dispersed, and the

unprecedented tenth term as this was being written. His greatness will be told for generations, yet he lives humbly among us as a civic servant.

"As appreciated as he is here, he is even more recognized nationally. He served as the president of the National Conference of Mayors and has received every major award that group presents," Duffy related. "And yet he would never tell you that. His vision for Charleston goes out a hundred years or more. Nobody else could have made us a world city."

Duffy recalled some of the early influences that made him appreciate his upbringing in the Charleston that had been mostly forgotten.

"I had great mentoring. Father Hubacz was a family friend, and he looked out for my brother, Larry, and me. He gave great advice. He hailed from Boston by way of Poland. I had the utmost respect for this personable and selfless priest," Duffy noted. "He was always there for my family.

"Sister Jerome was my dad's aunt. She taught biology at Bishop England and mentored many others than myself," Duffy added. "And you know, she was one heck of a good teacher as well."

Duffy's earlier influences had him convince his family to allow him a path to a Catholic seminary. He attended St. Charles seminary in Catonsville, Maryland, for two years. In time his brother, Larry, would join him there.

"We had a very religious household. My parents attended daily mass. We were there with them, and we naturally had great respect for the church," Duffy explained. "So going into the seminary was a natural course."

His sister, Mary Ellen, also took a religious path, eventually taking orders as a Catholic nun.

In time, Duffy returned to Charleston and to Bishop England High School.

"Though I had sincere intentions, I realized that the life of a priest would not suit me. The lessons I learned and the perspective that experience gave me in life was priceless," Duffy concluded.

Other Charleston experiences followed. Most of Duffy's friends are quite struck by his expressive and companionable Irish humor. He became the defining reason in a previously docile Irish community to explore roots and celebrate with Celtic pride.

"My father was openly and proudly Irish before anyone really celebrated their Irishness. He had a marvelous singing voice and bellowed out the old tunes. He could play the piano, the harmonica and the spoons. We all knew the words to all of the songs. My mother's father was also a Duffy—nonrelated. So I had the Duffy name on both sides—one from County Donegal and the other from County Tipperary. My wife Kathy's mother was an O'Brien whose people

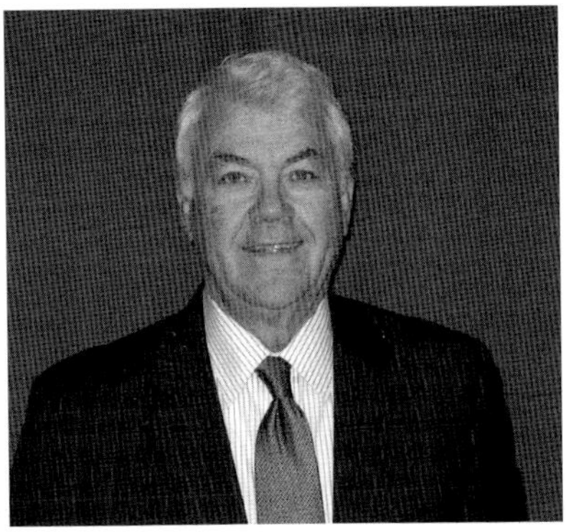

The enjoyment of friendships is accentuated whenever Judge Michael Duffy brings his invisible gavel. Duffy holds impromptu court with laughter and song. *(Photo by son Patrick Duffy.)*

were from Galway. So my children are saturated with the Irish lineage," Duffy stated. "They are doomed to be happy!

"I loved being Irish, because it was such a prideful thing in my own family. Once, when I was a cadet at The Citadel, I got in trouble for showing up to formation on St. Patrick's Day wearing a green shirt and white shamrock," Duffy recalled.

The political science major nonetheless followed his academic pursuits on to law school. His vigilance for the protection and reverence of The Citadel cannot be measured. It is one of his many passions.

"I loved The Citadel for what it meant, for the challenges it presented and for the deep and lasting friendships I have enjoyed. There is no place quite like it," Duffy contended. "It will always be a part of me."

There were others at The Citadel that appreciated Duffy's role there and beyond. His class of 1965 has become an exceptional assembly of successful graduates who developed the iconic Missar and Murphy bronze statue that has become the rallying point for the football Bulldogs. It sits directly in front of the Bulldogs' locker room at the Altman Athletic Center. Joseph Missar and Frank Murphy were two standout class of 1965 teammates who later perished in Vietnam. It was Duffy that emceed the unveiling event before a large group of classmates and others in 2005.

Another learning center on The Citadel campus was developed with funds raised by the class. Mike Duffy spearheaded the effort.

His class of 1965 further began sponsorship of The Citadel business college's annual awards dinner. This formal event recognizes business leaders from all over the country. The "old gang" of Michael Robinson, Jimmy Kerr, Mike Duffy and another dozen class of 1965 supporters are always there in earnest.

The Citadel is as much a part of the Charleston culture as shrimp and grits or she-crab soup. The resurrection of Irish culture would take some effort.

The Irish heritage of Charleston needed a refresher course before Mike Duffy developed his Gaelic jaunts and held his local Irish court. That spark of renewed interest came from his friend Jerry McMahon.

"Jerry McMahon went to Ireland in 1976 and ended up there for a time playing rugby. He convinced me to see the old country about five years later. We formed the Irish Historical Society in 1979 and raised the Irish flag over Kooksie Robinson's store that year on St. Patrick's Day. We have since moved that ceremony to city hall," Duffy recounted. "I went back over to Ireland another dozen times or so and made fine friends. McMahon has been as much as me. He is the man singularly responsible for the twining of Charleston with our Irish sister city of Ennis, County Clare."

Duffy had a trip planned within weeks of this interview. It was to be three days of golf surrounded by another six days of what I surmised would be the invisible gavel of another Duffy local court proceeding. It was upon his return that the stories from others rolled out. Rainy weather had forced the erstwhile golfing Charlestonians inside for a series of impromptu Duffy "hearings."

Duffy's diligence in assisting the growth of the Charleston Irish culture will soon culminate with the building of a Charleston Irish Memorial at the foot of Charlotte Street. The memorial will incorporate some of the great Charleston Irish family names with a park setting and some informative Charleston Irish history. Duffy and others have been planning the memorial for more than a decade. Together, they have raised nearly four hundred thousand dollars. It will become another of the significant contributions to the makeup of what is a wonderful mix of founding cultures that became the magic that is Charleston.

Duffy recalled an old saying that dates to another early Charleston Irish mayor, John P. Grace.

"It was said that Charleston was 'owned by Germans and run by Irish for the benefit of everyone else,'" Duffy revealed. "I don't know that that is so, but it sounds right from where I'm sitting."

And it was from where I was sitting that I was privy to the private court proceedings of the legendary Judge Patrick Michael Duffy with his invisible gavel—of Irish stock, but blatantly of Charleston.

Adjourned—for now.

By 2016, Judge Duffy was enjoying senior status at the federal court, his wife Kathy's retirement, travel with friends and valuable time with his four children and the grandchildren. His interaction with friends is usually highlighted by his sincere concern for others. Regardless of any major or minor matters he may personally weather, his first question is always directed to see how others are faring. A caring man, he has become an iconic judge who commands a most personable courtroom.

One is allowed to laugh, even in federal court.

The Sergeant at Normandy

Carl Cannon

It seems that everyone of the baby boom generation knew a World War II veteran with a story to tell. The most interesting tales were the ones from the marines at Iwo Jima or the tank commanders in North Africa. They were proud stories all. This generation is the most venerated among the living, not because of age, but for accomplishment in the face of undeniable adversities. Indeed, they have compelling reports. None of those wily veterans who made it to the ripe ages that 2011 hosted could best Sergeant Carl Cannon. He landed at Normandy on D-Day.

"When I jumped from the transport with ninety pounds packed on my back, I landed in a sink hole another LST diesel engine had made on the bottom," the spunky eighty-nine-year-old recalled. "I was way over my head and weighted down. I didn't panic. I began to walk up the slope under water until I could get my head out and breathe."

The five-foot, six-inch tech sergeant got to the shore amidst enemy fire. He signaled for his men to follow him to establish a beachhead. The invasion had many casualties. Among the mortal losses was his best friend, Eddie Rolling. It would take Cannon a lifetime to find his friend's grave.

Carl Cannon was born in Collins, Georgia, on August 14, 1921. After attending Lexington High School in Collins, Cannon joined the United States Army in 1940. Within four years, Cannon had demonstrated great proficiency in his endeavors and earned the rank of technical sergeant, his rank level when he landed at Utah Beach on June 6, 1944.

"The army is built on the backs of good sergeants," he stated proudly.

Cannon was a member of the Fourth Infantry Division, Third Army, under the command of General Theodore Roosevelt Jr. Cannon's direct command as a member of a mine-unit detection team was Captain George L. Mabry of Clinton, South Carolina, who was later awarded a Medal of Honor for gallantry in battle at Schevenhutte, Germany. Cannon revered the captain in later years, because he led the men valiantly with a minimum of casualties.

Some casualties did not stay that way. Carl was one of them.

Cannon was injured by a German antipersonnel mine explosion in July of 1944, earning a Purple Heart and spending two weeks in a field hospital with a severe injury to his right foot. However, upon learning that his unit was moving out and that he would be transferred upon his medical release to another unit, Sergeant Cannon left the field hospital with a tightly bandaged foot—finding an opening under the side of the tent—to join his unit. These were the boys he felt responsible to lead. He fought through the hedgerows and small towns like Pouppeville and Sainte-Marie-du-Mont—all the way to Paris in early August. He was among the first American troops to liberate the city. He continued fighting beyond Paris to northern France, Belgium and the Siegfried Line and ultimately all the way into Prague, Czechoslovakia (now the Czech Republic). He was in Regensburg, Germany, when VE Day (Victory in Europe) was declared. Having achieved his rank as master sergeant by this time, he had walked from the Atlantic Ocean at Normandy over eleven hundred miles into Prague in less than a year. He refused to ride in a Jeep, because, as he noted, "my men walked, so I walked."

Sergeant Cannon remained in the United States Army for thirty-two years, including other combat duty in Korea (1950) and as an observer in Vietnam (1967). He retired in 1972.

Cannon came to the Charleston area in 1952 to be stationed at Fort Moultrie. The fort was decommissioned in 1960 and turned over to the National Park Service. Cannon's fondness for the community led to his adoption of Charleston as his permanent home. He was married in 1950 to Stella Louise Johnson. Together they had one child, Rick, in 1955. Cannon's wife, Stella, died of cancer in November 1986. She was the love of his life. Cannon never remarried. He lived by himself at the home he and Stella had purchased in 1962. On February 15, 2006, Cannon moved to Ashley River Plantation assisted living community in Charleston (West Ashley).

As Cannon had entrusted the author of this essay to assist him with that move, it became a proud honor to serve this American hero. With my two oldest sons, we were able to move his most meaningful career treasures to his

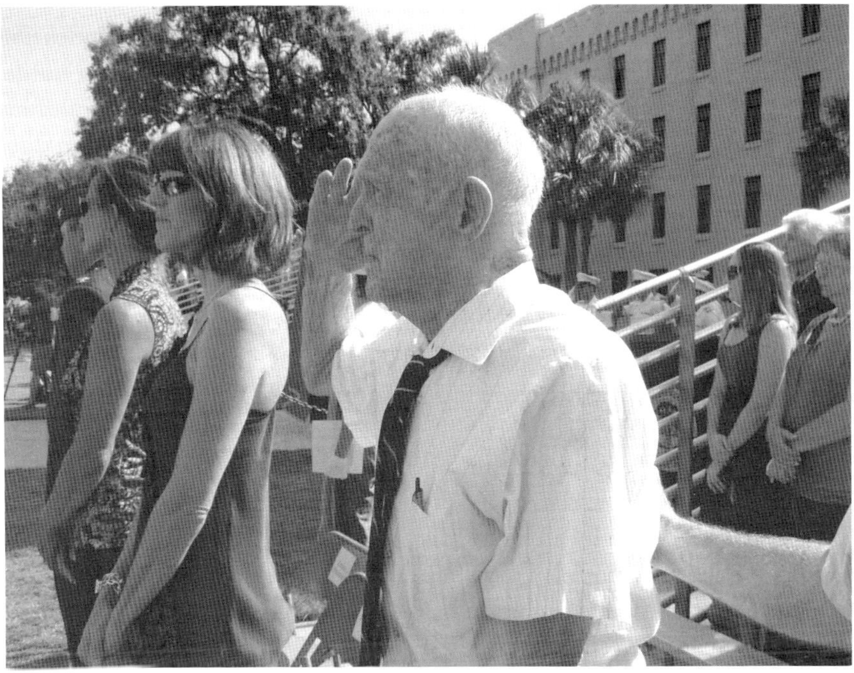

The sergeant at Normandy, Carl Cannon, salutes the United States flag at a Citadel ceremony in 2009. *(Russ Pace)*

new Ashley River Plantation home. There, he regaled the ladies with stories of France, Germany and Korea.

Sergeant Cannon related the exact details of his wartime stories proudly, giving much credit to his superiors and reverence to the men he led as a sergeant. Fifty years later, Cannon returned to Normandy for the first time to find the grave of his best friend, Edward J. Rolling, to no avail. In June of 2004, Cannon again returned to Normandy for the sixtieth anniversary of the Operation Overlord landing. At this time, he met the U.S. Joint Chiefs of Staff chairman, General Richard Myers, who dispatched staffers to assist Cannon in finding his friend's final resting place. The grave was found, and Sergeant Cannon gave a sigh of relief that he could finally come back and visit.

Cannon also met former French president Jacques Chirac on this visit. Proudly, Cannon had received the highest French award, the esteemed Croix de Guerre, for his participation in the liberation of Paris. Over his career, Cannon received sixteen military awards for his valor and bravery. He routinely wore eight of these medals when dressing for an occasion in his

"No, sir, I was lucky. I just have some trees on my fence and some shingles missing. The good Lord watched over me," he replied. "I just came by to see if you needed some help. The McDonald's is closed, probably for a few weeks."

Stunned by this sincere show of selflessness, I was taken aback.

"Well, Carl, we're going to be very busy, but the claims will have to be taken by our staff. They are licensed. Do you know a place that's open for lunch? We could pay you to get it," I offered this option, knowing he would be happiest with the duties that sergeants follow in due course.

Sergeant Cannon retrieved food with ice and sodas from a Kentucky Fried Chicken he found that day. They had a generator. We were operating the office from a gas generator ourselves until the electricity was restored two weeks later. The diminutive retired sergeant returned every day at about eleven o'clock. He took orders, brought ice and drinks daily and occasionally brought a potted plant for the ladies in the office. They loved him dearly.

I never forgot the unsolicited assistance I had received from this retired army sergeant. It came at a time when every small act of charity meant so much to each of us.

As the years passed, Sergeant Cannon continued to visit us every few months. Sometimes he would bring candy or some small token with him. His reception by the ladies of my office was warm and genuine. The men appreciated him as well for what he meant to our country for so many years of service.

It was on one of those visits that I mentioned the fifty-year anniversary of the Normandy landing. He brightened up.

"You know, Mr. Tom, I've always wanted to go back and visit my best friend's grave," he said in wistful tones. "But I just can't. I owe too much and need to pay off the house mortgage."

It had been eight years since Stella had passed away.

"Mr. Cannon, if you're in good walking shape and you want to go, I might be able to help," I offered, thinking of the many organizations in Charleston that might step forward.

After several funding and travel suggestions, he left my office with instructions to get an updated passport.

In time, I found a few organizations that would help, but they would volunteer sums of fifty dollars or less. This was not the avenue of success I had anticipated. I had decided to call a friend I had met two years earlier in Paris, Stephanie Delarue, a tour guide. Another acquaintance, a Charleston travel agent, found some discounts. Considering timing and the flexibility of dates, Stephanie and the travel agent were able to piece together incredible savings and even freebies to get this American hero back to Normandy. It would cost only fourteen hundred dollars. I placed it all on my American Express card, rationalizing that he had done at least that much service for our office five years earlier. Sergeant Cannon was going to find his friend. He was ecstatic when I told him.

Over the next few weeks, he arose daily to walk purposefully several times around the inside expanse of a local shopping mall. He wanted to be ready for the opportunity. He wanted to walk however far it would take to find his friend's grave.

"I'd walk eleven hundred miles again if I knew it would take that distance to find him," he told me. "He would do the same for me." Sergeant Cannon was approaching his seventy-third birthday.

I took him to the Charleston International Airport on a Thursday and retrieved him on Friday of the following week.

The trip went off without a hitch—except that the friend's grave was not to be found. Sergeant Cannon was so close, but yet so far from the accomplishment of his mission. He was distraught. He told me of his travails.

It was when he had reached a point of despair that a young French schoolteacher approached him with some two dozen fourth graders in tow.

"*Excusez-moi, s'il vous plaît,*" she started.

Sergeant Cannon doffed his beret.

"Ma'am, I cannot understand a word you're saying. I can only speak English," Sergeant Cannon replied courteously.

"You appear to be an American veteran. Were you among those that landed upon our beaches?" the teacher asked in anticipation.

"Yes, ma'am, I landed at Utah Beach on June 6, 1944," he stated proudly.

"If it is not any trouble, would you mind if my young students asked you about that day?" the teacher inquired.

Sergeant Cannon consented, and the children were instructed to sit. They sat in a semicircle on the grass in front of Sergeant Cannon's bench. The students began raising their hands and asking questions in French. The teacher translated the questions. Sergeant Cannon proudly shared the chronology of the invasion, from his jump into the hole made by the boat diesel engine, through his friend's death, to the liberation of Paris. The children were spellbound from hearing the living history. After some thirty minutes of translations, the children rose upon the teacher's instruction. They formed a single line. They shook his hand or curtseyed. They simultaneously gave the same remark to the very polite old soldier.

"*Merci pour sauver mon pays*," they each said with a slight bow of the head.

Sergeant Cannon looked to the teacher after the first few repeated the words. He was puzzled by the remark and looked to her for a translation.

"*Merci pour sauver mon pays*," the words resounded.

"I do not know what they are saying, but they are polite to say it. Please let me know what I should say back to them," he asked of the teacher.

"They are saying, 'Thank you for saving my country,'" she revealed. "And it is best that you accept their thanks and mine as remarks that are overdue and understated."

Sergeant Cannon thought of his friend and started to sob as he continued acknowledgement of the children's greetings.

When they were through, he had taken out his handkerchief to dab his wet eyes. It was then that the teacher lined the children up to depart. He saluted them patriotically, as if saying "mission accomplished."

As they started away, the teacher turned to see him slump back into the bench, overcome by the moment. She, too, uttered the departing words.

"*Merci pour sauver mon pays*!"

His friend had not died in vain. He had made these schoolchildren appreciate a sense of unity in a country of progress made possible by the sacrifice of others.

Sergeant Cannon was back breathing the air that swelled in his chest that day. It was the air of life that was the first breath from a near drowning before the battle was fought. It was the stench-of-death air that accompanies an assault in spontaneity, voracity and harsh reality. It was the sweet air of survival he ingested deep into his lungs that first night after taking the beachhead. It was the same beach air that propelled the lungs of the then septuagenarian to pause and sob, then gather his demeanor for a cane-aided walk back. He steadied himself and headed to the comfortable room a French family had provided, gratis, in Colleville-sur-Mer. He had saved their country, too.

It was not until his return visit on June 6, 2004, with the help of aides dispatched by General Richard Myers, that Cannon found the grave of his friend. Sergeant Cannon was nearly eighty-three years of age when he found the grave, sixty years after the incident.

The grave was a white cross like the others so perfectly lined and manicured. Sergeant Cannon removed his trademark beret, said a few words out loud, then paused and returned the beret to his head. He then moved his feet together, standing in his best military posture, and saluted his friend. A better and more meaningful salute would not be made that day, for it had been building in its spirit and purpose for six decades.

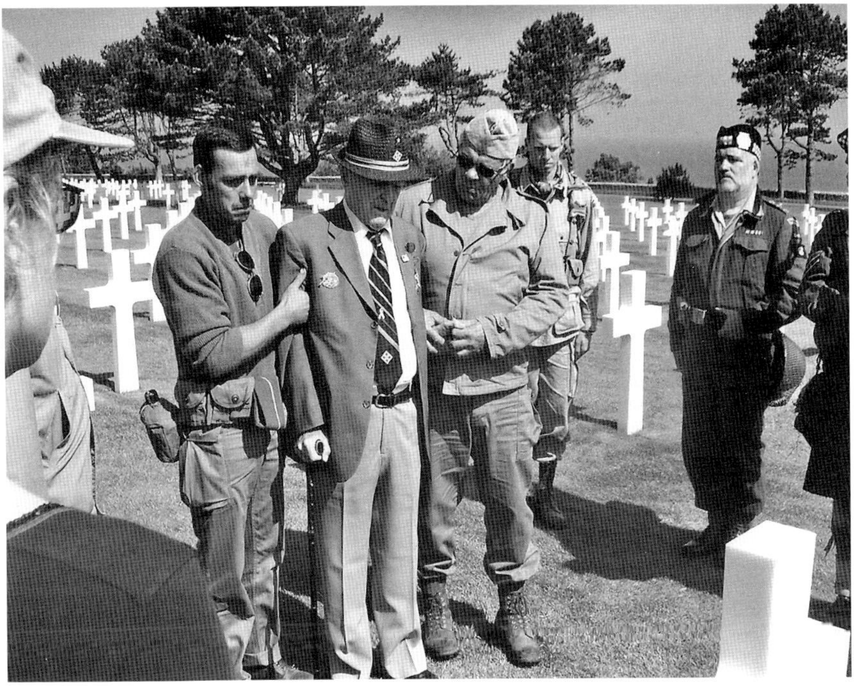

Sixty years after the D-Day landing at Normandy, Carl Cannon finds the grave of his best friend, Eddie Rolling, with the help of General Richard Myers's directive to his staff. Cannon met then Joint Chiefs of Staff chairman Myers on June 6, 2004. *(Stephanie Delarue Calligaro)*

Just a few years ago, the good sergeant stopped by to speak with me in my private office. I was immediately concerned.

"Carl, is everything all right?" I inquired.

"Mr. Tom, I've been thinking. I have no reason to be buried here," he stated solemnly, with his beret in his lap. "I want to be cremated."

He continued as I lost a sense of comfort in my office chair, realizing the stark consideration of what my role would be in this morbid decision.

"I would like you to consider the favor of taking my ashes to Normandy to be spread on Utah Beach," he followed. "I want to be a part of that day forever, because it is what my life has been about all these years. I could have easily died there, like my friend. But the good Lord had other plans. Will you give me your word that you will do this for me?"

I was caught in the moment of something so incredibly serious that I had a lump in my throat. But I knew his heart and what it meant to him.

"Of course, Carl," I replied. "It would be my honor." I certainly wanted to put his mind at ease and at the same time give him the high level of respect he deserves.

In trying to raise the conversation back to the lighter side, I added, "Carl, I don't mind doing just as you ask me, but would you mind if we wait until you die?"

He broke out in laughter. It was the capstone of a serious conversation with a serious responsibility. He stood up and again saluted the ersatz colonel. I returned my Citadel-learned acknowledgement. He left, assured of my commitment to him.

It is with a deep sense of responsibility that I accepted the charge from Sergeant Cannon to return his ashes to Utah Beach. When that day comes, I will command two ceremonies. One will be as he directed. An urn will be emptied after a prayer and a pause of silence for a true American hero. Then I will return to the grave of his friend, who paid the ultimate price of freedom's quest. There I will salute the white cross that is symbolic of a sacrifice by a man I have never known. I dearly hoped that the timing of these two related events would be well into the future.

Being Carl Cannon's friend required some responsibility, but it will never amount to the level he imparted to his fellow countrymen.

Not long after I interviewed him for this book, Carl Cannon, "the sergeant at Normandy," passed away at 4:30 on the morning of September 4, 2011. It was the same time of the morning when that historic invasion started, more than sixty-seven years ago. And so it would be that the ashes would be returned and spread upon the honorable others that perished at Utah Beach on June 6, 1944. Salute the sergeant.

Everybody's Cousin Arthur

Arthur Ravenel Jr.

When Arthur Ravenel Jr.'s name is mentioned, Charlestonians automatically think of the endearing term he calls everyone he meets—"cousin." In Charleston, there are two categories of residents—"beenyas" (or "been heres," the native population) and "cumyas" (or "come heres," the moved-in population). It would not be surprising if the cumyas actually thought that we were all double first cousins. So "Cousin Arthur" would naturally fit any predisposition one would place upon the children of the pluff mud.

One would surmise that Cousin Arthur never met a man he didn't like. It would seem that the description has a reverse theorem. How could anyone on God's green earth not like Arthur Ravenel Jr.?

He has a deep Charleston drawl and a wide, toothy smile, and he looks you in the eye to shake your hand. His serious demeanor has no partition that divides it from his down-home, fun-loving side. He's in that mode naturally. He is charming, charismatic, introspective, helpful and courteous—all with the same gleaming grin.

My mother's first cousin was indeed a Ravenel. Cousin Emily turned ninety-six in February of 2011 and passed away in May. She had hosted a Ravenel family reunion for the past thirty years. "Cousin" Arthur was usually there. That's where he was actually everyone's cousin. Being around family suited him more than his other domains. That's where he felt he could, in his words, "get down to serious business and have fun."

Ravenel served in the United States House of Representatives for eight years. He served in the South Carolina Senate for six years in the early 1980s, until his stint in the U.S. House took him to Washington. He came back to his roots in the South Carolina Senate and served for ten more years before retiring. Well, at least all of the cousins thought he was retiring. At the age of seventy-nine, Cousin Arthur was elected to the Charleston County School Board. He felt a passion to resolve some pressing issues the school board had encountered. He stayed four years, retiring from public service for good at the age of eighty-three. For now, at least.

"The political life brings on conversations of great and small meaning. Some of the smaller ones were in Washington, and some of the bigger ones were in my back yard," Ravenel reflected. "So I have no great expectations beyond those of doing what's best for others."

The Ravenel name is one of the major service lines in the formative substructure of Charleston history. They arrived here in 1686. Cousin Arthur would be quick to point out that he was not on that particular ship in 1686, but his ancestor René Ravenel was. René left the French town of Vitré, near the Normandy coast, and boarded a ship in London. René was chasing a pretty French Huguenot lady named Charlotte St. Julien, who came to Charleston on the same ship. He fell in love with her, and they married that same year at Pompion Hill Chapel in Berkeley County, just outside of Charleston. That church still exists and predates the American Revolution. Over the next 325 years, that marriage has resulted in a line of over seventeen hundred progeny. One thousand, seven hundred Ravenels—no wonder he calls everyone "cousin!"

"My cousin William Ravenel is with General Dynamics. He did all of the research to find that information for the family," Ravenel asserted. "Don't you know that was a tremendous amount of work?"

Imagine that—another Cousin Ravenel doing a lot of work.

The family Ravenel propagated nicely. Some were merchants, some were doctors, others farmers. One in particular brought his scientific genius to the world. It was St. Julien Ravenel who gained fame as an agriculturalist by devising both water and fertilizer remedies for fields with depleted nutrients. He is credited with breakthroughs in physiology and natural history. He was the one person who saw the benefit of the phosphates that were available in the Lowcountry for other uses.

Oh yeah, and the low-profile torpedo boat was invented in Berkeley County, in 1862, by that very same St. Julien Ravenel. This cigar-shaped innovation was called the David class of semi-submersibles. The St. Julien Ravenel house accents the White Point Gardens end of East Bay Street, where the tour guides tell incredible tales of Ravenel prowess. Most are

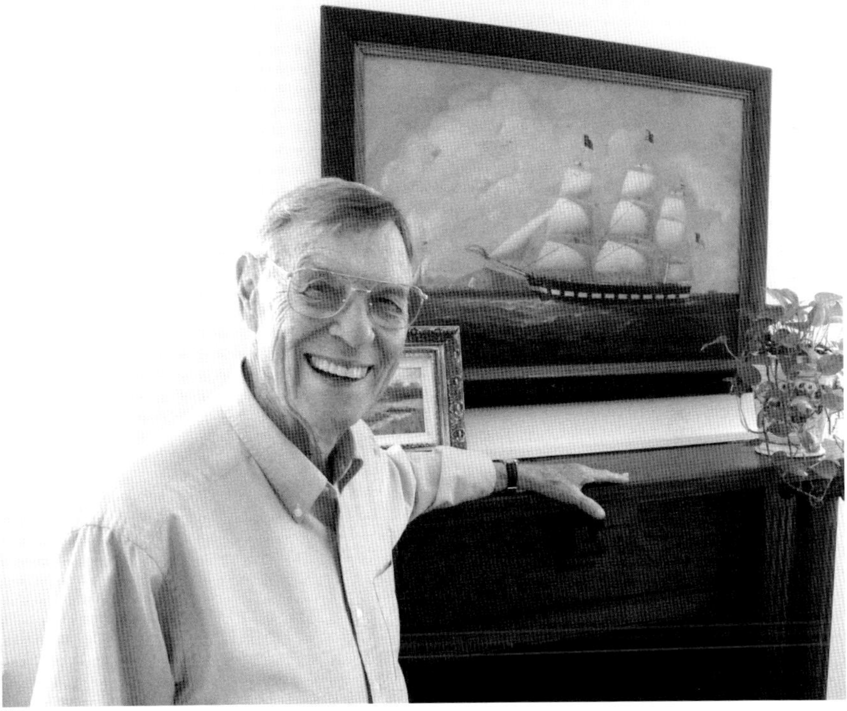

Arthur Ravenel Jr. relaxes at his residence in front of a painting of the *John Ravenel*, a family merchant ship shown at the Port of Naples in the mid-1800s. *(W. Thomas McQueeney)*

injected with hyperbole, with the likely exception of what they may conjure about Cousin Arthur.

"I'm not sure my ancestors came, as others did, to Charleston out of religious fervor," Ravenel assessed. "But they came nonetheless, and I'm still here."

Indeed. He seems to be everywhere.

Ravenel has distinguished himself in ways other than politics. It was he who led a group of French Huguenot–lineaged Charlestonians to resurrect the ministry and congregation at the famous French Huguenot Church in 1983. The church parish dates to 1687,[31] with several bands of natural and mankind-induced troubles stunting its growth. The Gothic church was still standing when the parish disintegrated in 1950, yet the church still held an annual spring event for the French-descendent community. The 1983 reemergence came three hundred years after its inception. The current church was completed in 1845. There were two fires, a revolution, a misnamed "civil war," more than a dozen hurricanes and an earthquake. Three centuries can do that to that to a church. Ravenel just had to look in the phone book for the handful of Huguenot names not related to him. You see them on street signs, neighborhood maps and even book titles. They flow from the school-taught French inflections as Huger (YOU-gee), Mazyck (ma-ZEEK), LeTellier (la-TELL-yer), Beauregard (BO-re-gard) and Manigault (man-e-GO). Other prominent names include Porcher (POOR-Shay) and Gaillard (GIL-yard). The French lesson by itself cannot encompass the entirety of the subject "Rav-en-EL."

Similar to the natural adversity of the venerable sandcastle-like church, Ravenel has had a few setbacks. He lost a run to become governor and a few other high-profile elections (mayor of Charleston, South Carolina Senate and U.S. House special election). It was never for lack of energy, ideas and enthusiasm. It may be that those in the hinterlands didn't understand his "Gullah-Geechee" accent. It's just the normal way we pluff-mudders express ourselves. Everyone else sounds different.

Ravenel was one of the originals—along with lifelong friend and college classmate James B. Edwards—to resurrect the South Carolina Republican Party. Both Ravenel and Edwards graduated from the College of Charleston in 1950. They forged a trail. In 2011 South Carolina, the Grand Ole Party has taken a convincing foothold in state and local politics. They're the "in" crowd.

Ravenel's relationship with the former South Carolina governor Jim Edwards went back further than most knew.

"We were in the third, fourth and fifth grade together at St. Andrew's School," Edwards recalled. "We were great friends. Arthur was the best marble shooter around, with those long fingers and a good eye. My mother was a teacher and taught Arthur in the seventh grade. She always said Arthur was very bright and had a keen mind. I was reacquainted with Arthur again when we became classmates at the College of Charleston."

Indeed, it was Edwards's third association with Arthur Ravenel that changed South Carolina. That's when Ravenel and four others visited Edwards at his dental office on Gadsden Street after hours and talked him into chairing the local Republican Party. It was a propitious meeting for both of them. Edwards later served as the secretary of energy under President Ronald Reagan and also served brilliantly as the seventeen-year president of the Medical University of South Carolina.

Both of these lifelong friends went on to tremendous careers that changed the state and especially the Charleston community. Ravenel's signature on one particular change of legislation may actually impact the entire nation.

In a time when every piece of legislation is superscrutinized by the media, Ravenel has become even more significant in his retirement. It was partially his early support of a legislative initiative in 1955 that the now-relevant right-to-work law was enacted. This is a major national and statewide item currently. As a member of the South Carolina House, Ravenel found good reason to champion that particular bill.

"Those little strikes were meant to better conditions. However, they didn't do that. They held the employers hostage—and in some cases put them in a noncompetitive situation," Ravenel opined. "We felt it was union muscle trying to undermine corporations and, in turn, the ability of workers to feed their families."

Over a half century later, the Boeing Corporation is being put to task for its sound business decision to grow outside of its previous union-burdened state of Washington. The other Washington (D.C.) has a justice department that has initial reservations it is studying. Hold the phone. The suit is presently filed by union backers to force Boeing to give up its almost-completed South Carolina site. It argues that Boeing has operated to punish the unions by opening a plant in South Carolina. This brings into light a major constitutional question. Can the federal government dictate where a corporation can locate its manufacturing facility? The right-to-work law of South Carolina will be further scrutinized by those intent on forcing union oversight upon industry. Some media opinion contends this issue may reach the United States Supreme Court. There is bound to be a wreck of three trains in the train yard of intention. The trains will be named "Union Specific," "Federal Expression," and "Working Progress." Let's hope the switchman operator has the sense of an Arthur Ravenel Jr. and those trains can roll on the same track under the name "Majority Opinion."

Ravenel's work in the public arena then rolled forward and now is the basis of bringing in more than four thousand jobs to the area from Boeing alone. There have been many others—like BMW, Mercedes, Westvaco and Michelin—that have come to South Carolina. South Carolina attracts corporations, and they find the added value of agreeable weather, a thriving port and an enterprising workforce to their benefit.

There were many other bills, commissions and public forums this iconic Charleston figure endorsed, endowed or endured. There were matters of the old navy yard (vacated by the U.S. Navy in 1996), the ports, the roads and bridges, public education and laws to protect our citizens. He's done it all.

Ravenel's pragmatism went back many years. He had a familiarity with livestock, especially cattle. He played football when there were no faceguards. He worked daily on the family farm. He had infused character with responsibility and always remembered where he started.

"West of the Ashley was out in the country and known then as St. Andrews Parish," Ravenel recalled. "When you crossed either bridge from the peninsula, you were clearly out of Charleston and in mostly farmland. The peninsula was Charleston, and Charleston was only on the peninsula back then. And everybody knew everybody."

Ravenel enlisted into the United States Marine Corps upon his eighteenth birthday on March 29, 1945. The stint in the marines went way beyond the farmland. Propitiously, his training at nearby Parris Island and subsequent transport for the planned invasion of Japan in mid-1945 were literally cancelled by a seminal event, the bombs of early August. Hiroshima and Nagasaki brought an end to the war and with it a new mindset for Ravenel. The young marine was just beginning. He found work at the north area paper mill. That mill made itself known when the infrequent northwest winds wafted across the Charleston porticos with a familiar and potent sulfuric stench. His hourly wages of $1.57 couldn't tip a good shoeshine today. He persisted earnestly. But he had other plans.

From a farming background of growing cabbage and potatoes, Ravenel entered the postwar world wide-eyed. He wanted to grow other commodities like friendships, family and influence of the political system. He matured. The economy was promising. He married and started a family. He earned his degree through the new G.I. Bill. In short time, he began a love affair with politics. After losing his first attempt at a South Carolina House seat in 1950, he showed resilience by winning in 1952. People were his portal for politics. He knew people, and his gregariousness was his most outstanding asset. He was easy to approach. He was…like a cousin.

"You could only win as a Democrat in those days. After I left the statehouse the first time, I got involved with the Barry Goldwater campaign for president in 1964. I became one of the early Republicans and lost elections trying to get a seat in the South Carolina Senate," Ravenel recalled. "Eventually, I wore down the voters and won!"

Ravenel's homespun humor finally won out. Among his more familiar campaign postures was his chant to local voters: "I'm for you so be for me!" The saying came off perfectly in the Ravenel parlance. No other candidate could say it with the proper accent and correct inflection. It was simple; it promoted his personality, and it endeared him to his constituents.

The farmer turned soldier turned statesman rode the political rollercoaster to its conclusion of a career in the service of others. Yet, a few generations from now, few will know the Arthur Ravenel Jr. story of timely guidance to his beloved Charleston, his diligence in caring for his home state of South Carolina and his bonus of service to the nation. They'll all think he was a contractor.

You see…there is this bridge.

The Arthur Ravenel Jr. Bridge rises elegantly above the low brow of the Holy City's profile. The numerous church steeples are the spikes that frequently exceed the level of the trees. The bridge punctures the sky twice at 575 feet with distinctive elongated diamond towers. But the bridge is much longer than it is high. It accommodates eight traffic lanes and has resolved the long-term difficulty of traveling north and south on Highway 17. It is a magnificent convenience well beyond its monolithic aesthetics. It accommodates bicyclers, walkers, joggers and spirited tourists with long-lensed cameras. It may well be the signature of Charleston—every bit as indelible as one would recognize other emblematic structures of other world cities.

There's the Eiffel Tower—some 500 feet higher and having no purpose whatsoever—that heralds Paris. It attracts travelers vertically. There's a big lady with a flame that has only ornamental prowess in New York Harbor. The Statue of Liberty is diminutive at 111 feet tall, but it says "New York" loud and clear. As large as it seems, it is only one-fifth of the height of the new Arthur Ravenel Jr. Bridge (completed in 2005). The Washington Monument (555 feet)[32] is an obelisk that does not even fully invoke Washington. Obelisks are more common than torch-bearing ladies. So you might find the U.S. Capitol (289 feet) as the symbol of the City of Gridlock. If you placed the Statue of Liberty on top of the U.S. Capitol and then added our very own People's Building (built as the highest building in Charleston in 1911, requiring the city's first elevator), those three structures would still not reach the height of the Arthur Ravenel Jr. Bridge! And you'd get in trouble for moving any of them from their present sites.

There's a statue of Christ the Redeemer in Rio de Janeiro, and it intimates a strong sense of protection. It is 120 feet high with arms reaching 98 feet across. And then there's that famous opera house in Sydney, Australia. It is 221 feet high, or one-third the height of Charleston's soon-to-be-famous bridge. Besides being a background for a tourist photo, the opera house is well utilized for its purpose of artful performance. It is moving, but it doesn't move anyone.

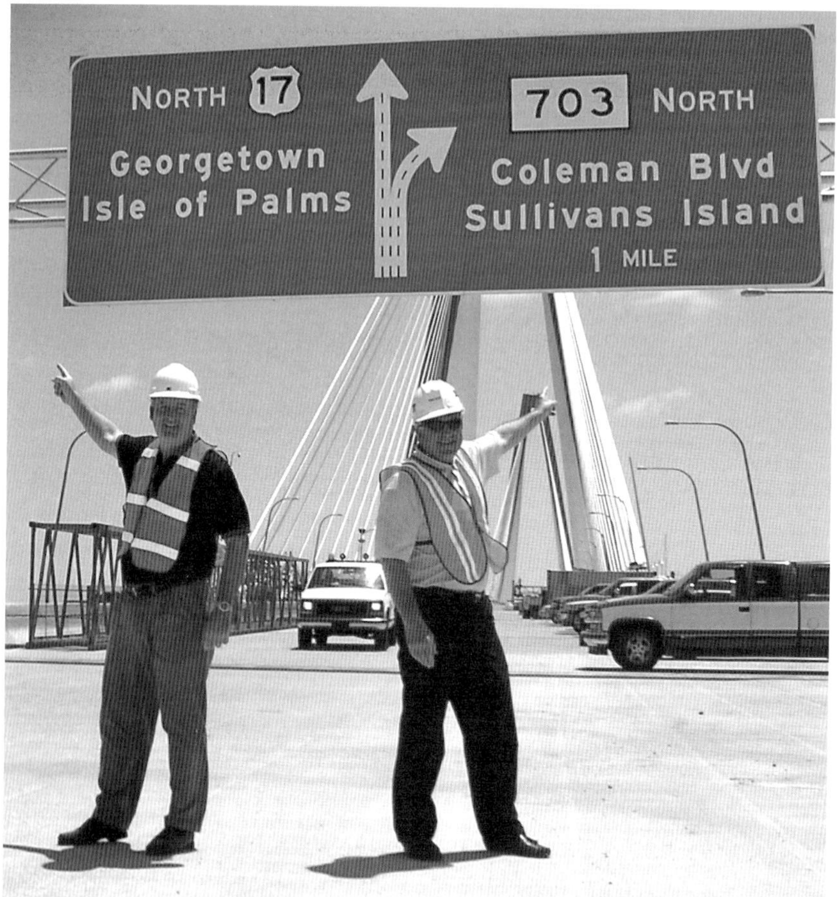

Tommy McQueeney (*left*) and Les Robinson point the direction to be taken to get home over the new Arthur Ravenel Jr. Bridge in the spring of 2005. In a matter of months the bridge was completed, well ahead of schedule. *(Photo by Tommy Eiserhardt)*

None of these world icons actually route people into the convenience of modernity. Yet they light up our minds with identity.

The coming century may prove or disprove many theories, challenges and prognostications. It would not be overstating the significance of the Arthur Ravenel Jr. Bridge to forecast its rise to becoming the identifying edifice of the world's burgeoning new star, Charleston. It dominates the skyline as well as the future of Charleston. It has made life in the Lowcountry infinitely easier. It is our symbolic spirit.

Bridges connect. Charleston has connected. It is on the minds of travelers, entrepreneurs and corporate moguls. Its charm is not just the weather and the historic palmetto-lined avenues. It is enriched by its people. They are the Welcome Wagon on steroids.

"I'm glad my name is attached for one reason—that bridge is the only thing in Charleston nobody complains about!" Ravenel allowed. "It has been a blessing for all concerns. It has been free of criticism, and I like that…believe you me!"

Getting that bridge built took decades of planning work by many important personas, most notably Arthur Ravenel Jr. There were dealings with the local municipalities, with the state General Assembly and with the feds in Washington. All had to be coordinated. That's what Ravenel does best. The total package of $631 million was procured—nearly $1 million per elevated foot.

"When I was reelected to the South Carolina Senate, I prioritized the bridge, because the one we had was about to fall down," Ravenel recounted. "We created an infrastructure bank in South Carolina. We also received help from my friend Senator Fritz Hollings in Washington. The balance was done with federal loans and local support. We had the momentum to finally solve the financial puzzle. It was built a year ahead of schedule, saving even more taxpayer money."

The simple Ravenel homestead that sits out overlooking Charleston's deep harbor is where this remarkable man has lived for decades. The small elegance the fenced home captures is usurped by the view from his short dock. The Old Village in Mount Pleasant has a spattering of finger-like protrusions to the boundlessness of the water's edge. The horizon never moves, but the waves ripple, and the seabirds are omnipresent. Dolphins roll and plunge in the distance. A few cargo ships saunter by, along with the silent sailboats that tack for wind by reading the ripples. Cruise ships have found us. They see us as the place of the tall, double-masted bridge. They see it first.

The Arthur Ravenel Jr. Bridge is the highest fixed-span, cable-stayed bridge in the Western Hemisphere. It is the new star in the Charleston sky. It has marked a new age of Charleston. The stars that rise behind it are there because it is there.

Likewise, it would not be spurious to identify the star that has already risen, Cousin Arthur Ravenel Jr.

The Unchurched Now Churched

Pastor Greg Surratt

Seacoast Church is a happening place. The Sunday service starts with the visual of a stopwatch countdown. There is anticipation in the air. Those attending will leave as poignantly different people in varying degrees from whence they came. The selfless souls within the worship team are mindful of timeless rock stars in their impressive range of talent. The Scottish vocalist has a tonal quality reminiscent of the 1960s pop singer Donovan. An expectation of the Christian version of "Hurdy Gurdy Man" or "Catch the Wind" would seem in order. The drums, keyboard and acoustic guitars lead into song transitions.

There is a syncopation of metronome-like clapping as the female vocalist steps forward to command the high notes accompanied by a refreshingly harmonized background. Her angelic voice hits the vibrant pitch of the known stars named Celine, Mariah and Beyoncé. All comes to a crescendo. There is a melodious lifting of hearts and eyes to the Creator. In the dim of the lights, the band dissipates and the pastor humbly appears.

Star power seems to elevate the visual and hearing senses. A vertically challenged man is confidently perched on a stool, as wired as Garth Brooks in concert. In an instant, he is the focal point of all lighting. He has a goatee instead of a cigar, but would otherwise be a midlife version of George Burns. Think *Oh God! Book II.* Pastor Greg Surratt may even be funnier. He is simple but charismatic, self-deprecating but insightful. He has a "with-it" wit. The gearshift lever from hilarious to serious never grinds.

Surratt's Seacoast Church boasts more than a dozen campuses where people assemble for his weekly messages. It is contemporary, yet thousands of years old. He applies things like Twitter, *American Idol* and mocha frappuccino to the teachings of the Old Testament sewn into the time of Christ by way of Luke or Matthew. The beauty of a revelation tapestry is completed in perhaps twenty minutes. After music and communion and even more sounds from the cherubim, a meaningful closing prayer is offered. It reminds us profoundly of the magnificence of God and that all things are possible. The exodus from the church to the parking lot is brisk to enable the police-aided traffic control to wave out fourteen hundred from the 9:30 service and wave in eighteen hundred for the 11 a.m. service. Those leaving will go forth as recharged Christians spurred by the uplifting words of a small and humble servant. He is the reverend and the pastor, but everyone just calls him Greg.

There is but a smattering of empty seats at the 9:30 service. And that's not the big one! Some thirteen thousand will attend all the weekend services on all of the campuses. That number more than doubles with electronic outreach. The Seacoast service is video-streamed to another fourteen thousand cyberspace attendees in places like Germany, Iraq and Afghanistan. It can come into every home that has a computer. Seacoast is one of the most successful electronic churches in the world.

Surratt is a founding board member of ARC, the Association of Relational Churches. It's a wonderful acronym that gives the sense of reaching up to the heavens. Ostensibly, ARC churches are reasonably recent phenomena. Seacoast Church is a perfect example. In a time when European churches are diminishing, American churches are growing. How do they do it? They attract the largest group of potential worshipers available—the unchurched.

"It is in the Scripture," Surratt shares. "'Righteousness exalts a nation' [Proverbs 14:34]. Equally, righteousness exalts a city. Good people make a good environment to live in. The Gospel is about forgiveness of sin. We are all sinners. Good churches help a town to be good. We discovered a couple of things here. People seem to stray away from churches at college age and come back, if they come back, when they start having kids. We also compete with other things here that are difficult—the beaches and golf, just to name a few. We try to give young people an important seat in our church. We don't treat them as our future or as even in a role of our church of the future, but as the church of today."

Seacoast Church on Long Point Road in Mount Pleasant is one of the fifteen largest megachurches in the United States. It was started in

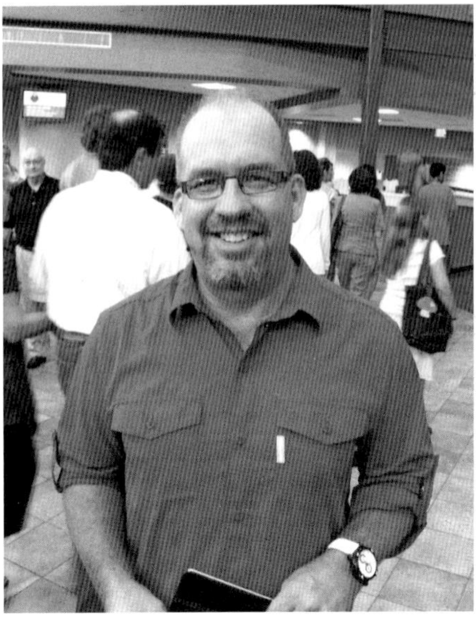

Reverend Greg Surratt has endeared himself to the Charleston community by just being himself and teaching the words of scripture as they apply to antiquity as well as to contemporary mores. *(W. Thomas McQueeney)*

an apartment complex clubhouse two dozen years ago. The visionary progenitor that is Pastor Greg Surratt is an honest and humble, even reticent, servant to the greater glory of God. He was a high school wrestler in Columbine, Colorado, near Denver. He became a youth pastor in Colorado before pastoring a church in northern Illinois for eight and a half years. He's married to a lovely lady he adores, Debbie. They have four children and nine grandchildren. His father was a pastor. His sons are assistant pastors. They are from obviously good stock and would be giants on the set of *The Wizard of Oz*. It is easy to discern Surratt's love of people and his passion for his mission.

Surratt's 2011 book titled *Ir-rev-rend* would best detail his unconventional journey to a conventional place—a life center stage on Sunday in front of thousands. He's the Greg that one would picture more in the middle of a "con-Greg-ation" than leading it. But he's up front, because he's incredibly "Greg-arious." Poking fun at himself is his natural way to stay real in his book—and in his life. It is a quality enjoyed by all.

"Did you hear about the guy who got the award for being the most humble? When he accepted the award, they had to take it away from him!" Surratt joked.

He looks like anyone other than a pastor. He wears blue jeans and comfortable golfing or gardening shirts, usually untucked. Eyeglasses assist his vision, though his bright blue eyes are soulful and engaging. They are mirrors to his casual and happy nature. His personality consumes moments. He is quicker than most to the humor in a statement—mostly something he realized was funny just after saying it. His wide range of interests includes golf, digital photography and the wondrous technology of an iPad. His daily motivation is the person in front of him, a verse from scripture and some random vignette of God's world, like a bird nesting or children being handed an ice cream. He reminds you of that outgoing and entertaining neighbor with whom you enjoy chatting in the driveway for twenty minutes. There are volumes of happy and touching chapters in his repertoire. Even being in Charleston is a chapter to be titled "The Divine Providence and Delivery of the Family Surratt."

"While in Illinois, I was sensing God's plan and felt it was leading me to plant a church in a large city. I immediately thought of Denver," Surratt related. "In my way of hearing God, I sensed no peace in that direction. During that time, I received a call from Pastor Fred Richard of Northwood Assembly Church [in North Charleston]. Fred is a wonderful man and is married to my cousin. His elders had prayed, and he said to me, 'You should come here.' He wasn't even aware of my inner sense. So Debbie and I came to visit Charleston. We were blown away. It was maybe February, but it was like springtime. We toured downtown, ate in one of those incredible restaurants and did the whole tourist thing. We were smitten. When we got on the airplane to return, we both thought, 'This is fabulous,' but we didn't feel that the East or the South were in the cards for us. We got back to our snow and ice and thought and prayed for about three months. But all I could think about was Charleston. It was pulling at my heart. My father and my uncle didn't think Charleston was right for us and didn't think we'd like being in Charleston. But I thought that maybe God was telling me that Charleston was right. In essence it would mean going from pastoring a church to becoming an assistant pastor at another church. That was a change for me, but I accepted it." The Surratts packed up and headed to the place they both had not imagined as their destiny. It was in the wrong time zone and the wrong latitude, they had thought. But it had the right heartbeat and the right attitude.

"When we started Seacoast in 1988, there were less than thirty thousand people in the entire Mount Pleasant area," Surratt recalled. "Now there are about seventy thousand. We were able to put a calling team together for a weekend to call nearly sixteen thousand phone numbers. We just asked two questions: One, what church do you attend? If they had a church, we thanked them and advocated their continued attendance. We were not here to take away from other churches. Secondly, if they had no church, we asked them to consider joining us and told them our service times. As simple as that sounds, it led to our growth and the spreading of God's word. We told them what we knew, that the grace of God is an irresistible force."

However, Surratt's timing could not have been worse.

"We had back-to-back tragic news stories [both in March of 1987] going on about other pastors in other communities that made our job difficult," Surratt conceded. "First Jimmy Swaggart had just undergone a highly public moral failure. Then, the PTL Club and their pastor, Jim Bakker, had another moral failure that developed at the same time. Both of those events gave a poor first impression of trying to build contemporary evangelical congregations. That made things most difficult in 1988. Then, of course, we had Hurricane Hugo here in 1989. So the church would have to be challenged very early to survive."

There were other obstacles, but none to compare with the auto accident of 1988 that nearly took the lives of two of the Surratt children.

"It was three weeks after we had arrived in Charleston. My parents were visiting, and we had decided to see Charles Towne Landing," Surratt related. "I still have never seen Charles Towne Landing. There was roadwork, and a truck ahead had stalled. We had stopped in our van where they were building the I-526 and I-26 interchange. A semi truck behind me did not see that everyone had stopped and plowed me full bore into a concrete retaining wall."

"My daughter that I thought was dead was brought back to life by nurses from three cars behind us. They were both on their way home from their shifts and happened to be there. My son Jason was unresponsive and unconscious. My father had broken his back. Debbie and I were the only ones in the car not seriously hurt. I remember thinking that things like this happened to other people, but not to my family. You can't imagine our fears and concern. It was all in God's hands."

The injured were transported to the Medical University Hospital. In a matter of weeks, all were treated and released, except son Jason. He was still in a coma.

"I remember standing with my arm around Debbie, all alone and looking out of the window of the ninth floor across the top of Charleston. I was thinking, 'Why did we come?' But Charleston's wonderful people came forward. With the blessing of Fred Richard, others came. I sensed the peace of God. And then the happiest day of my life arrived when my son Jason opened his eyes and smiled at me."

There's a good chance that Pastor Greg Surratt senses the peace of God daily.

"We've found Charleston to be a special place. It is everything advertised and more," Surratt explained. "There are so many gracious and friendly people here, and so many have stepped forward to become a part of Seacoast, especially in our ministries. You really do understand why Charleston is such a great destination and why growth is constant. My family loves it. God gave me a supernatural love for Charleston. I love this city!"

The ministries now take an army of volunteers.

There are small groups for women, for men, for singles, for students, for divorced members and for just about every permutation under the sun. If you can't find a small-group identity at Seacoast, it doesn't likely exist…but it could if you wanted to start a small group!

Seacoast has "The City" as well. "The City" is the online network of Christian-centered members who may want to share inspiration, prayer and even humor. It is the "gracebook" in a style of Facebook.

There are numerous prayer groups. They meet at private homes mostly, but you might easily stumble into one at a Starbucks. That may be a backdoor tribute to Surratt's admitted addiction to the magic brew.

"I first got hooked on Starbucks in downtown Charleston," Surratt stated. "I guess you could say that now I'm a daily addict." That wonderful laugh followed.

Surratt has seen so much that has been positive in the meteoric, almost exponential growth of Seacoast. He gave insight to why he is appreciative and those mentoring influences that have meant so very much to him.

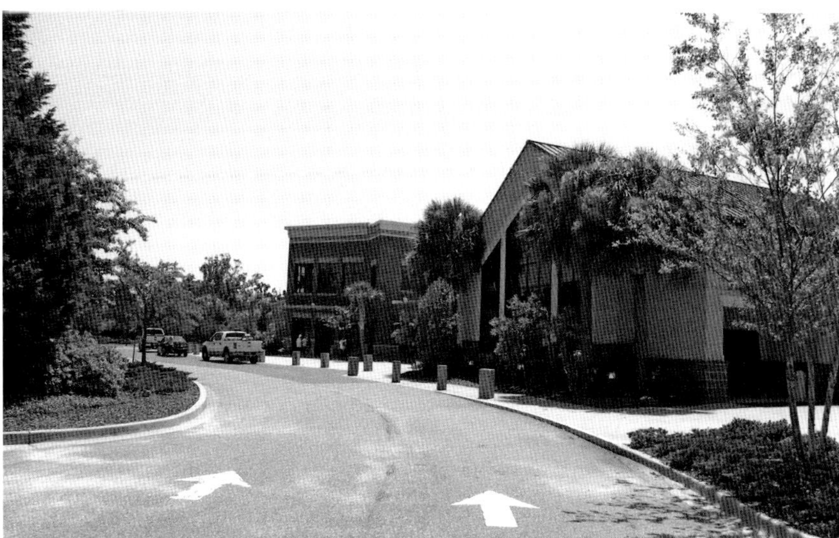

Sunday services at Seacoast Church place the modern facility into the top fifteen megachurch congregations in America. *(W. Thomas McQueeney)*

"I have been blessed. My father was a pastor of a small church back in Denver. He never had much but always gave every bit of what he could," Surratt remembered. "He gave people money from his own pocket. When someone might suggest that he was conned or that the person wouldn't use the money for food, but for alcohol, my dad simply replied, 'We're going to err on the side of generosity.' This is as true with grace as it is with other resources from God. The money is a resource, and it all comes from God."

"Fred Richard has been a forever influence on me. I can never thank him enough for his prayers and his faith in me. Fred brought me to Charleston," Surratt added. "He is a special friend and a great man.

"From afar, I've had the fortune of friendship with Pastor Rick Warren from Saddleback Church," Surratt noted. "There were so many things I have learned from his leadership and humility."

Seacoast once boasted a second Pastor Surratt. Geoff Surratt, after much prayer, was called from his role of assistance to brother Greg to serve at the famous Saddleback Church in the Los Angeles area. Geoff Surratt is now the pastor of church planting and resides in Huntington Beach, California. The brothers Surratt are now the coast-to-coast proponents of works in progress—the churching of the unchurched. Only their longitudes differ.

"Geoff is one of the smartest people I know," Surratt conceded. "He has brains like you would not believe. He was the one that thought out the multisites and the campus growth and so much more that we do here that has turned out so well. When he first came up with the idea to rent a building, bring in music and do the sermon by video, I told him he was crazy. As it turns out, he's the real brain, and I'm the idiot. That became our multisite formula. My brother has been one of the very great blessings of my life. He's doing a great job, and though we miss seeing him as much, we talk often."

Failures have been the initial phase of success. The exuberance of something new and passionate taking place on the far side of Charleston's preeminent bedroom community caught on. Throngs brought masses and multitudes. The building was too small. New surface parking meandered to the woods, over hill and dale. An approved expansion was completed, doubling the main church capacity. A large formal chapel was added. More assistant pastors assisted the pastoring. Auxiliary services included age-group daycare for attendees. Just the organization of activities and availabilities would take high-level management on the order of a few White House chiefs of staff or the like.

Then, even this massive church was too small. More Sunday service times were added. There was even a time when Surratt begged some of the midmorning service attendees to consider an earlier or later time so that the overcrowding would not pack the lobby and create a fire hazard. A plan was made for yet another major expansion out of necessity or, better said, out of prosperity.

Mount Pleasant has the atmosphere of a town, not a city. In fact, it is the Town of Mount Pleasant. A further review of population growth shows an increase from less than seven thousand in 1970 to seventy thousand in 2010. That's no town. It incorporates old neighborhoods like the Old Village and Bayview Acres into an infrastructure that has not fully anticipated the steroids of gated-community girth. The powers that be were not given to stark changes or large industry. Simply, the Town of Mount Pleasant was not ready for Greg Surratt and Seacoast. The healthy growth of Seacoast Church became analogous to becoming a Mount Pleasant industry. The town reached into its past to determine its future. The town council denied a plan of further growth to the burgeoning megachurch. It seemed like Pastor Surratt had hit the wall. He prayed.

The first step that appeared to be failure was chameleon-like. Things changed.

"Failures reaffirm your humility," Surratt keenly observed. "I can remember in Illinois delivering a big meaningful message. After the service I greeted those leaving and perhaps a hundred people thanked me, but one man came up and said he had no idea of what I was trying to say. That overpowered the hundred that had smiled and thanked me. I realized I needed to apply lessons to the worshippers simply and thoughtfully. I had to pull down the barriers. My failure led to the personal adjustment that gave me a chance to communicate better.

"In the case of building a bigger church, I was distraught over the barrier that was put up. I prayed," Surratt continued. "I then realized the barrier was not a building permit. It was reaching people with the message. We had to find a better and more effective way to do that. The failure in getting the building permit approved turned into the success of multisites and even online video streaming. We only have humble successes in life through God's love. Ultimately, my success will be when I stand before God and he says, 'Well done, servant.' I mess up like everyone else, but I've learned to apply God's grace. We are all just trophies of God's grace. If you humble yourself, God will lift you up. Failures reaffirm your humility.

"The issue of getting a permit was something I judged then as a bad result," Surratt confided. "I'm slower to judge what happens as either a good or a bad label. The future decides that."

Technologies augmented the reach of the megachurch.

"When you think about it, there will always be a one-on-one aspect of relationship with Christianity," Surratt said. "The multisite was birthed out of desperation in a pretty package. Advances in technology allowed this next level of reaching people. Technology is much like the microphone. The microphone changed the way you reach a number of people in a gathering. The new technologies are the extension of the microphone to even more people who want to hear God's word and the teachings of Jesus Christ, his Son."

If it's Sunday, regardless of the means, they are still tuned into Pastor Greg.

Those incredible music people will watch the stopwatch countdown and invite a fully engaged worship service to begin by standing and singing out. There will be blissful renderings in divine chords of hope. The pastor will comfortably elicit the strength of God's word in today's circumstance. He will make you laugh, make you examine your own conscience and make you think of the wondrous gift that our Savior, Jesus, has given. All things are forgivable. He might interject that a ball out of bounds will still cost two strokes. There are no aisle theatrics, no histrionics and no blatant pleas for financial support. In fact, new guests will be asked to not remit tithing by a friendly reminder from an assistant pastor's closing prayer. He'll petition, "This one's on us." And next week's crowd will be bigger than this week's.

Pastor Greg Surratt has made Mount Pleasant and Charleston and South Carolina and the world a better place. His technologies reach even beyond.

In March 2016, Seacoast Church announced plans to nearly double its worship congregation capacity to 2,400 seats. In the twenty-five years since Seacoast came to its spacious Long Point Road campus in Mount Pleasant, it has built twelve satellite campuses. Many services are video-streamed. On any given Sunday, the church may have as many as twenty-five thousand attendees, nearly half attending at the main building.

Almost like the biblical "loaves and fishes" story, the Surratt family has multiplied. Greg and wife Debbie "begat" four children, who then "begat" fourteen grandchildren as of 2016. Surratt continues to preach and humor crowds, the overflow serving as a testimony to his spiritually driven effectiveness.

The Charity of Understanding

Glenn McConnell

Somewhere between a battle reenactment and a risen submarine, Glenn McConnell has busied himself with the intricacies of state government. The brilliant lawyer and orator is a staple of South Carolina, like seine casting nets on the coast or fresh peaches in the upcountry fall. He is the ultimate arbitrator, leader and statesman. There will be roads and buildings in South Carolina that bear his name one hundred years hence. In fact, those already exist.

McConnell's physical presence is visually contrary to his life experience. He appears considerably younger than his birth certificate would indicate. He has a full head of darkened locks and the clear enthusiasm of a voracious college student. He exudes passion for his profession and a relentless zeal for his most intriguing avocations. A portrait artist would wisp simple strokes of burnt umber to capture the depth of his eyes in his most pensive pose. He has a gallant demeanor, both confident and comfortable.

He has witnessed the metamorphosis. Another of the children of the pluff mud, McConnell remembered his Charleston roots.

"My father, Samuel McConnell, was a contractor. I was only a small boy when we moved from Byrnes Down on Highway 17 West Ashley all the way out to St. Paul's Parish," McConnell recalled. "We were at a place called Live Oak Plantation down Sauldam Road. That old house is gone now. The high school I attended, St. Paul's, is torn down as well. For a time, I attended Rantowles Elementary School—just two rooms with three grades in one and four grades in the other. That's gone now, too."

That background would not have predicted the rise of one of the Charleston area's major political emissaries ever. McConnell took his seat in the South Carolina Senate in 1981. Since then, he has exemplified statesmanship by being deftly articulate, punctiliously engaged and imaginatively enterprising. He has selflessly built coalitions that have benefited the citizens of South Carolina for more than three decades. His Senate peers elected him as the Senate president pro tempore in 2001. In that role, he meticulously adheres to proper decorum and procedure whilst leading that august body in a mesmerizing array of legislative actions. But that is not all he does.

Besides his duty of leading the state senate, he is active in his church, the Church of the Holy Communion—a stone's throw from the medical complex on Cannon Street and Ashley Avenue. He's served as a delegate to the Republican National Convention three times. He's been a member of the South Carolina Bar since 1972 and is active with the Exchange Club of Charleston, the largest exchange club in America, with 270 members. He's the chair of the Hunley Commission and has been since its inception. He is proud of his Scottish descent and his membership in the South Carolina Historical Society. McConnell has been an active member or has assisted more than a dozen other community and statewide volunteer functions. His participation in Civil War–era reenactments has been broad and energetic. Those forays have made him a member of four reenactment units simultaneously—the Marion Light Artillery, First Connecticut Light Artillery, the Twenty-seventh South Carolina Volunteer Infantry and the Nineteenth Indiana Volunteers. All are based in the accurate rendering of history. These attachments have built national friendships along with a keen appreciation for chivalry and valor.

McConnell has multifaceted interests. He was a driving force behind the recovery, preservation and what will be the eventual display of the *H.L. Hunley* submarine. The *Hunley*, a Confederate-built submersible, represents the first successful use of a submarine in a wartime action. It was on February 17, 1864, that the *Hunley* sank the Union ship *Housatonic* in the Atlantic Ocean off Charleston. The *Housatonic* was a sloop holding nearly 120 tons of supply cargo. But the *Hunley* never returned. That singular incident changed naval warfare forever. McConnell's role became vital in the careful coordination and transformation of the "sea bottom to see it now" chronology.

"There are several opportunities that came from that experience," McConnell recounted. "First and foremost, it is a truly incredible engineering and management feat. To have reached back one hundred and thirty-six years and bring the *Hunley* back into civilization intact required incredible management skills and the application of new technologies untested before. The next fortunate event was the engagement of Warren Lasch. It was a happy day to meet this gentleman and what he has meant to the entire enterprise. He and the team he assembled set the bar on how to recover and preserve marine artifacts. They effectively changed that entire process with their work on the *Hunley*. In partnership with Clemson University, there has been an enormous scientific breakthrough in metallurgical preservation because of the *Hunley*. The science of the subcritical metallurgy procedure has resulted in the process of taking salt out of metal at a rate as much as fifteen times faster than was ever accomplished before. That new process may change other areas of science well beyond the *Hunley*."

Warren Lasch, a transport executive, with McConnell activated the Friends of the Hunley, a nonprofit organization that has benefitted the enterprise in addition to advancing the science of submerged recovery and preservation.

"The process of removing salt from metal has so many other contemporary applications," McConnell continued. "Clemson's Restoration Institute is studying applications that could assist in the maintenance of the wind turbine project we will soon see off of South Carolina's coast. It will help us to obtain and maintain the clean energy of the wind. Other *Hunley*-inspired science has also helped in the science of recovery following the 9/11 terrorist attacks on New York's Twin Towers. It was our use of gamma rays in the preservation of DNA for the *Hunley* that was again applied in postdisaster New York."

The technology that grew from the laboratory at the Warren Lasch Conservation Center is compelling in other ways. McConnell expounded upon the impact.

"What they've found in their experiments with the Clemson Restoration Institute research is that there may be a way to reengage building materials that have lost their usefulness. This would be a major breakthrough. All of this happens here because of one restoration project that the world has watched for fifteen years—the *H.L. Hunley*."

Beyond the technological leaps that have accompanied the *Hunley*'s recovery, there has been a worldwide leap of interest. *National Geographic*'s specific attention to the process, along with the historical implications, has captured world imagination. Documentary films have been shown in other countries. In addition to the scores of thousands who watched the historic recovery as it passed the harbor and bridges in Charleston, another crowd estimated as high as 150,000 attended the procession of the last funeral honoring those brave soldier-sailors who stepped the heroic one pace forward. The vignettes of the subplots included the heartwarming story of the gold coin belonging to the *Hunley* commander, Lieutenant George Dixon. The coin had a bullet indention from the battle of Shiloh in 1862. That coin was thought to have saved Dixon's life. It was given to him by his girlfriend, Queenie Bennett, of Mobile, Alabama. The story was thought to be bogus—that is, until the coin turned up among the *Hunley*'s most incredible artifacts early in the conservation process.

In ways that the information generation has advanced the world capacity for knowledge, the profound meaning of information has catapulted Charleston's identity by way of the *H.L. Hunley*. The *Hunley* says Charleston.

It is surely not the same Charleston that existed prior to the *Hunley*'s discovery and recovery in 1995—and especially in the decades leading to the event. The peninsula of Charleston was the axis of a compass to all who lived there. But unlike a compass, there were only three directions. McConnell details his youth by the directional designations.

"All points of identity were from the inside looking out from Charleston then," McConnell detailed. "You had the north area, east of the Cooper and the West Ashley area. The West Ashley area included James Island, Ravenel, Johns Island—just about anyplace in that direction you reached by crossing the Ashley River Bridge. Now, it's different. All of those places have better-defined identity.

"Just since the time I entered the senate in 1981, much has changed," McConnell continued. "You and I have deep Charleston accents. Very few people in Charleston have Charleston accents now. Other changes are felt from the loss of some small businesses I enjoyed for years. For instance, Robertson's Cafeteria was family owned. They had that legendary tartar sauce. It's never been replicated. They also had a fantastic crab casserole and a dessert called a Huguenot tart. It had nuts, etc., in it. I haven't seen those things since Robertson's closed down. I suppose they're gone forever."

There are things that are not missed in McConnell's lament.

"The most dramatic change I've seen is the redevelopment of the City of Charleston, block by block," McConnell noted. "Instead of rat-infested, empty and overgrown tenement and warehouses, we have beautifully restored offices, homes and restaurants. I credit Joe Riley for what he's done and the Charleston Historical Society and their peers for staying the course. They saved our footprints in time. People come from all over the world to see the beauty and history of Charleston today. That was accomplished by great planning and leadership.

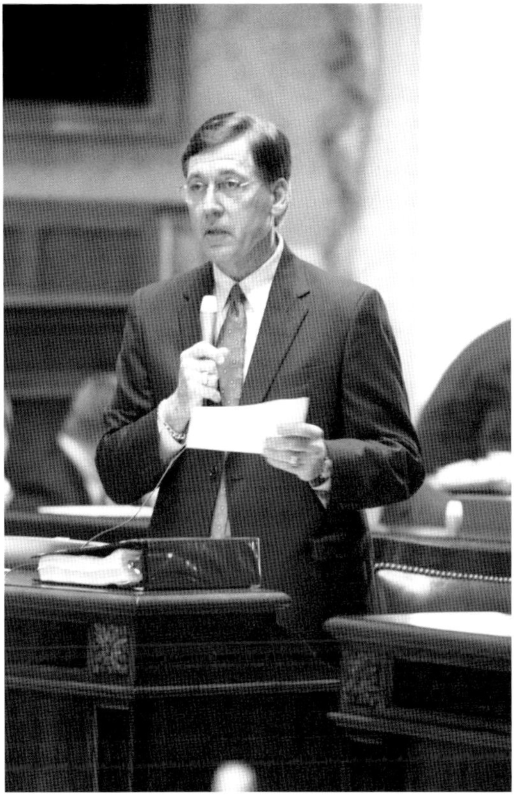

As president pro tempore of the South Carolina Senate, McConnell has gained the profound respect of his colleagues, his constituency and so many others in the state's General Assembly. *(Courtesy of the South Carolina State Senate)*

"Other events impacted Charleston's spectacular rise," McConnell pointed out. "The Spoleto Festival put Charleston on the world map for art and music. The rest of the world watched helplessly as Hurricane Hugo in 1989 made a direct hit on Charleston. Yet, the city came away better than it was before. It took a wonderful community resiliency to do that. The navy yard and naval base closures in the mid-1990s would have normally crippled a community. It made Charleston, if anything, stronger. Now you can cite the addition of Boeing as a major player in not only Charleston's economy, but the state's and region's as well. And I really think the raising of the *H.L. Hunley* did much to bring international attention again to Charleston. That episode still stands as one of *National Geographic*'s highest-rated shows. It is the only statewide attraction on the incline in attendance. That says a lot in a down economy."

McConnell's other avocation is related to his persistence in preserving cultural history—of all cultures. In the McConnell world, that relates to a reverence for the courage of his personal ancestry, especially as that relates to Confederate-era history. His lifelong pursuit of the insights and mindsets of those slowly recessing past generations of Charleston history persists. It is not politically popular in some quarters to be proud of one's Confederate heritage.

"I urge people to look at that era from the eyes and brains of that generation and not through a contemporary prism," McConnell explained. "We should understand the context of the times. Certainly we would not agree with slavery or any other injustice. People who stood in their shoes back then saw a world in flux. Those Confederate soldiers felt that they represented order. There was even the sense that failure to win freedom and their distinctive way of life in the South would subject them to perhaps massacre, punishment for civil disobedience or other atrocities. They saw the North in prewar times as having an insatiable appetite for tariffs on the backs of Southerners.

"There should be a charity of understanding that exists between opposing, but respectful viewpoints," McConnell offered. "We should never be embarrassed about our ancestors and what they stood for. It was different times and different views. No one should use an existing standard to quarrel with the history of the past. We should not let others seduce us into anger. Emotion brings division. It's that charity of understanding we should adhere to in order to reconcile differences in every culture. By example, the War Between the States did not solve problems to the extent some would suggest. It did not elevate the rights of women to vote or give other freedoms later realized, even to African Americans."

McConnell is not just whistling Dixie. He has been proactive in preserving other cultures than his own, especially as it applies to South Carolina's African American population. As chairman of the African American History Monument Commission, he was one of the major proponents of a monument on the statehouse grounds that extolled the many sacrifices and accomplishments of African Americans across the history of South Carolina.

McConnell had a strong opinion on the matter. "Our state capitol grounds should speak to everyone's history. We already had monuments to liberty and states' rights, but we were missing civil rights—an incredibly important major event in history. That monument today is near the senate building. It's a wonderful and deeply meaningful addition to the statehouse grounds."

McConnell's sense of service to others was fostered through the initial influence of his father.

"I didn't really appreciate it until later in life, but my father had some great advice that he repeated often," McConnell remembered. "He'd say, 'Never get mad enough to cost yourself money.' Another way he'd put it was more profound. 'When you wear your emotions on your shoulders, your backside is before the world.' That's a polite way of putting it."

McConnell's experiences through St. Paul's High School and his undergraduate work at the College of Charleston, where he graduated in 1969, have served him well. The college had less than 450 students then. It has 11,000 now. In observance of McConnell's dedication to the institution, some students are lodged at the Senator Glenn F. McConnell Residence Hall at the corner of Wentworth and Coming Streets.

Proficient in the world of academia, McConnell obtained his law degree from the University of South Carolina in 1972. He practiced law full time over the next few decades while concurrently taking his seat in the state senate. His command and articulation of language, coupled with a control of accentuation, made him into one of the great orators of our time. His impassionate stance on matters from fiscal conservatism to attracting major industry to the state is based in reason and researched statistics he is able to recite as support. He is a throwback in oration to John C. Calhoun or even Jimmy Byrnes.

McConnell has a special reverence for those who have served his role previously in the South Carolina Senate.

"Marion Gressette taught me the history of the senate and the need to preserve the institution with great care," McConnell said. "He was a believer in the art of persuasion and, also, the art of deprivation.

"John Drummond taught me about teamwork," McConnell added. "And he felt we should always work to rise above division to make a decision.

"Marshall Williams was another wonderful mentor for me," McConnell continued. "He really didn't subscribe to all the parliamentary devices so much as he led by his fun-loving personality."

McConnell is now the study in process and the mentoring influence to others.

The Glenn McConnell legacy seems to be rooted in three large political and cultural crossroads. He will certainly merit scholarship by coming generations because of his adroit guidance of the South Carolina Senate, now into his second decade of leadership. The special care it takes to lead in difficult times cannot be overestimated or quantified by its daily toll. Secondly, McConnell will have his name attached forever to the reclamation, recovery, restoration and proper presentation of the *H.L. Hunley* to the world. The technologies that followed the process will themselves become legend. It would not be of great revelation to cite that his third contribution may be the most powerful. He will be remembered always for his ability of discourse in the preservation of cultural diversity. He will be the man who turned the future by revisiting the past with a profound sense of the charity of understanding.

When the College of Charleston began a national search for its twentieth president to take charge in January 2015, it needed to look no further than to one of its most distinguished alums. Although the job competition was at the highest level, South Carolina's sitting lieutenant governor was chosen. He summarily stepped away from the political arena to meet the challenges of higher education. McConnell succeeded George Benson in what had been the college's next trial of creativity.

Funding for every state higher education institution's annual budget has steadily diminished since 1994. Most state colleges receive less than 10 percent of legislative support toward their annual needs. There is also very little designated to address capital improvement projects.

The college had recently changed athletic conferences and was in the midst of a debilitating financial crisis. McConnell would be the best choice to manage for success.

A 1969 graduate of the college, McConnell attended when there were fewer than 500 students enrolled at the historic and quaint George Street icon. The college enrollment has mushroomed since, topping off at 11,500 during the 2015–16 school year. With graduate students, the number is closer to 15,000.

McConnell, a traditional conservative, would need to overcome an undercurrent of much of the faculty entrenched in adverse ideology, some of whom had vociferously challenged McConnell's politics. Personable and sincere, he navigated much of the initial vitriol well.

Glenn McConnell had been known over his lifetime as a taskmaster with vision. He demonstrated that innate quality in his governmental responsibilities. He reasserted his willingness to handle every college concern with appropriate priority and decisive action at the College of Charleston. As a major force of the peninsular Charleston economy, the College of Charleston will continue its academic reach and impact within the expert guidance of Glenn McConnell.

He will achieve much, and given his character, he will do so in a confident and quiet manner.

A Change of "Status"

Sheriff Al Cannon

Al Cannon understands the exigencies of the Charleston area but has reservations about efficiently protecting the future that his observations have entailed. He's concerned. The circumstances of Cannon's youth and those of today's youth are worlds apart.

"Young people that have no sense as to the value of human life are lured and attracted to the alternative of 'status' as we know it," Cannon explained. "I knew 'status' as someone with honor and courage, or a student that excelled or an athlete that gave his or her all. Today's youth associate 'status' with material things. To them, 'status' is a car, money, a girlfriend, a gun, expensive sneakers and bling. Our generation was tied to a family, a neighborhood, a church or a high school sports team. We were, in a sense, a village moving forward.

"That saying that 'it takes a village to raise a child' misses a major point," Cannon continued. "It takes a village idiot to believe that. It is parents who must have the primary responsibility to raise a child. The sense of a village influence is only for indirect mentorship. Direct mentorship must always come from the parents—not the teachers or the guidance counselors, but the love, care and discipline of parents.

"So many of today's youth—at least the ones I see—have a fundamental problem. They have no fundamentals," Cannon expressed with concern.

James Alton Cannon Jr. grew up in the north area of Charleston before there was a North Charleston. He advanced his self-worth by hard work and even higher goals. Cannon may be the most overqualified county sheriff in America. Yet he relishes the opportunity to work in America's finest community to make it a better place for all. He has passion for his profession.

Cannon is tall and physically fit. He is attentive to details; a set of enthusiastic eyes dart in response. His passion for his profession is not only exhibited within its shielded law enforcement emblem, but within his fervency to stay moves ahead in the crime game. He anticipates, and he reacts.

Cannon and his wife, Wallis, live on the Isle of Palms and have raised two children, Al III and Sara. Al III followed his dad into law enforcement and is currently a deputy sheriff in Greenville, South Carolina.

After his graduation from the now-defunct Chicora High School, Cannon later enrolled at the College of Charleston. There he completed his bachelor of science degree before entering the University of South Carolina. His next graduation earned a master's in criminal justice, then his law degree from the same college. He is a member of the South Carolina Bar Association. Cannon entered the air force and served as a translator, owing to his fine abilities in learning Russian, at a time when learning Russian was crucial in the intelligence world. Cannon kept a reserve role in the Air Force after his initial four years of active duty. That role took him all over Europe and into the Middle East on many occasions. His specialized abilities as a law enforcement expert made him a valuable resource in parts of the world where chaos reigned. He retired in 2006 as a full colonel. Oh yeah—and he's been the elected sheriff of Charleston County for two dozen years.

The immense task of patrolling Charleston County wears out cars as well as manpower. The annual $56 million budget pays for protection from the South Santee River (past McClellanvile on Highway 17 North) to Edisto Island up to Edisto Beach. Tasks in addition to policing criminal behavior and domestic violence reach over to illegal immigration, traffic oversight and other growing concerns in the county. The position comes with extreme responsibility and a mandate of duty personified.

"The economy is not the central factor in crime rates, as most people think," Cannon stated. "Mobility is the biggest factor. In times past, a person in North Charleston was likely to commit crimes in North Charleston. Now that criminal may rob someone in Awendaw or Ravenel. And criminals can congregate with their crime partners by cell or texting. The most disturbing change is that giving up is not what it used to be. They watch these shows with incredible chase scenes and decide they can wreak havoc after a crime. It's another thing they think that gives them status. There are more confrontations now—and even ambushes. There is also the new fad of 'suicide by cop.'

"'Suicide by cop' is a hardened criminal's way of brandishing firearms in the face of overwhelming police containment so that the criminal will invite a firefight. These types of criminals are usually violent and often on drugs," Cannon continued. "They want no part of prison, and many times have already spent considerable time in prison.

"I've noticed a unique connection with New York City to Charleston crime," Cannon continued. "We've seen many who break the law here that flee to New York to hide with family there. And when they get in trouble in New York a year or two later, they come back here. It seems that there are more crime-cultured individuals here than ever with New York connections."

They'd be much better off staying in New York. Sheriff Cannon's reputation as a hardliner who does his homework gives him an upper hand. He is adept at removing criminals from society and protecting the peace for those decent citizens he is sworn to defend.

He prides himself in knowing the neighborhood as well.

"I grew up in what was a lower-middle-class or upper-lower-class family. My dad worked hard and was responsible," Cannon reflected. "He worked his career at the navy yard—a blue-collar guy. My mother, Margie Cannon, eventually became a magistrate. They both spent many hours pitching in so that my brother, sister and I could have better opportunities. Mom was a magistrate for twenty-six years. She died in 2007.

"I played basketball at Chicora High School for Coach Ray Graves. Coach Graves was a fine player for Coach Norm Sloan at The Citadel. He'd turn the heat up in our gym for home games, I remember. He kept us in physical shape, and we'd run the other teams out of the gym," Cannon recalled. "Coach Graves was a mentor to me. And so was Gary McJunkin, who has spent his life coaching kids on the playgrounds. He's been a fantastic role model for kids wanting to learn sports."

Gary McJunkin spent fifty-five years of exceptional dedication to north-area playgrounds and especially Dixie Youth Baseball. McJunkin has coached literally thousands of children and gained a wonderful reputation for pitching in with volunteer physical labor to improve the ball fields. Very few of Cannon's contemporaries were not mentored by Coach Gary McJunkin.

Cannon's lifetime love of baseball came naturally. Cannon has seen his own son and his nephew go through the playgrounds and graduate from The Citadel. His nephew, Chip Cannon, played baseball at the famed military college.

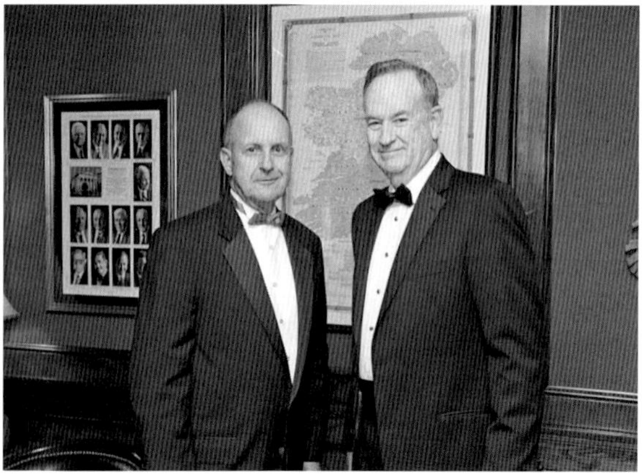

Sheriff Al Cannon with FOX News talk show host Bill O'Reilly in 2011. Cannon has served Charleston County for more than twenty-four years as sheriff and, as such, has been instrumental in implementing several effective programs that have reduced crime and made the county among the safest in America. *(Courtesy of the Hibernian Society of Charleston)*

"Ralph McCullough was another gentleman that inspired me. He was my tort law professor at South Carolina," Cannon added. "He was a great instructor and helped me to work towards career goals. I worked for him after my first semester. He's currently the provost at Charleston School of Law."

Cannon became engaged in the practice of law enforcement. He pursued that career in vehemence and is now one of Charleston's most recognizable public figures. It's best to see him at events, not as an event that causes him to see you.

He rarely forgets a face or a name.

"You pay attention to detail in law enforcement. Especially your training," Cannon continued. "One of my most harrowing experiences was the simple task of serving papers at a residence early in my career. A huge guy came charging at me through a screen door with a butcher knife. Had I not stood aside at the protection of the doorframe as I had been trained, I would have surely been stabbed. Because of the proper training and paying attention to such a small detail, I was able to pull my firearm quickly enough to subdue the large man and have him then surrender."

It's the difference between being a blood spurt and an expert. Sheriff Cannon qualifies himself in other enlightening matters beyond the routine of everyday policing activities. For years, he has been advocating the consolidation of police forces with local municipalities.

"Crime is blind," Cannon emphasized. "That mobility factor changed the game. As a citizen of the area, we often live in one community, work in another and have dinner in yet another. Crime is now the same. What benefit is it in having the world's greatest police chief in Charleston and your wife being murdered while Christmas shopping at the Northwoods Mall parking lot in North Charleston? That happened. It's just a sample of many crimes that are in other jurisdictions away from the victim's home jurisdiction.

"Only police and politicians pay any attention to lines," Cannon offered. "It's a very evolved problem with an archaic structure. Lack of mobility reduced crime rates way back when. Mobility increases them now. Today's criminals are inundated with propaganda that extols violence. The culture of violent crime is glorified with movies, TV and lyrics to music. And the spread of crime throughout multiple jurisdictions makes it most difficult to identify, solve and apprehend. Coordinating the departments as one agency would be a game changer."

It seems it's all a matter of perspective.

"If you're traveling abroad or well away from here and someone asks you where you're from, you say Charleston. If you're in Charleston when asked, you might say James Island or Mount Pleasant. If you're being asked by another Charlestonian, you might name your high school," Cannon explained. "That's your hometown identity, but it's always a different answer, according to who's asking. What that really says is that when we are away from here, we do not signal a competition. We're all from Charleston. We're proud to be Charlestonians. It's the best place ever. The competition begins when we're here. We have our lines to protect. And that's silly. That criminal doesn't care."

Cannon makes more sense as a pragmatist than any politician. And that is precisely why this simple but effective change is not likely to happen anytime soon. He is a well-trained, passionate and overqualified county sheriff. He is not a politician by any stretch. Cannon tells it as it really is and is willing to stand the criticism. A good sheriff does that.

"When you stand up and exercise some leadership it offends some people and inspires others," Cannon opined. "It's a pack mentality. You lead in order to accomplish at a winning pace. Some are inspired and catch up. Some drag along and complain and yet others stop altogether and criticize, saying the pace is too fast and the leader is wrong for them."

The step-back look at the consolidation argument leaves little argument. Cannon is correct in every assessment, and there are more. In addition, there would have to be a cost savings to the taxpayer. Crime labs would be consolidated. Record keeping could be centralized, dispatch streamlined, SWAT teams and their resources unified and more effectively orchestrated. Specific training for specific community concerns would be better performed together as a regional or countywide force than a separate force for each large municipality and the duplication of resources and facilities. Currently, Charleston County deputy sheriffs traverse several other jurisdictions to patrol the remainder that is not overlapped by a municipal force. The waste of fuel and vehicular depreciation are factors. Even the simple task of reconstructing an auto accident becomes difficult if the accident is at the border of two competing jurisdictions.

But it's not all about money. It's about service. A consolidated force would seem to better serve the entire community. Perhaps the blindness of crime could "see" the difference as well.

The same old arguments against police consolidation are conflicting wage structures, turf wars for the politicians and otherwise politics as usual.

To approve a consolidation plan would seem to be a matter of getting the decision makers that are from Charleston when they are away from Charleston to be from Charleston when they are here.

"Some of the things that tax police departments now that were not as evident in the past are things like hostage situations," Cannon cited. "Historically, the police quickly gain containment of the perimeter. We bring in SWAT and negotiate. We identify the victim and the hostage and then determine the motivation. Time is our greatest ally. The longer we can negotiate, the safer the victim becomes. Short situations are usually bad for the victim. So to lengthen the negotiation is an asset. It takes tremendous knowledge, experience and manpower to manage a hostage situation to a successful conclusion. However, today it is far more complicated. What appears to be the traditional hostage situation is something else entirely. There is no negotiation.

"Those situations are more prevalent than before, from the Columbine massacre to the Amish school shootings to the Virginia Tech shootings," Cannon said. "A well-coordinated and specially selected police team could best be developed and trained in a large county consolidation. In these rapidly evolving situations, there is no time for the traditional approach. Time is not on your side. Time is against you, and the chances of making a mistake are great."

Sheriff Cannon remains ever diligent in his role. He has top-level captains and lieutenants. He expertly delegates for the best of reasons.

"I want my people to be the best. That includes making proper decisions in times that are intense," Cannon proudly revealed. "When I traveled to the Mideast with the reserves, I had to know that Charleston County was every bit as safe as it was when I was here. And that is an accomplishment for which I am well pleased. I work with fine professionals that I trust."

Cannon's executive assistant, Brenda Hoskins, has served the department for thirty-five years. She is most appreciative of the sheriff's leadership skills and compassion for others.

"Sheriff Cannon has a heart for the elderly," Hoskins intimated. "If one of the elderly citizens calls here and asks for the sheriff, he'll go to their home to see them. He does it because he cares. He's an honest, good man, and he gives all of us the tools to get the job done. He trusts us and gets out of our way. I don't know of anyone who really knows the sheriff that doesn't really respect him and like him."

Hoskins continued, "He is an avid reader. His wife, Wallis, tells us that he rarely watches television, that he much prefers to read. It makes you understand why he is so incredibly intelligent."

It is apparent that Sheriff Al Cannon is engaged with the spectrum of subtleties that can influence both the commission of crime and it's antidote, his police department. He reads the journals and the books. He keeps his eye on the media, the trends, the communications and technologies and, most importantly, the identified criminal elements.

His status of integrity, diligence and intelligence will prevail over the pseudo status of those bent on crime. His status is based on enthusiasm for the work ahead and the honor of serving a community he loves.

The Wind in His Sails

Board of Zoning Appeals Chairman Lenny Krawcheck

Being a Charlestonian comes with responsibility. You see it daily when a tourist asks for directions or when an editorial is written in the *Post and Courier*. The homegrown citizens—the children of the pluff mud—take Charleston seriously. It is a matter of municipal pride. It is also a matter of concern for our future.

Lenny Krawcheck grew up as much on the harbor as he did on the harborside. He has resided at his Colonial Street address since childbirth. He's had a lifelong affinity for sailing races. The former national Y-class champion sailor reads the ripples upon the water to get a sense of the wind. He is adept at the direction, speed and intensity of what is to be expected in front of him. This simple ability has served as the pulse of Krawcheck's rhythm. It has guided his judgment and intuition and enabled his accomplishment.

"My proudest sailing moment was winning the Y-Flyer nationals here in Charleston in 1991," Krawcheck noted. "I had a bit of a home-court advantage."

Krawcheck has been a regatta participant since his youthful days in Charleston. His expertise in the sport is sought by other yachtsmen of every age. His knowledge of sailboats, the elements, currents and racing strategies is perhaps unsurpassed in the Charleston sailing world. He serves as the fleet captain of the Charleston Lightning Fleet. His competitive zeal and sailing know-how keep him engaged in the sport currently.

Krawcheck knew about other things than tacking against the wind. He was an outstanding student and athlete at Charleston High School, where he played basketball under the legendary Coach Morris Finkelstein. Finkelstein was one of his early and memorable influences.

"Coach Finkelstein's work ethic was very special. He demanded your best effort and had an attitude that you never stopped fighting," Krawcheck recalled. "He taught us honor and integrity. He was a taskmaster. He was firm, but fair, but always told us that the world is not always fair."

Morris D. Finkelstein was a longtime coach at the High School of Charleston who passed away in 1994. The High School of Charleston closed down in 1982, though the main columned building remains as a prominent historical edifice on Rutledge Avenue near Calhoun Street.

Krawcheck's high school friends included Charlie Jaques, Benny Varn and Beansey Frampton. Varn was a fine tennis player who went on to play at The Citadel and coached tennis at Wofford. Frampton played at Presbyterian College, and another friend, Paul Scarpa, played tennis and later coached at Furman University.

"Varn was in my neighborhood. We rode bicycles from Moultrie Playground all the way to Hampton Park to play baseball. We thought nothing of it," Krawcheck retold proudly. "We played where there was a game—Moultrie Playground, the Horse Lot or wherever. Buzzy Newton has been a lifelong friend and lived near us as well. We'd all go to Colonial Lake and take out rowboats. I can remember first attaching a sail to our rowboat to navigate the lake."

Joseph T. "Buzzy" Newton III became president of Piggly Wiggly Carolina in 1979. This Charleston-based grocer and food distributor has had a tremendous impact upon Charleston's growth and development and is known for his generous support of the community.

"We'd play tennis and football, basketball and softball," Krawcheck noted. "It was a different pick-up game every day. We'd bike over to East Bay Playground and play those boys over there as well.

"Saturdays came, and we went to the movies for a dime. We had a half dozen choices, and they were usually all westerns," Krawcheck reminisced. "You had the Gloria, the Garden and the Riviera, the Majestic, the American and the Palace. If you had a nickel, you could get popcorn."

A bright student, Krawcheck spent time at Duke University and the College of Charleston, where he received his bachelor of arts in history.

A College of Charleston mentor, Professor Puryer, was the dean of the history department and talked the young Krawcheck into pursuing a law career. Krawcheck did just that. He was accepted at the prestigious Tulane University School of Law in New Orleans. He lived away from Charleston for the only extended time in his life but earned his law degree and returned to Colonial Street. It was in New Orleans where his new wife, Townie, gave birth to two of their four talented children.

Upon returning, Krawcheck set up a small practice on Broad Street. In 1965, Morris Rosen, a successful lawyer, mentored Krawcheck. Rosen was of great influence to Krawcheck's career.

"Morris Rosen is a fine man who took the time to assist me every opportunity that came along," Krawcheck recalled. "I can't imagine what path my life might have taken without the guidance of this brilliant and caring man.

"There were not that many lawyers in Charleston, contrary to popular belief," Krawcheck asserted. "There were five new lawyers starting that same year in the Broad Street area. That was a lot. There were only seventy-five in the entire Charleston Bar Association. Within two months, I knew them all.

"Morris Rosen stepped forward and helped me. Others, like Gedney Howe Sr. and T. Allen Legare, were advisers, and I learned much from them. There were others, like J.C. Hare and Lawrence Stoney," Krawcheck recounted. "The tight associations of Charleston lawyers in the mid-1960s were compelling. They were all good men, extraordinary lawyers and civic minded."

Krawcheck has an established practice and shares the eponymous firm with attorneys Lydia Pruitt Davidson and Lydia Brooks. Their historic two-story State Street office is cozy and exquisitely furnished and spreads out over both floors. The vestigial law books line the walls in defiance of a click of a mouse button to an updated computer program. Both exist in harmony.

Krawcheck became proactive in service to the Charleston community early in his career. He was elected to serve in the South Carolina House of Representatives from 1967 to 1970. He served on the Tri-Centennial Commission—the board that ushered in the beginning of Charleston's fourth century. After establishing a repertoire of law services in private practice, Krawcheck was appointed chairman of the City of Charleston Board of Zoning Appeals by Mayor Joe Riley in 1979. He had served on that board for a time a few years earlier. Krawcheck has currently chaired this essential Charleston authority uninterrupted for thirty-two years. It is in this role that most Charlestonians are familiar with Lenny Krawcheck. That board is the reason Charleston remains diligent in its intense regard for its preservation, adaptive use and livability.

"Charleston is a difficult place to apply zoning, because so much of the city was built before there was a zoning ordinance," Krawcheck assessed. "Most buildings do not conform with setback and parking requirements. We have to deal with that and apply reason. Because we start off with an unusual situation, variances are often required for use of a property."

Zoning isn't always about what you see, but is often about what you don't see.

Krawcheck relates the point. "I can sometimes turn the corner from Colonial to Tradd and see ships coming in, crossing the harbor as you look down Tradd Street. There are other wonderful corridor views, especially on East Bay Street. Those views have to be protected for coming generations. It makes this city both beautiful and unique."

There were seminal moments in the zoning decisions that Krawcheck remembered. One was the final approval of the Omni Hotel project that would become today's Charleston Place.

"The inception and impact of that hotel was an absolutely positive change to Charleston," Krawcheck explained. "That hotel turned out to be high quality, with fine materials and design. It brought in visitors that we would not have otherwise had. It anchored that area and began to change Charleston for the better." Some thought it would have a negative impact on preservation, but he feels it has had the opposite effect.

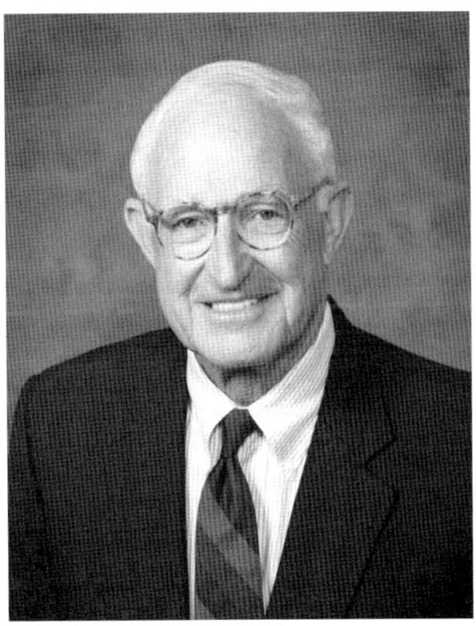

Lenny Krawcheck has served the community, especially the peninsular area, with his common-sense approach to new construction projects and renovations of earlier edifices that fit the character of America's most historic city. *(Krawcheck family collection)*

"And it brought in a revitalized King Street with it," Krawcheck continued. "When you stop and think of it, the King Street retail area that runs now from Spring Street to Broad Street is perhaps the premier retail street in the country."

Krawcheck's point is profound. King Street is low profile, with short blocks and only two traffic lanes. The length he describes is about a mile and a half long and features an abundance of uniquely Charleston shops, restaurants and boutiques. There are bookstores and sushi bars, antique emporiums and jewelry retailers. Mingled in are major national players like the Apple Store, Banana Republic and the commensurate number of Starbucks. It is the easy walk of a mall, but outdoors in Charleston's famously agreeable weather.

Lest ye consider Manhattan: Sure, there are canyon-like boulevards of long blocks and wide lanes of traffic in Manhattan. There are throngs perusing the spacious glass windows, regardless of the austere winter weather and incessant loud traffic. There's Broadway and Fifth Avenue and the run up to the park at Fifty-ninth. No jaywalking allowed. It's New York, the center of the universe. But Manhattan ain't Charleston!

Krawcheck's insightful point is that the quaintness and variety that King Street offers is unlike anywhere else. King Street, Charleston, is an experience unto its own—unmatched, unrivaled and unencumbered by what does not belong. Proper zoning, preservation and common sense do that.

In his long tenure in this sometimes-testy role, Krawcheck has demonstrated finesse well past his insight. One of his fellow board members, Michael Robinson, describes the famous Krawcheck personality.

"For certain, Lenny is a true Charlestonian, but even more importantly, he is a consummate gentleman," Robinson stated. "I have served on the city's Board of Zoning Appeals with him for more than twenty years, and his ability to calm potentially volatile hearings is artful. I have seen, on numerous occasions, citizens clearly upset over issues in their particular cases, leaving the hearing with the feeling that they had won, even though that was not the case, due to Lenny's very calm, caring and persuasive delivery. I have told him that he has all the attributes of an Irish diplomat—the ability to tell a man to go to hell and make him believe he will enjoy the trip."

Krawcheck has a daughter in New York with whom to compare notes. Sallie Krawcheck is his second child. The oldest daughter of Lenny and Townie Krawcheck, she's well known in New York and points beyond. You might know her as the former CFO of Citigroup and recently the head of Global Wealth Management of Bank of America, which includes Merrill Lynch. Her Charleston roots and fine upbringing serve her well. As her father aptly relates, "Sallie is so much like her mother and our other three children. They all have the same qualities. They believe in hard work, and they tell it like it is even when it's not popular; but importantly, it is truthful."

Kenny Krawcheck, the oldest, is a lawyer practicing in Charleston. Johnny Krawcheck is a lawyer in Atlanta, and the youngest daughter, Elizabeth Krawcheck Rodgers, is also a lawyer and a trust officer with

Wells Fargo in Charleston. Papa Krawcheck exudes the confidence of what he and Townie have produced to the world. The Krawcheck offspring are pursuing careers in truly professional pursuits. Lenny Krawcheck should be quite proud.

Lenny Krawcheck came from fine Charleston stock as well. His father, Jack Krawcheck, owned a fashionable menswear store on King Street. Jack Krawcheck's opened in 1922 and gained a reputation as a top-quality clothier. They carried distinctive men's business suits and ties, trousers, dress shirts, tuxedos, shoes, hosiery, wallets and belts. They even had fedoras. It was a King Street fixture until it closed in 1995.

The Krawcheck name became idiosyncratic to Charleston. It still is. It will continue to be.

"I have been lucky in many respects," Krawcheck noted. "My children have done well, and I'm living the life I wanted to live in the city where I grew up."

Attorney and zoning board chairman Leonard "Lenny" Krawcheck has not only done well for himself over a lifetime, he has read the ripples in the water and predicted the wind in Charleston's sails. He has expertly directed a course of which we can all be proud.

Reverend Tony Thompson Reformed

The little church at 51 Bull Street has a new pastor. The Reverend Tony Thompson was sent from a flourishing parish in Summerville to revive an edifice in decline that has an even more desperate need in membership. Nine parishioners attended his first Sunday service.

The Holy Trinity Reformed Episcopal Church had extensive wood rot and a failing pier system dating from its construction in the 1880s. The church needed new paint perhaps ten years ago. There were also leaks from the ceiling, cracked windows and a front brick wall that had begun a perilous-looking lean to the sidewalk. In short, the church needed both physical and spiritual work.

"That's why I'm here," the beaming new minister said. "If this were not a dire challenge, I would still be in Summerville."

Indeed, even the demographics were antiquated.

The Reformed Episcopal Church has its national headquarters in Philadelphia. The movement is less than 140 years old. It was a mostly Caucasian initiative that has, in time, transcended race, especially in the South. Reverend Thompson's nine attendees are all African American on this Sunday, but the church is not intended to be of any color. It is a fundamental movement to the basic teachings of the Bible that brought these peoples together, most associated with the *Book of Common Prayer*.[33] It is a passion for Christian teachings actually rooted more in the Catholic theology that preceded the 1534 establishment of the Church of England that underscores its mission.[34]

Reverend Tony Thompson's Summerville ministry is different. That exemplary church has a fine blend of race, youth and enthusiasm for the future. The seminary that abuts the church produces the future leadership nationally of the Reformed Episcopal Church.

Tony Thompson has been selected to orchestrate the miracle of miracles. Upon first glance at the little clapboard church at 51 Bull Street, the Southeastern Diocese of the Reformed Episcopal Church has chosen the right man. He is trim, bright and energetic. His sermons are seated in finely organized cross-references from Old Testament to New. His voice resounds in the simple acoustics that this austere chamber has provided orators for 130 years. He intersperses comprehensive prayers with a strong a cappella voice tempered by a simple foot tap or rhythmic clap of the small assemblage. At fifty-eight, Tony will be the rising rock star of a renewed evangelical bent he hopes to bring to downtown Charleston. His immediate concern is not that he has only 9 dedicated attendees for his initial Sunday service or that the church is a structural nightmare. It is that the church only seats 150. His plans are God's plans, and in God's plan, he will need more space.

Over coffee after his fourth Sunday service (which I attended), we spent three hours talking about our common past, as uncommon as it was, and what can be the surge that uplifts this warm and historic church on Bull Street. His neighbors are mostly college students from the College of Charleston. He is two blocks from the college's impressive administration building, Randolph Hall. The college has done its own forty-year transformation to become a major force in regional liberal arts education. It has eleven thousand students. Its student population in 1970 was 470, or about two-thirds the size of Bishop England High School, where Tony Thompson and I shared classes. The college recently built its state-of-the-art library where Bishop England High School once stood. In so many ways, the college may serve as a template for Holy Trinity Church. It may also become a vital piece of its salvation. There is a dynamic at work here. It may be these young students who bring a renewed vigor to a calling, but first they have to be called.

Just forty years ago, I was somehow in tune to the abbreviated and profound words that Tony espoused in our infrequent conversations. Perhaps I knew he would become a leader and that he would be inspirational. Tony is the only member of the Bishop England Class of 1970 that became a pastor. We had several other classmates of promise, but Tony was the only delivery. There were Catholic priests in both the class ahead of us and the class behind us. Tony is our only cleric.

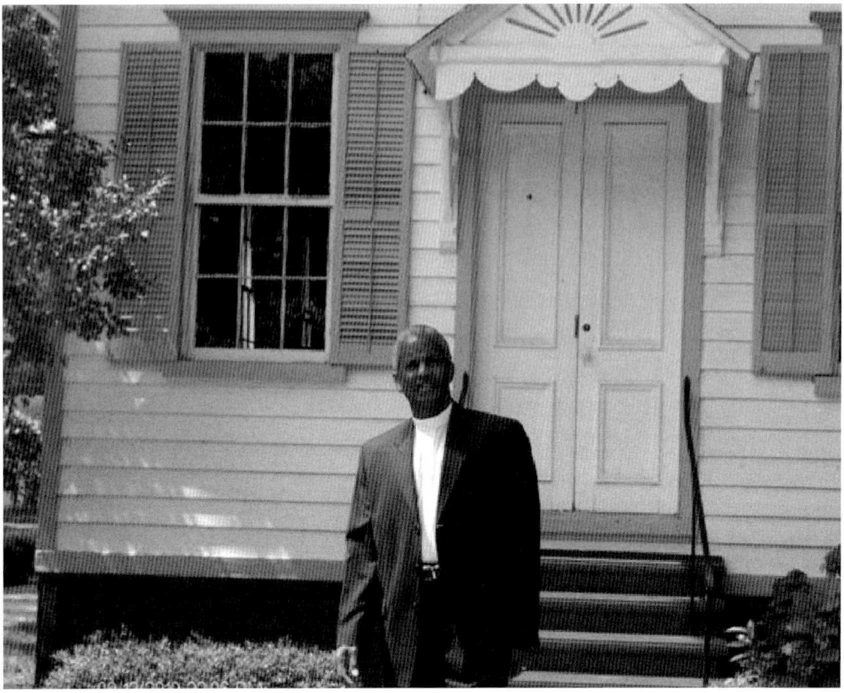

Reverend Anthony Thompson, with assistance from the beneficence of José Rueda, took on the monstrous project of renovating the 135-year-old Holy Trinity Reformed Episcopal Church. *(Thomas Russell McQueeney)*

The Reverend Tony Thompson began his spiritual journey less than a dozen blocks away. He attended Immaculate Conception Catholic School. This association fed this minority parochial school into Bishop England High School at the nexus of the absurdities accompanying public school integration. Bishop England High School graduated its first African American student in 1965. There was not a newspaper article or protest or celebration. It was just another graduation of a fine student from a private Catholic school with strong moral and ethical values. Other minorities of great note followed.

Tony Thompson came from a semi-Catholic household and continued his education at the historically black Benedict College in Columbia, South Carolina. His background included twenty-two years as a drug and alcohol abuse counselor with the Charleston County Police Department. There he had seen the depths of social malfeasance and misdirected lives. And it was there that he had first professed a well-placed trust in his Creator and Savior.

His new path took him to the Cummins Reformed Episcopal Seminary in Summerville. His entire adulthood had been dedicated to the shepherding of care and assistance to his fellow man. It had ultimately brought him to a place of utmost trust in the divine. It was the divinity—a Holy Trinity—that embraced the little church at 51 Bull Street that would determine where, what and how he would proceed.

The history of the congregation parallels the history of the church building. The Charleston County Public Library offers some insight from the works of Robert Rosen, who catalogued many of the structures in the Bull Street area. Though most of the Bull Street edifices date from the early 1800s, the Holy Trinity Church was a later addition. Indeed, Denmark Vesey, a free black who was vilified by whites and honored by blacks, lived at the single-story house at 56 Bull Street.[35] It dated back to 1805.

A breakaway group from the Calvary Protestant Episcopal Church on Line Street initiated the Reformed Episcopal Church in 1874.[36] They acquired the site (then numbered as 49 Bull Street). An unusual event occurred in 1880. At a full cost of one thousand dollars for materials and even design costs, the assembly raised the church in three weeks![37] It must have been like the traditional barn-raisings that predominated newer communities in the American Midwest. The simple structure was laid out in symmetry, with clean lines and an inviting double door centered on a covered portico. It was built on low piers and roofed with tin. The original structure had no plumbing or electricity. The ten large, plain windows sat opposing each other along the clean, wooden exterior. There were no colorful lead and cut-glass biblical inlays—just the outside viewed from within. Not much has changed.

I spoke about how nice it would be to have stained glass windows that worked the light into a prism and reflected the greatness of the Almighty. The windows had been simple glass panels for 130 years. Somehow, Tony and I both felt that the Charleston Board of Architectural Review would never allow such a change. That was one area of restoration that we would not need to consider. In a way, the windows are a microcosm of the church itself—no distortions, nothing fancy, just the way it is. These windows were painted shut a few restorations ago. The sills may have a greater volume of paint than wood.

Tony's wife, Myra, is most supportive of her husband's new mission. His three children are off to life as it happens. Their adventures seem to always lead back to Tony. He is their answer to the world that sometimes thwarts them. He's been a stalwart mentor of that which is right. It is all he ever really knew.

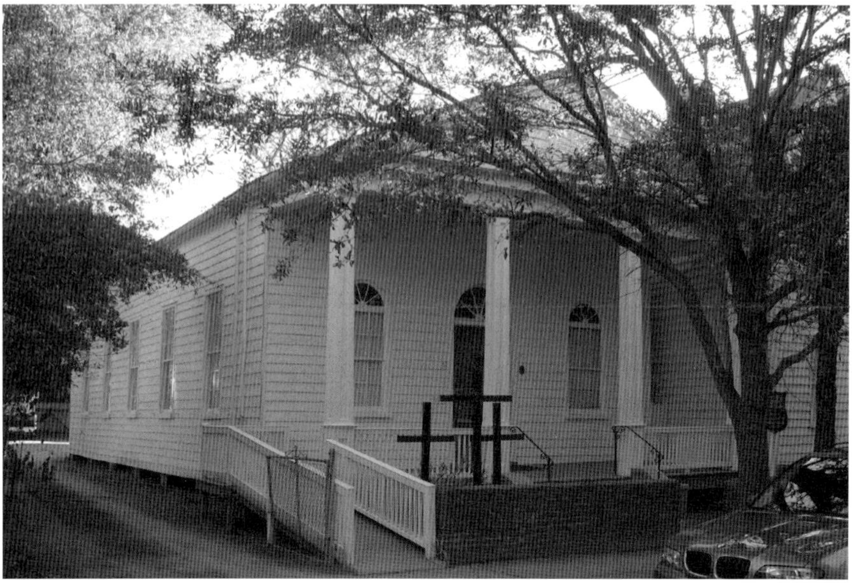

Holy Trinity Church at 51 Bull Street was built in 1880 over three weeks at a cost of $1,000. Its renovation is the seed for its revival. *(Photo by Charlotte S.)*

Tony's uncle and his cousin come to his service often. They are exceedingly proud of Tony. Family matters. They believe in him, and they believe a better day is to come—both spiritually and physically for this stark, wooden structure that defies time.

The roof needs sanding and primer. With new metal paint, the elements will be sealed out for another twenty years. Some elements need to be sealed in.

Tony noted that a building fund had been started. There may be a few hundred dollars in the fund, not even enough to file for a permit. It would not appear that this dilapidated old church would have an opportunity to resurrect itself. It had experienced the unholy trinity of doom—no money, no parishioners and no passion for the cause. The Holy Spirit would need to intercede. Or maybe Tony and I could recruit angels?

It was in medieval Avignon that angels were said to have inspired a shepherd to do the unexpected. Bénézet, the shepherd, described his motivation as words from the heavens during an eclipse in 1177.[38] The angels appeared and stayed to attend his flock whilst he built a bridge to cross the Rhone River. The civil authorities refused to help him. I suppose they thought him unstable. He moved a large, rounded stone into place and announced it as the bridge's foundation. He toiled alone for many years and completed his task before he died. Miracles happened in the process. Bénézet was beatified and sainted. That stone bridge had suffered many floods and natural disasters through the centuries. The stone arches are built as a pathway to what would become, 140 years later, the Palais des Papes—the Palace of the Popes. Indeed six popes were in residence in Avignon from 1309 to 1371.[39]

As one who was most interested in this story and the history of the papacy during its only time away from the Vatican, I traveled to Avignon. There is a park on the west bank that gives one a fine view of the Pont Saint Bénézet and the palace beyond. There are benches there to sit and hear the wide river rush by or enjoy the constant breezes that pulsate through this natural setting. It is here that I sat and reflected upon a saint I had not studied in my many years of Catholic tutelage. His time was a time of devotion few of us could imagine. My mind leaped to the sheer magnitude of his ambition and challenge as he rolled that first large stone into place on the opposite side of the river. Surely this holy man had to envision the result before he began the quest.

A local man with a disjointed English accent told me that Saint Bénézet had built the bridge stone by stone for nearly thirty-five years. He said the enthusiasm the saint exhibited for the project was rumored to be a long and contrite act of penance.

"Perhaps so," I thought. If a hand-built bridge could free one from the burdens of sin or even temptation, it would be because the search for stones and mortar disallowed the time for these haphazard dalliances. We should all build bridges.

An eclipse or a whisper from the heavens or the appearance of angels to fully comprehend the power of the Holy Spirit and the goodness of mankind was not forthcoming. Whether this saint had built this bridge as penance or as a divine instruction, the view from that west bank of the large, Roman-arched remnant was spiritually compelling. It would be my recollection of this experience that aligned my thoughts to Tony Thompson's little church on Bull Street. There would be no large boulder to be rolled forward, just a list of essentials to repair. Idleness is the devil's workshop, is it not?

Building a future would require rebuilding the past. Yet, this small congregation needs the promise of tomorrow. The church would need renewal for its own rebirth. With the inspiration of Saint Bénézet and the blessing of the Reverend Tony Thompson, the promise of tomorrow would be bridged from the dedication of today. A wide river could be crossed, stone by stone. Holy Spirit Church will be revived.

There is a spirituality that pervades all space. This church exudes the Holy Spirit's anointment. There is the warmth of the small congregation. There is the gentle demeanor of those within the performance of every Sunday's responsibility. There are those inside who righteously serve the Lord and respectfully assist the pastor. These are the fertile seeds of what these patrons are to be and what the church is to become.

The interior had lost some of its lathing and finish. Some has already been patched. Some has held through the time. Other pieces have fallen from the constant contraction and expansion caused by the sweltering Charleston summers and the infrequent cold snaps that ruin our morning golf plans. They could be repatched and repainted. The time of carrying stones to get to the other side had begun.

Other work will be delicate. The church must awaken. Lead-free coatings are needed both on the exterior and interior. More paint will come off than will need to go on. The joists are solid. Some of the piers under the church have crumbled and will have to be rebuilt. New bricks and new mortar are gathered. That's a start. This undertaking will level the floor and align the pews from their current lean downward to the wall. Everything begins with a solid foundation. The chandeliers will need to be refinished. The windows should be repainted and cleaned. The pews will be painted and varnished anew. The flooring will shine. The railings will sparkle. The altar will invite prayer with the excitement of its reinvigorated pastor. He will be renewed as well. God has shared his smile through the Reverend Tony Thompson.

In the rear yard of the church building, there will be a garden. It is inspired by that view of Avignon from the park across the river. It will be a place of benches, foliage, water, flowers and the imagined scents of creation. This will be a place of meditation. It will feature tea olives, azaleas, camellias, jasmine and honeysuckle. There will be a statue of great inspiration chosen for its beauty by the pastor. It will be the centerpiece of the meditation garden and will be elevated above the sound and renewal of water.

The church is for the congregation of believers. The garden is for the world. The church and garden will uplift tomorrow's tomorrow.

Tony Thompson and that little church on Bull Street have a lot in common.

On the evening June 17, 2015, during the Wednesday night prayer services at the Mother Emanuel AME Church in Charleston, a lone gunman entered the rear of the church. He sat for a while before pulling a gun and murdering nine innocent victims. His announced intention was to start a race war. One of the nine murdered in the church was Charleston's newest ordained minister, Myra Thompson. She read the scripture that evening from Mark. Her husband, Anthony "Tony" Thompson, had been assisting her with her topical homily. He would have been there to enjoy her achievement had it not been for his responsibility to lead Wednesday prayers at the Holy Trinity Reformed Episcopal Church on Bull Street, just five blocks away.

A precious life was ended prematurely. A soul departed. Reverend Anthony Thompson was immediately summoned. In the whirlwind of the aftermath, the world media, the captured gunman and the national public outcry, Myra Thompson's lifeless body laid within the jurisdiction of the FBI. Services could not be arranged in a timely manner until investigative evidence was completed. Tony Thompson was in deep despair. He had lost the love of his life.

As a friend, I called Tony on Friday morning, just thirty-six hours after the brutal murders. We shared words, pauses, tears and grief. Somewhere among the difficult words, I asked him about the garden in the rear of his church property. He mentioned that Myra had a habit of entertaining the grandchildren there while waiting for him after Sunday services.

The reference to the garden gave me an idea to introduce something meaningful for Myra from our classmates. They turned out at the Holy Trinity Church the next day. I had called McCarthy's Monument Company to order a simple marker that read, "Myra's Garden." It produced the marble marker and left it out that evening for retrieval.

Together, the Bishop England High School class of 1970 reworked the soil, cleared broken bricks, repaired the fence, fixed the fountain, planted new and vibrant flowers and mulched the entire site. Curious neighbors enthusiastically joined in. The front of the church grounds was replanted as well. Afterwards, we gathered near the garden to pray for Tony and Myra.

I received an e-mail from Tony Thompson after his Sunday services. He said that his parishioners were astonished at the beauty. He added that that Myra would have been proud and told me that he had offered blessings to those who pitched in and did the laborious work in stifling ninety-degree weather. It was a most difficult time. Services, which many of us later attended, were still to be conducted.

Tony Thompson had not only bridged our class, but within days, he would also bridge America. At the arraignment for the accused and confessed murderer, the presiding judge asked him if he had any questions or wanted to say anything. At first, he hesitated—as he had instructed his children to remain in control and to not speak.

"It was as if I were touched by God to say something. I arose and the words just came out," Tony Thompson recollected during the Wednesday evening prayer vigil at the Mother Emanuel Church one year later. There were no plans to speak at the arraignment, and no words were prepared. Media was present from every major network.

Slowly, he turned to the captured source of the horrific crime, Dylann Roof, who had driven in from a Columbia, South Carolina suburb to perpetrate the heinous tragedy: "I forgive you. My family forgives you. We would like you to take this opportunity to repent….Do that and you'll be better off than you are right now."

With those selfless words, Tony Thompson set the tone for the entire community to come together. Other families of other victims followed. A spirit of forgiveness pervaded. A slogan of "hate cannot win" emerged.

I was humbly honored to be invited by Tony to speak in the Mother Emanuel Church at the one-year anniversary. I cited a passage from scripture, Revelations 7:14:

> *These are they that come out of great tribulation.*
> *They have washed their robes*
> *And made them white in the blood of the Lamb.*

I then read a tribute I had written honoring the nine victims:

NINE

Where gentle persons gathered for peace
And prayers were offered to an amazing God;
Where rains had cleansed and sunshine followed—
The locals dawdled; tourists awed.

Within the historic and sacred temple—
Where Moses spoke through an old ragged page.
And the Lord and Savior of all humanity
Heard the wails of sudden rage.

Away from the altar by the darkness
Stood the temporal abomination.
The celestial angels swirled aloft
Climbing in timeless exaltation.

Higher and higher they soared above,
Their golden trumpets divined.
Under the cover of God's pure love
His brilliant countenance shined.

Wherever they walked, they served.
Wherever they spoke, they lifted hearts.
Where their martyred heads lay rested now—
The warmth of Truth and Mercy imparts.

When I stop and consider how Charleston has changed in just the five years since I authored the first edition on this book, I cannot help but think of an ageless lesson. It emerged from the worst tragedy I had witnessed in my more than six decades roaming the Holy City. Reverend Anthony Thompson, in a time when divisiveness had become all too prevalent, spoke up for humanity. He changed the predictable to the amazing. He internalized his personal anguish and handed his life to God. Through God's inspiration, he delivered words that changed fate. In my own little way, I became enlightened and happy that God sent this great and humble man into my sphere as well.

For Our Following Generations

KITTY ROBINSON, EXECUTIVE DIRECTOR,
HISTORIC CHARLESTON FOUNDATION

In the 1690s, there was a bastion of the walled city shaped much like an arrow point. It sentineled threats of danger and heralded incoming ships bringing imported goods. It faced the southeast quadrant of the rest of the world on a vector of Charleston's famed harbor. That salt marsh–lined deep harbor more often attracted prosperity.

The Granville Bastion protected the most accessible corner of North America's only English-walled city. The walls fully enclosing the sixty-two-acre settlement only existed for forty years. The Spanish and French threats subsided, and the Native American population was considered among the most hospitable on the continent. Charleston grew quickly through trade, industry and labor. By the 1730s, most sections of the brick, wooden and earthen walls created the city's first notable landfill. Some harborside fortifications along the Cooper River remained until after the American Revolution.

The walls were well planned. They protected not only the lives of those in containment, but also their commerce, culture and edifices. The walls were eventually considered obsolete—more barriers to those inside than protection from those outside. After the walls came down, the city flourished anew.

Generation by generation, the city of Charleston advanced its fortunes. Merchants and chandlers and plantation owners developed their estates. Opulent houses were designed and constructed, church spires were erected and the community broadened architecturally. Each generation's architectural vision reflected the prevailing design trends. There were reigns of the Gothic summits, the Federal period of simplicity and the Greek Revival period of columnar grandeur. Italianate, Victorian and Georgian styles stood arm in arm, blending to form picturesque streets. The city of Charleston is beyond beautiful and would seem to have been ordained. The ambience remains. The treasures of the past have not been treated as a museum exhibit, but retained and respected in memory of the citizens who created them and lived within.

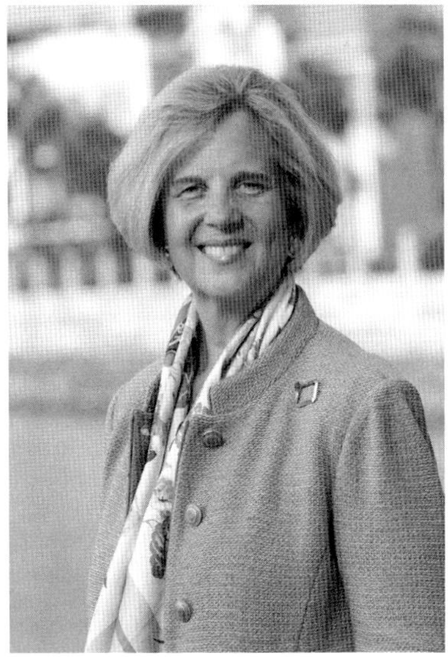

The executive director of the Historic Charleston Foundation, Kitty Robinson, focuses efforts on the preservation of all things Charleston for our coming generations. *(Courtesy of the Historic Charleston Foundation)*

The care of such treasures was increasingly difficult for two centuries. The strife accompanying war, weather and wallet anemia took its toll. The adage of Charlestonians that were "too poor to paint and too proud to whitewash" may have saved the city we know until a focus on preservation became the natural order. Enter the Historic Charleston Foundation, now directed by Katharine S. "Kitty" Robinson.

Historic Charleston Foundation (hereafter referred to as the Foundation) was founded in 1947.[40] All its missions are designed to motivate, educate and preserve. The Foundation promotes volunteerism and seeks solutions for threatened properties of significance by seeking potential funding sources and preservation-minded buyers. The Foundation does extensive historical research and provides guidance for appropriate preservation methods. The Foundation even developed a preservation plan that has been codified and updated. If you can't readily find one, look on the mayor's desk.

"I started my career as an interested community volunteer," Robinson explained. "That was thirty years ago, and I was a newcomer to Charleston. I became the executive director of the Foundation in 2000, having long admired the reputation of the Foundation. I inherited the great work of so many others and became a part of that work through osmosis."

Robinson is enthusiastic about working amid the excitement of preservation. She is proud of the Foundation's headquarters building, the

Captain James Missroon House at 40 East Bay Street. Fittingly, the Missroon House sits atop the Granville Bastion that once served as the sentinel for threats as well as opportunities for Charleston's prosperity. The Missroon House serves the same function today.

The imposing, two-story structure of old Charleston brick sits alone as the first building on East Bay Street at the High Battery overlooking the harbor. The building features exemplary Flemish-bond brickwork with European-style lintels and the original interior woodwork. The house was built in 1808 and was named for its second owner, the seafaring Captain James Missroon.

Robinson is delighted to give impromptu tours of the house to guests. She is courteous, responsive and enlightening. Tall and gleaming, with the vigor of a teenager, she is a Charleston lady once removed. She exemplifies Southern hospitality in her voice and manner. She grew up in Montgomery, Alabama, the first capital of the Confederate States of America. Her Charleston-native husband is Randal Robinson, whose twenty-eight years of active duty and reserve contributions afforded him the title of brigadier general, United States Army, retired. Fittingly, the Robinsons live in a fine Charleston house that dates to 1872. The great Charleston artist Alicia Rhett captured their four children in exquisite portraits. They love the timeless setting and enjoy the feel of history from all perspectives. They have immersed themselves in the Charleston culture.

"We adore the city and all that it has to offer," Robinson exclaimed. "There exists here a collective community fervor and pride. We profoundly enjoy the combination of preservation and people here. It is like no place else."

The Historic Charleston Foundation benefited from tremendous long-term leadership that started with the late Frances Edmunds (1916–2010), a legend for her foresight. The Foundation is famously helpful and informative. It has no formal membership, yet it has many constituents. It is a thriving nonprofit that profits every citizen of the Holy City.

"The seminal point in the preservation of Charleston was the creation of its historic district in 1931," Robinson explained. "The Board of Architectural Review was created to protect the architectural integrity of the city. The historic district has since grown in every direction. We have distinctive neighborhoods such as Ansonborough, Harleston Village, the French Quarter, Mazyck-Wraggsborough and others that are all protected by the B.A.R."

With the recognition of historic boroughs came the identity of individual neighborhoods and an appreciation of their distinctive houses and gardens.

Through research and preservation of historic and architecturally significant dwellings, others in the neighborhood gained respect and even market value.

"The names that we still see on streets and buildings are the essence of the history of Charleston—Middleton, Drayton and Gibbes, for instance," Robinson stated. "We appreciate all the components of our city—a living city with active churches, houses, public and private gardens. Charleston is now more 'discovered' by others, yet it retains its natural culture, character and pride.

"We established the nation's first revolving fund to finance preservation, the Edmunds Revolving Fund," Robinson noted. "Through this fund, we can purchase a threatened property and stabilize it to mitigate any further damage caused by the elements. We then sell it to a preservation-minded buyer committed to fully preserving it. We use the sales proceeds to replenish our revolving fund for the next project."

Historic Charleston Foundation was established as a vehicle to preserve and protect the history, culture and architecture of the city. Other entities have also played prominent roles, notably the Preservation Society of Charleston (established in 1920),[41] the city's B.A.R. and the Board of Zoning Appeals.

"Many outstanding citizens and other prominent institutions through the years have joined in the effort to keep this city's unique character and culture intact," Robinson indicated. "Beyond the unparalleled efforts of Frances Edmunds, I would add the likes of Mayor Riley, Ted Stern and Peter McGee as preservationists of note."

The first preservation plan, a wide book of illustrations and documentary information, sits near the executive director's desk. Its most updated version, an effort to commemorate the sixty-year impact of the Foundation, is a spiral-bound, thick "bible" of historic preservation. It is the pivotal source publication for direction and emphasis upon the principles of conservancy within the field. The newer version even addresses the details of Charleston interiors.

"We partnered with the city for 50 percent of its development, and it received from the National Historic Trust the highest national award for a preservation plan," Robinson explained.

"There was discussion about a gala event to celebrate our sixty years of work that would have culminated in 2007," Robinson detailed. "Yet we all thought that the celebration should not be just about us. It was always about Charleston and the people who live here. So instead of spending money on a fabulous party, we used those funds to renew our dedication to the

Condon used this structure to gain a largely humanitarian view of life by accepting the flow of tides from austerity to prosperity. In an unfortunate twist, the austere tide came first. His father became somewhat unstable and, for a time, was not available to assist in the great responsibility of providing thirty daily meals. Much of the burden was shifted to Tommy and his barely teenaged sister, Anita. His mother showed great courage and resourcefulness. Tommy took a job busing tables in a small bar and eatery near the minor league ballpark, just a few blocks from his home. It was this experience in Jimmy Dengate's (an Irish neighborhood establishment) that gave Tommy his bottom-up view of the restaurant business. The proprietor of the same name kept the weekend and after-school job open for Tommy until he finished high school and joined the United States Army as a field corpsman.

The nearness of other tragedy lurked. Condon's career in the military was shortened by the hostilities of the Vietnam War. Under enemy fire, he took a fall and broke a vertebra in his lower back. A troop transport helicopter—a Chinook—landed near, just after a call was made for a medical relief helicopter, called a Medevac. Condon was asked if he wanted to be evacuated by the troop transport commander. In severe pain, he relinquished a place on the immediate transport to wait on one that, in his assessment, may have taken much more time to arrive, if at all. The second helicopter had the medical equipment and personnel attendant needed for his condition. He gambled. As he laid facing skyward and the troop transport climbed to nearly one thousand feet, an enemy shell hit its mark and the helicopter he painfully scrutinized as immediate relief was destroyed. All on board perished. He grieved for the horrific loss of lives. Condon's medical discharge did not erase the nightmare memory of that fateful experience.

"I made a critical judgment while in pain. I really felt that the Medevac that was called would respond and that I would get immediate treatment. But lying on my back and seeing the Chinook destroyed is something I'll never forget. They were guys I had just talked to—husbands and fathers—gone in a flash," Condon remembered. "It brought home the deep meaning of life to me and the price others have paid in service to our country."

After returning to Charleston, he channeled his attention to career objectives. Through associations he made in his formative years, Condon secured an opportunity to attend mortuary school. During subsequent training and apprenticeship in Birmingham, Alabama, Condon met a vivacious and equally outgoing young lady named Sandra McCormick. They married in 1971. Condon's timeliness in courting Sandra did much to bring a centered and stable life back to Charleston. Together they raised three daughters: Tracy, Tyler and Chris.

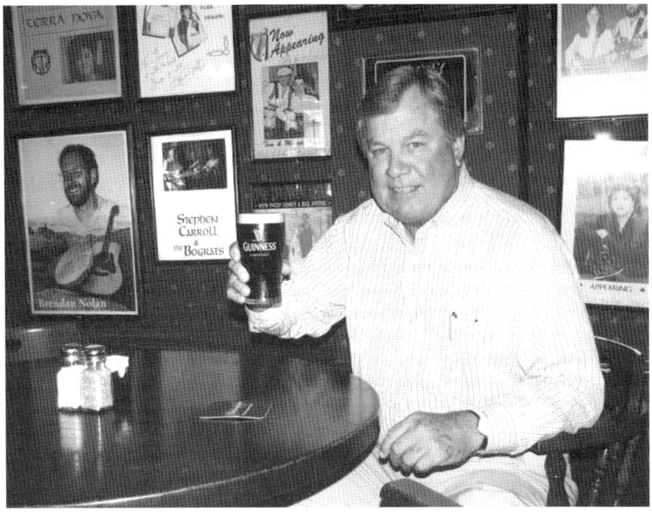

A dual citizen of the United States and Ireland, Condon has tapped more than just his family roots. *(Joan Perry)*

After a short stint in the practice of mortuary science, Tommy and Sandra agreed to a contract for concessions on the U.S.S. *Yorktown*. Eventually, Tommy Condon, Skipper Condon and David Forbes formed CFC Foods, Inc., in Charleston. They looked for other opportunities. The concession success was followed by a foray into a downtown restaurant, appropriately named Tommy Condon's, to mirror the early neighborhood success of an Irish pub with home-cooked, Charleston-style meals (remember Jimmy Dengate's?). This was closely followed by a seafood venture (A.W. Shucks) and eventually the Italian cuisine of Bocci's. The Condon brothers brought in a longtime friend, Carl Forsberg, who had a sound CPA background. His judgment complemented the Condon brothers' business sense and vision. Condon went on to develop restaurants in downtown Richmond and in Washington, D.C., near the Pentagon. Both restaurants are named Siné (Gaelic for "This is it!").

"We started the *Yorktown* concessions together. Tommy was working at McAlister's Funeral Home, with a side job helping Helen Dengate, Jimmy's widow, after Jimmy passed away," Sandra Condon recalled. "We catered to the Boy Scouts mostly on the *Yorktown*. We asked Skipper (Tommy's brother in Baltimore) to join us. Eventually, David Forbes came as well."

The Dengate-Condon connection has continued as well. Young Jimmy Dengate has been much like a brother to Tommy Condon and continues to work with Condon in his namesake Irish pub.

"We were lucky, I suppose," Condon explained. "Charleston was ready for something different. I had the background of Charleston staple meals like fried chicken, butter beans, rice and even shrimp creole. I had learned the restaurant business working at Jimmy Dengate's all of those years. We brought in live Irish music and authentic pub furnishings directly from Ireland. Finding the right spot near the [City] Market was also important. People could walk to Tommy's from their hotels."

The enterprising Condon kept several business friendships strong in the Republic of Ireland (through his many visits to that country). Proud of his Irish roots, he sought and gained dual citizenship in 1996. He returns several times a year to his favorite Irish community of Ennis, County Clare. Through the efforts of friend Jerry McMahon and Condon, Ennis has officially become Charleston's sister city in Ireland.

The Condons trace their sequencing to two branches—the department store Condons and the bakery Condons. The department store Condons have been prodigious in supplying the city with merchants and lawyers and a recent two-term elected state attorney general, Charles Molony Condon. First cousin Tommy Condon initiated this statewide political campaign at Bocci's restaurant in 1993. The bakery Condons have been no less prodigious.

Condon is unpretentious, a fine listener and an advocate of great assistance to the needy. He takes a bicycle to and from his office on State Street, when the weather allows. He enjoys his gin games at the Hibernian Society when his schedule permits. There, he surrounds himself with his best friends who are there to banter and keep egos in check. It is at the Hibernian Hall on Meeting Street that he rose to the most esteemed office of president, serving a two-year stint from March 2002 through March 2004. Yet, humility will not let him enjoy the earned honor of being a portraited past president. He earnestly joined the Hibernian Foundation to make sure others receive opportunities he never had—assisting others in funding to attend college. Condon also served as chair of the Southern Conference NCAA Basketball Championships when they first came to Charleston in 2001. He was a member of the Patriot's Point Foundation board, which assists the National Medal of Honor Museum on the *Yorktown*. He knows what it takes to be a hero and understands the tenets of service and sacrifice to others.

"Tommy is the most honest and personable person I know," extols his wife of forty years, Sandra. "That's probably why I love him so much."

Tommy Condon has made substantial financial and personal contributions to the Charleston community. He is not unique in this endeavor. But his story is unique in so many other ways. That ubiquitous tide of austerity has ebbed. It is through ages of growth and prosperity, tempered by the cycles of recession, that he remains steady in his diligence. It is Charleston that will—presently and in posterity—catapult the legend that is both the restaurant and the wide-eyed personality, fondly and forever known as Tommy Condon's.

The Time of Jim Rigney

It is likely that you, the reader, know more about the man I knew and considered an acquaintance than I did. Jim Rigney was someone I admired from afar, knew in passing and now hold an elevation of insightful regard for in his aftermath. The man I speak about was a pseudonym to you. I knew him by his legal name, James Oliver Rigney Jr. It was the name that was called out at our graduation from The Citadel in 1974. You, perhaps, know him by what would be his real name to a reader, Robert Jordan. Yes, *that* Robert Jordan.

In the small circle of revered authors attempting the mind-expanding trade of fantasy, Robert Jordan thrived. He did so by his incredible appetite for knowledge, his orderly sense of drama and his legendary discipline for the challenge. He did not come by these traits by anointment, but rather by inurement. The man who was to become Robert Jordan was an American hero. He was hardened by the exigencies of life itself in our common birthright of Charleston. His rise from the pluff mud of the Lowcountry and through the swampy jungles of Vietnam were simple footnotes to his later notoriety. He was awarded the Bronze Star and the Distinguished Flying Cross with oak leaf clusters for his selfless gallantry. As a helicopter machine gunner, he lived through two tours of duty against all odds. You see, the role of a machine gunner on helicopters in Vietnam was given mostly to rookies. Very few veterans of this assignment existed.

To be sure, Charleston has a fine literary pedigree. William Gilmore Simms was considered the poet laureate of the Confederacy. Alexandra Ripley wrote a sequel to *Gone With the Wind*, titled *Scarlett*. Contemporary author Pat Conroy is among the major novelists of our time. Dubose Heyward wrote *Porgy* and collaborated with George Gershwin for America's seminal opera, *Porgy and Bess*. Frank B. Gilbreth Jr. was our very own columnist with the pseudonym Ashley Cooper, but he also wrote the powerful and poignant *Cheaper by the Dozen*. There were many others of great note. The author we knew as Robert Jordan was a man dedicated to a genre that required otherworldly imagination.

Jim Rigney lived, it seemed, for our enjoyment.

I mention that you as a reader may well have known Jim—Robert Jordan—better than myself, because I know it to be true. I would cringe to admit this fact to his soul mate widow, Harriet McDougal, who was also his editor. The quality and volume of Jim's work has been lauded by the masses. It has been favorably compared to the only other great fantasy writer of the past century, J.R.R. Tolkien. Jim Rigney was the one living legend in my midst. I knew him. I admired him. I liked him. I chatted with him. I never read his work. I didn't read Tolkien either. In every context, it matters that I have not read a single word of Jim's *Wheel of Time* series. This faux pas can be corrected. And if God grants me the selfishness of time that I can command as mine alone, I will read the complete *Wheel of Time*.

In a way, my qualification to even utter the great Charleston name of Jim Rigney is by default. In 1991, our Citadel class chairman (for the class of 1974) stepped down. I was asked by what is now The Citadel Foundation to take the role on for the benefit of the college. I did so intrepidly. I did not find out until later that others had been asked but declined. My father always said it was a good thing that I wasn't born female. I never learned how to say "no."

As I took on the role of coordinator, informant, fundraiser and scheduler for my class of 385 graduates, I was drawn to a few anomalies. The numbers and strength of a class had heretofore been its cadet graduates. Jim was a member of "V" Company—the name I assigned to the veteran military students who graced our hallways. Three of our top five donors—year in and year out—had been from my inherited extra company of grads, led by Jim Rigney. Another anomaly existed. Our class contributed on a lower-than-normal percentage. We were underachievers. This couldn't be! I had to reassert my belief that we were among the greatest in the annals of the school. Jim would become the centerpiece of that braggadocio going forward.

A final anomaly was that there had not been an estate-type gift given from my class. In my twenty years of responsibility, I have not been the catalyst to change any of the anomalies, but I can point to one person who changed all three.

Jim Rigney led our class annually in contributions. He inspired others. All that I could do, as chairman, was to bring a little light to the subject. I interviewed Jim for a class newsletter. He gave back large sums to the department of engineering. He contributed beyond the call to the Daniel Library. He wrote hefty checks with more-than-sufficient zeros that followed a generous starting digit. I did not ask him to do so. It was in his heart. The interview inspired others to do the same. The wide gulf of would-be class contributors was bridged by the actions of Jim Rigney. His selflessness and humility became inspirational to all. Our numbers grew; our impact rose. In little time, we had a class hero—not so much by his notoriety as by his generosity. The bulwark of an estate-sized giver was established. Others followed. The unfortunate result of Jim's untimely passing also changed the third anomaly. He had inspired us as a class, and the rejuvenated cadet graduates stepped up to assist the veteran graduates. Other leadership in giving developed. Outside of the readership of this poignant essay about my deeply respected acquaintance Jim Rigney, no one had known about his other impact upon his alma mater, especially The Citadel class of 1974. Jim Rigney made me into a person that I would not have been without his shoulders to prop me up. And I thanked him often and sincerely. I wished that I could have thanked him more.

Upon the occasion of our twenty-fifth reunion in 1999, I personally asked Jim if he would be so kind as to join us. We had a live band and well-appointed accouterments at the Swamp Fox Ballroom in the Francis Marion Hotel. Jim came. I think he may have done so as a favor to me. He arrived in vogue. A blustery evening from a Charleston November produced Jim attired in an overcoat with cane and pipe. Sporting the beard that was his trademark, this amazing author and brilliant man looked more the part of a returning Confederate veteran from the century prior. Jim had panache by the throat, no doubt. I was somewhat personally conflicted. I had asked him to attend and felt responsible for his enjoyment of the event. We chatted over a few hors d'oeuvres, and I served more or less as an attaché to introduce this humble man to so many classmates that wanted to shake his hand. I admit that I wanted to see them raise their brows and perhaps genuflect to his deserved place in our collective regard. My conflict was to stay with him as the introducer or to grab the microphone and announce his presence. My

"I sold cars after classes as a veteran student at The Citadel," Baker noted. "I also taught G.E.D. courses and worked as a bouncer at a downtown bar. I pretty much did all of these at the same time to pick up a few extra bucks. Selling cars was sometimes a challenge, but I always knew that there were cars that fit people better than others. I just put man with machine."

He does a pretty good job of putting people together as well. He told a story of flying his friend, Judge Sol Blatt, up to North Carolina a few months ago on his private plane. The judge went with Baker as an undisclosed special guest to see a World War II buddy that Blatt had served with and had not seen in sixty years. John Blaney Williams was Baker's friend who once casually mentioned that he served under Blatt in the navy. Baker put two and two together. Williams was deeply moved and quite surprised to meet the honorable federal judge in a Clinton, North Carolina, restaurant. The ninety-one-year-old Williams was shocked to see his former ranking officer walk in after six decades. The two old soldiers enjoyed stories they had both almost forgotten. It was a spirit-lifting encounter that Baker had arranged.

"Just to see them over laughing and telling about each other's families was touching. That was the greatest generation catching up, and the rest of us got out of the way," Baker recalled. "And when the judge was ready to go home, we all shook hands and headed back for the plane."

Who else but Tommy Baker would have pulled that one off?

Baker grew up in old Ansonborough, at 49 Chapel Street. His parents moved to Mount Pleasant, and Baker enjoyed the spread of life in the quiet of the area nicknamed Hungryneck. He finished Moultrie High School as one of the three Fifty-third Rifle Company marine aviation hopefuls. Baker joined the U.S. Marine Corps with plans to qualify for aviation school. His four years of service took him to Okinawa, Japan, and to the Quantico, Virginia, training base. He also spent time at New River and Camp Lejeune. Baker returned to Charleston in 1968 and propitiously met then Citadel baseball coach Chal Port while playing for a local league team, Richter's Dry Cleaners. Port played on an opposing team. The coach talked to Baker about bringing his baseball skills to The Citadel. He did so and played center field for the Bulldogs.

"Some of the players thought I was an assistant coach at first. I had pork chop sideburns and was a twenty-two-year-old freshman that did not have to have the buzz cut," Baker recalled. "I can remember a Citadel official calling me over and telling me I had to get a haircut and shave my sideburns if I wanted to continue representing The Citadel. I knew that I was not required to do so, but I did what he asked, because I loved The Citadel and loved to play baseball."

Baker had a postgraduate opportunity to work with a friend up in the aforementioned Clinton, North Carolina, area. They opened a small car dealership. Along with the good friend, Bill Johnson, Baker began to amass a small empire of auto dealerships in Greensboro. They obtained franchises for Nissan, Hyundai, Mercedes, Pontiac, Cadillac, Lincoln-Mercury, Mitsubishi and Infiniti. He sold his Nissan dealership to basketball great Michael Jordan in 1988.

Baker used his largesse to help others and was one of three founders of a long-running golf tournament near Raleigh to assist the Duke University Children's Hospital. The other two founders were former North Carolina State head basketball coach Jim Valvano (who passed away from cancer in 1993) and current University of South Carolina head football coach Steve Spurrier. Spurrier was coaching at Duke University when the golf tournament was founded twenty-seven years ago. The tournament continues to assist the Duke children's hospital. Baker once served as their board chairman.

"At the twentieth tournament, I got a hole in one on the eighth hole!" Baker proclaimed. "And wouldn't you know it, the prize was a new car, a G35 Infiniti. After enjoying the shot for about ten seconds, I donated the car to the hospital."

After fifteen years of healthy business growth, Baker made a major decision. He had been visiting old friends in Charleston and had an innate desire to move back. He could not entertain the instinct to move, given his time commitments in North Carolina. So he did the unthinkable. He sold every one of his North Carolina dealerships and came to Charleston with a wealth of knowledge and an idea how to reinvent himself at the business he had learned to orchestrate. He started by contracting the Mercedes-Benz franchise.

"It was all about priorities. I was in an executive OPM [owner/president/manager] program at Harvard in Cambridge, Massachusetts, from 1986 to 1989. I didn't get to see my family as much as I wanted to, and I missed them deeply. The course actually helped me put things into perspective. We came to Charleston to visit a few times and really didn't want to leave. Our children were growing up, and I was on the road," Baker recounted. "So I decided to give up the bird in the hand. It was a tremendous financial sacrifice, but we realized that our family was more important. I sold every one of the North Carolina dealerships and moved to Charleston in 1988."

Baker met his wife, Vickie, through a stockbroker friend. Vickie was also a sales associate. He romanced her for ten whole weeks and then married her. Baker had distinctive tastes and recognized Vickie was his ultimate sale. It

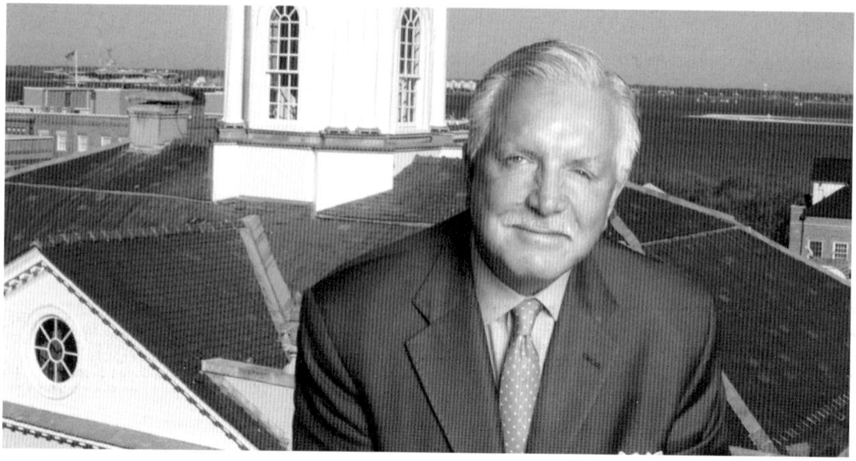

Tommy Baker came back to his hometown just in time. The carriage footstools had all been sent out for repair, so he sent a loaner car to the bluebloods. The horse carriages have all been retired. *(Baker family collection)*

was a whirlwind relationship that has now reached twenty-one years. They have three children and two grandchildren.

Character counts. Coming back was coming home. Baker recalled the experience of Charleston as a youth and young adult.

"I had a wonderful childhood," Baker stated emphatically. "I pumped gas, bagged groceries and paid ten dollars a month to Richard's Menswear. They'd let you charge just about anything if you paid them just ten dollars every month. I was easy-going, cocky and confident, because I always had good clothes.

"We were essentially lower middle class—all of us. Nobody really had anything in Charleston back then," Baker recalled. "I remember a banker telling me that there were not five true millionaires in all of Charleston. So we all worked while not in school, and our leisure consisted of dressing neat with nice, simple clothes and Weejuns to go dancing at the Old Side on the Isle of Palms. I remember that I could only afford to go out one night, because I didn't make enough money to go out both Friday and Saturday.

"We shagged to the beach music. Everybody had to know how to dance. And that place would get the best live bands ever," Baker continued. "There was the Sea-Side and the Old Side. You could bring a half pint of liquor into the Old Side. And everybody went there. That was when you picked up your date from one of the old, drafty downtown houses where they only air-conditioned the kitchen and the drawing room. You couldn't afford to air-condition the entire house back then.

"We played half rubber on the beach," Baker added. "You could play all day long against the best half-rubber players in Charleston out at the Old Side on Saturdays to win the grand prize—a case of beer. My partner and I always seemed to win that beer. He could pitch, and I could catch, and we both could hit."

The fun guy that Baker has always been seems to refute his acquired passion in later life. He teaches college students. He does so as an adjunct professor of entrepreneurship at the College of Charleston. He simply loves the experience. It keeps him sharp and in touch with the burgeoning generations to come. Living downtown gives him the convenience of proximity and the perspective of assistance to the cause of education. His Harvard degree and outstanding business experiences have been a solid foundation for his course insight.

There is much more to Tommy Baker than meets the eye.

And so it was that the trappings of youth gave way to the seeming entrapment of the business world. Baker built his world on principles that he engendered into his entire network of luxury-car dealerships. He insists on personal service, with a classy, low-pressure sales force well trained in every nuance of the high-end vehicles. He extends every possible courtesy, to include one of his very favorites—hydration. Everybody is asked if they would like bottled water, a soft drink or a cup of coffee. Being in his enclave is akin to being at the Hilton or the Four Seasons in plain view of the Motel Six. The customers feel the difference.

Baker himself exudes Charleston. He still has his loafers—without socks. His appearance is crisp and his grooming impeccable. He is a very busy man, but the time he takes with the person in front of him seems to be as pleasant for him as it is for the person. He is welcoming, overt in his friendliness and attentive to every concern. His energy level originated with his appetite for late-night, Old Side dancing. He is an entertainer still. They call him the "Night Mayor of Charleston."

The venerable entrepreneur enjoys his friendships. He takes friends and clients alike to the finer downtown restaurants where one may find it difficult to claim propriety upon the final check. It is usually his to remit. He brings the corporate out-of-towners, a few college professors or an old friend he invited. It is in the downtown restaurants that he earned his now-famous moniker. The Night Mayor is often on the prowl. It's his way of doing business with those that have done business with him as well. He revels in the ambiguous anointment. Though his nocturnal forays are innocuous, his entourage has fun.

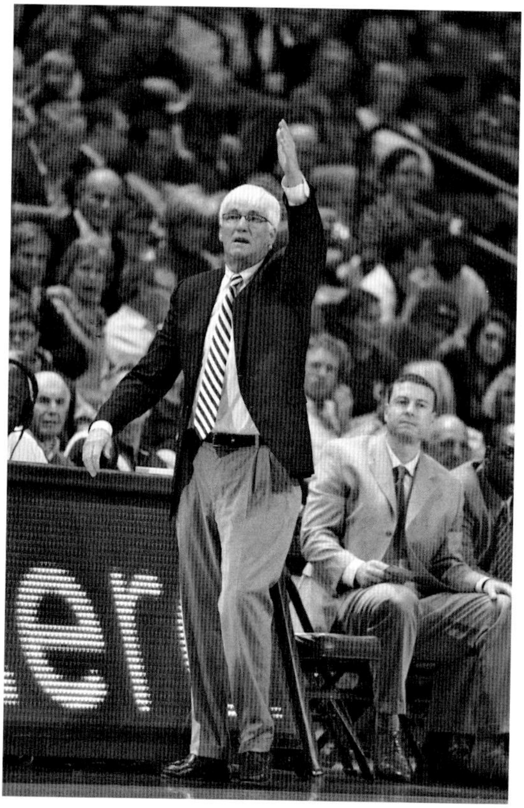

Coach Bobby Cremins came back to the career he enjoys after a six-year hiatus. Cremins has been a program builder and consistent winner at the NCAA men's basketball level. *(Courtesy of College of Charleston)*

Les Robinson," Cremins recalled. "But it wasn't until I retired from Georgia Tech that I really had the opportunity to spend much time downtown from my trips here when I lived in Hilton Head."

Cremins noted several changes to the community.

"Coming here permanently was a godsend—a mulligan," Cremins said. "You see that bridge to Mount Pleasant and you think to yourself, 'This is a nice place.' We've got the new arena. There are events to suit every taste. There's always something new and exciting happening in Charleston."

The adjustment is still in progress. Cremins draws upon his mentoring influences to get the most out of his players. He's had an impressive lot to draw from.

"Frank McGuire had so much class. I loved playing for him. He knew how to handle people. I watched him a lot. He knew adversity, and he handled that with class as well," Cremins asserted. "His first wife died of throat cancer. And you knew about his son, Frankie, with special needs. He handled the Mike Grosso situation in the best interests of the university first.

Coaches today don't do that. Frank McGuire did, because to him it wasn't about basketball.

"I could tell you as much about Ben Carnevale, Corky's dad. He was a great man. Then there's Al McGuire, not related, but who learned everything from Frank. He was like me, a New York Irish Catholic, first generation. He was quirky, but what a great coach and motivator," Cremins intimated. "And I have to add Coach Dean Smith with reverence. I looked up to Dean and coached against him all those years. He was tough to beat. He coached under Frank McGuire, too, and had McGuire's kind of class. There were others, like Jack Curran and my All Hallows grammar school coach, Jack Lyons."

Cremins coached in other roles. He was named to assist Lenny Wilkins with the 1996 Olympic team in Atlanta. They won the Olympic gold medal as "Dream Team II."

"That team was loaded with great NBA players. Winning the gold medal wasn't quite as easy as it was in 1992, but we pulled together and won," Cremins recalled. "In the process, I gained such respect for some of the players we coached. John Stockton was super. David Robinson was exemplary in representing America. And Grant Hill was an even better person than he was a ballplayer. There were others. They represented our country with pride and class."

The 1996 Olympics did not go off without incident. A man placed a bomb in a trash can to indiscriminately kill or injure others. A woman was killed and several others injured.

"It happened right next to our hotel, across the street from Olympic Park. The Dream Team spent time with some of the injured and family victims," Cremins recalled. "It really was a difficult time for those families."

Cremins takes what little time he has in the off-season to visit friends and assist organizations that raise money for a variety of needs. This period finds him checking on player grades, calling contributors to assist in a tennis fundraiser and catching up with friends like Les Robinson. He schedules a golf game two months ahead and books a flight to see a player in the period the NCAA allows visits. He is a multitasking dynamo.

His gregariousness is uniquely tempered by his spirited challenges.

"Do you play tennis? Let's play tennis," he offered. He'll engage all comers. "I'll bet I can beat you in tennis. Golf? What do you shoot? I can kick your butt. Let's play sometime."

His wife, Carolyn, has been his best fan and replicates his wonderful, outgoing personality. Carolyn Cremins is stunning, insightful and devoted.

She assists her husband by becoming a second mom to so many young players who are away from home for the first time. The two of them have been virtually inseparable since their 1973 marriage. They met in Columbia when Cremins began his career under Coach Frank McGuire.

It is when Cremins is entrenched in his full schedule that he realizes how much he enjoys it. He has reunited himself with his passion. He is back pursuing his purpose.

Bobby Cremins is back in his element. He is the dapper, white-haired gentleman who may be recognizable as Charleston's most prominent sports celebrity. He has become a proud Charlestonian and has taken what the city exports in friendliness to the extreme, from basketball court to basketball court in the hinterlands beyond the Holy City.

Just like his last tennis match or the last game he coached last season, Cremins advances his thoughts and plans to the column of "What's next?" The 2010–11 season amassed an amazing twenty-six wins. There are four key graduations, including Southern Conference Player of the Year Andrew Goudelock, who was drafted in the second round of the NBA draft by the Los Angeles Lakers. He's gone, and the win column for 2011–12 starts again at zero. So Cremins is recruiting the players that can bring him back to the top of the Southern Conference.

It's a recharged and motivated Bobby Cremins now. But the season will start without Murphy. Sadly, the aging retriever died shortly after Cremins's fifth season at the helm.

In 2012, Bobby Cremins stepped away from coaching after thirty-one years. He left the College of Charleston's men's basketball in fine shape with top-level recruits. They had won twenty or more games in five of his six seasons. His record at the College of Charleston was 125-68, amassing a higher percentage than he had either at Appalachian State or Georgia Tech. His entire coaching career record is 579-375. He is in nearly every sport's Hall of Fame in the states of both Georgia and South Carolina.

By 2013, the College of Charleston had left the Southern Conference to join the Colonial Athletic Association, giving broader exposure to the institution up and down the East Coast. The Colonial Athletic Association has NCAA Division I teams in larger markets, including Boston, New York and Philadelphia.

Cremins eventually moved back to his former home in Hilton Head and began a new and exciting career as a basketball color analyst. He also works with friends Les Robinson, Dave Odom, Terry Holland, Skip Harlicka and his South Carolina Gamecock roommate Corky Carnevale in another

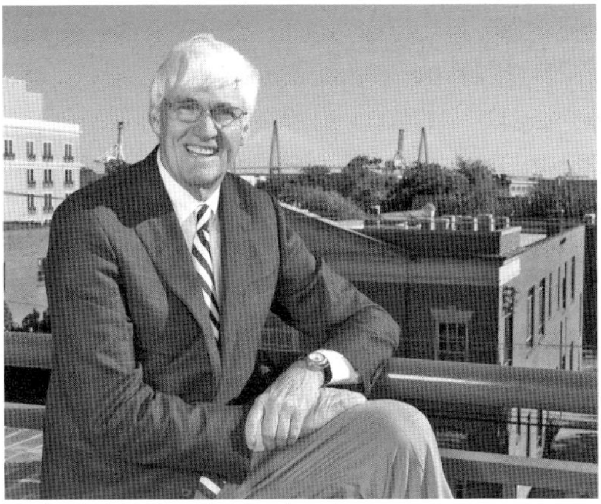

Born on the fourth of July: A gentleman, first-generation Irish-American and recognizable NCAA basketball personality, Cremins had accumulated 541 career basketball victories going into the 2011–12 season. *(Courtesy of College of Charleston)*

venture, USBA Basketball. These youth basketball camps are organized by Mark Thompson and are conducted in several U.S. cities, as well as in Puerto Rico and Canada.

Bobby Cremins has an inner voice that whispers. It tells him to appreciate others, enjoy his family and give back whenever he can. He comports his life accordingly.

Who Are Our Heroes?

Medal of Honor Recipient
Major General James E. Livingston

As a country, we revere our heroes. So many come to mind from childhood. They are legends we carry as a spark of eventual victory, a sense of quiet confidence and an example of overwhelming achievement.

The names roll like movie credits from generation to generation. Those that were my father's became mine. And those that are mine are known to my offspring. They are an epic enhanced, an epitome extolled and an epitaph edified.

Nobody could bring a team down the field like Johnny Unitas. Even his name signified the sense of "team." Willie Mays was as much an ambassador of the game of baseball as his on-field exuberance implied. He was the "Say Hey Kid." There were heroes of an era, like Roy Rogers and Dale Evans. It never mattered who played Batman. Likewise nobody that ever heard Ray Charles sing cared that he was blind. He was uniquely heroic for his challenges conquered and his talent. We hailed astronaut John Glenn and Olympian Bruce Jenner. Golf, anyone? How about Arnold Palmer or Annika Sorenstam? The movies? The "Duke" was John Wayne. Ingrid Bergman was once the ultimate leading lady. Now there is Julia Roberts. There were U.S. presidents admired, and there were those that gained fame as newscasters, like Barbara Walters and Walter Cronkite.

Surely these were among the best of the best.

Wrong. These were high-profile people with proficiencies for an avenue of entertainment, newsworthiness or sport. They were names in our newspapers or faces beaming back from the movie screen or television. They did not fit the definition of true "hero."

There are heroes in our midst. They are subtle, humble and camouflaged. They are single parents who build a family through exemplary responsibility. They are parents who team to instill the proper value system in the care of their children. They are teachers and doctors, firemen and carpenters. They are guidance counselors and policemen. They walk their everyday life prepared to make sacrifices in selfless ways to enlighten and support others. They are the real heroes. We do not celebrate them, though we may admire them from afar. They are more worthy than a baseball card or a hall of fame designation. They are everyday people of extraordinary experience. And you see them almost daily in our nation's military.

There are true, formal acclamations of military heroism. It is when a commanding officer pins a medal on a soldier for valor or selflessness or courage in the face of harm or almost-certain death. It is also a draped flag over a coffin when the ultimate sacrifice is patriotically made. This happens all too often. These fighting men and women do not perform for medals or acclamation. They do it to serve their country, their community and their family. They serve you and me.

Finding one amongst us is akin to finding gold in your backyard vegetable garden. Don't trample the carrots looking for it.

Major General James E. Livingston lives in Mount Pleasant. He is one of the acclaimed. He was bestowed the greatest of great honors, the Medal of Honor, for his valor as a U.S. Marine Corps captain on the field of battle in Vietnam. His Medal of Honor was presented by his highest commanding officer, President Richard M. Nixon. This sky-blue ribbon with service-specific medal is the highest military award and honor of our country. It is not given, but earned. Many times, the recipient is the spouse or parent of a real hero who did not survive to proudly wear the distinguished Medal of Honor and who may have died to save others. It was propitious that Jim Livingston survived for all concerns. He is the single best source of insight and perspective that the Medal of Honor Society may have. He also carries a heart flame of conscientiousness that protects the honor for the coming generations in his profound concern for societal balance.

The Medal of Honor Museum exists aboard the U.S.S. *Yorktown* aircraft carrier in Charleston Harbor. That small, digitally interactive museum extols the valor of scores of our country's real heroes—heroes at the pinnacle of heroism. There is a national Medal of Honor Society. Its membership is limited by criteria. Every living person that has earned the Medal of Honor, please stand up. Only a small room is needed, as the actual living count is only eighty-four. The living Medal of Honor recipient is rare, like the Siberian tiger or California condor. Yet we cannot place them in protective ecologies. They are a dwindling number that cannot likely be engineered to growth.

The Medal of Honor's museum location in the Charleston area is an excellent community benefit. However, the garage is too small for the Hummer.

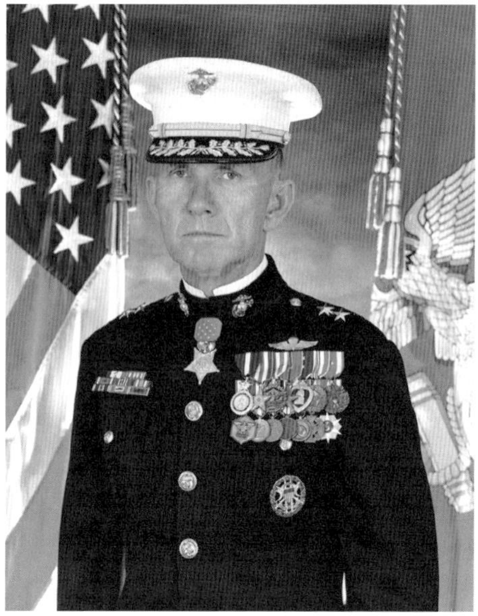

Major General Jim Livingston has devoted his adult life to the service of his country. His passion for America's success is evident in his everyday activities. *(Courtesy of the U.S. Marine Corps)*

"The National Medal of Honor Museum should be in a location of consequence to recognize all of our military, not just the Medal of Honor recipients. The noteworthy experiences of the military should be embodied within the entirety of the project," Livingston opined. "Charleston is on the world stage now. The museum should be representative of that context. It should champion those who have made the ultimate sacrifice. As a citizen, I am impressed with Charleston, but we are better than this. I would like to see the community rise to the level that the Medal of Honor and so many others in the military deserve."

Jim Livingston is perhaps the best example of Marine Corps leadership and confidence one might imagine. He is physically imposing and neatly trim. He conjures a steely resolve for what is right beyond the obstacles that would impair or inhibit others. He is true and direct. You know where he stands and for what he represents. There is no mincing of words. He has a firm handshake and looks you in the eye. Meeting him gives one the sense that there are other Jim Livingstons out there and that our country is all the more safe because of it. There is but one. And just as he had learned respect, leadership skills and service to a cause from others, so had he given. There are scores of disciples still serving in our brave military from the shadow this genuine American hero has cast.

"I learned from two great Southern Marine Corps commandants," Livingston intimated. "Louis Wilson was from Mississippi. When the marines were in great need of leadership, he became the commandant and brought the corps into modern standards as the pride of the United States military. He cleaned up the Marine Corps."

General Louis Hugh Wilson Jr. was also a recipient of the Medal of Honor for his valor in the Battle of Guam during World War II.[42] It was his leadership and sacrifice against an enemy force of superior numbers that earned Wilson the nation's highest honor. General Wilson died in 2005.

"Robert Barrow was from Louisiana. He continued the legacy of Louis Wilson and showed tremendous leadership when this country needed it," Livingston noted. "I would compare him to the great Stonewall Jackson—a man who made good decisions and led by courage and example."

General Robert H. Barrow followed General Wilson as Marine Corps commandant, served in three wars and was awarded the Navy Cross in Korea and the Distinguished Service Cross in Vietnam.[43]

Livingston had earned his Medal of Honor and lived to tell about it, despite his ordered protestations. Commanding Company E (Second Battalion, Fourth Marines) at Dai Do Village, Vietnam, in a response related to rescuing Company H, Livingston was twice wounded. A third company of marines assisted and launched an assault but was repelled by a massive enemy counterattack. Then Captain Livingston, wounded and bleeding, maneuvered his remaining men to halt the enemy's counterattack. He was wounded a third time and rendered nonambulatory. Selflessly and bravely, Livingston still commanded the battle and brilliantly evacuated his men from the field to more viable positions, only leaving the firefight—last, and with assistance—once his entire force had been positioned to safety. Now that's an actual hero. It isn't in the movies. Hollywood could not write this script for fear that an audience would not believe it. But this man lived it.

Livingston is concerned about America. Livingston cites leadership as a quality that our country so desperately needs in each and every generation. He had seen and experienced expert leadership during his thirty-two-year Marine Corps career.

"I've seen great leadership, and I understand what it takes," Livingston intoned. "General Bill Weise, for example, showed me practical leadership. He was the epitome of a combat leader. He understood troops and capabilities and the application of both. He was loyal and he was decisive."

It is this type of leadership, service to others and to country and the willingness of sacrifice that builds a community or a nation. Livingston mentions these same qualities in reference to what he hopes would one day be a world leadership center in Charleston.

"It can be done with focus from everyone," Livingston revealed. "A natural partner is The Citadel and all that it stands for in the education of young men and women of principle to become our next generation of leaders. There are corporations that could benefit, police departments, government, our entire military and others. The Medal of Honor Museum would be an inspirational piece of the bigger picture. Our nation needs leadership at every level."

Heroes are by nature selfless. The idea of a world leadership center would be about the future with a respect for the past. Livingston is much more concerned about the future for his two daughters, their husbands and his and wife Sara's grandchildren. The world leadership center could breed tomorrow's heroes.

It bodes well for all concerns that a Marine Corps major general and documented war hero is in our midst. He only retired from the military, not life.

"I first came to Charleston as a frequent visitor when I was at Parris Island in the mid-1960s," Livingston recalled. "I loved it. I came back to Parris Island in 1983. The Lowcountry always made me feel at home. We visited Charleston whenever we could.

"Once I retired in 1994, I started a business in New Orleans. New Orleans is a lot like Charleston, but bigger. We'd come to Charleston to visit Sara's two sisters, and we'd both agree we wanted to be here," Livingston offered. "So we went home and sold the business and sold our home quickly. We were moving before we could think twice about it."

New Orleans's loss is Charleston's gain. Livingston became energetically active in many local initiatives. He served on several community boards and became a featured speaker at banquets and graduations. He exudes enthusiasm and passion. He is a man of his word, and that word is unequivocal and direct. It's like a sergeant's command to wide-eyed recruits.

"I've lived all over the world. The U.K. has similarities to us but has a larger gap in the social structure. Australia is similar to our attitude with a big island nation, but yet different," Livingston stated. "And there are other democracies, like France and Canada, but none quite like us. In America, the strong sense of patriotism and abundance of opportunities separate us from the others. We are unique in that regard."

We are unique in the humility of our heroes as well. Livingston has not taken a moment to mention his valor or his service to America. He has not told of young soldiers saved by his decisive and courageous action. It is as if he was content with working a plan ahead in lieu of retelling of history past. He stays in a recruitment mode of encouraging and inspiring others to act patriotically and to love this country well enough to assert support for its future.

One could easily envision that the characteristics that make good leaders are inherent in the psyche of a hero.

"A number of years ago, there were those that wanted me to run for the United States Senate seat in Louisiana. Others wanted me to run for mayor of New Orleans. I considered everything but concluded that I have done my military service duty and that I could best serve America going forward by inspiring young people," Livingston said. "I know that my responsibilities as a citizen did not end with my retirement from the corps. In society as in the corps, we have to engage and we have to select the best potential leaders and teach them, train them and then support them."

Meanwhile, we have a natural resource in Mount Pleasant. He is an authentic and sincere, living and breathing, honest-to-goodness hero. He's not the poster of a drummer or the jersey of a running back. He is the real thing. He is a leader, and he has a great vision for the next meaningful project to keep Charleston on the world stage.

It would be easy for Jim Livingston to fully retire and enjoy the glory he has earned with a nice sunset, his lovely wife, Sara, at his side and a glass of wine.

"I'm a beer guy," Livingston related. "We have our pick of some of the greatest restaurants around. We go to the theater. We enjoy engaging others and completing good work. A sense of accomplishment for us goes a long way.

"Living here has been the best thing we could have done. We've met great friends. The community is outwardly friendly. It is so easy to find a comfort zone here," Livingston continued. "It has become one of the great national cities with its natural beauty, history, restaurants, activities and especially the attitude of its people. People reach out to you here."

The friendliest city in America could understandably be falling all over itself to reach out to Major General James E. Livingston. Charlestonians recognize the difference between pseudo-hero worship and the profound experience of meeting a genuine American hero. And he is *our* hero.

Major General Jim Livingston has embraced the Charleston community and has brought an iconic project to the harbor that may be lauded in the coming centuries. The National Medal of Honor Museum could mark Charleston Harbor much as the Statue of Liberty has welcomed ships to New York or the Sydney Opera House has identified "down under." It is a $105 million national project.

The massive financial commitment does nothing to dissuade a man who withstood an all-out assault of nearly ten thousand Viet Cong with an entrenched Marine Corps defense of barely two hundred men. Livingston reviewed the odds years later: "Two hundred U.S. Marines against ten thousand? I'd say that was a fair fight."

Coaching Life 101

Fisher DeBerry

It doesn't take long to appreciate a field planted with okra, Kentucky Wonders, lettuce, watermelon and tomatoes. Planting a vegetable garden is diligent, hard work. In Cheraw, South Carolina, during World War II, it was sustenance. The garden was a small field that Fisher DeBerry's grandfather meticulously kept and used to help feed the DeBerry household. Young Fisher DeBerry was sure he would carry on the family tradition someday. He tended that garden.

James Fisher DeBerry was born in the throes of America's Great Depression as the only child of a single mother in a household that belonged to his grandparents. That's who raised him. He was faithful in his attendance at the Cheraw United Methodist Church and proficient in little league and high school sports, and he prioritized his academic work. It was his grandmother's oversight and influence that motivated his upbringing. His abilities on the athletic field were special. He was a four-sport varsity letterman. Wofford assistant football coach Jim Brakefield encouraged DeBerry out of Cheraw High School in 1956 to come and play football and baseball for the Wofford Terriers. It was not without a great deal of consideration for The Citadel.

"Bud Watts was from Cheraw High School and a couple of years ahead of me. I went for a visit to The Citadel and stayed with Bud. Though it was everything advertised as a formidable challenge, and a tough decision for me personally, I opted to go to Wofford," DeBerry recalled.

Lieutenant General Claudius E. "Bud" Watts III, retired from the U.S. Air Force, became the president of The Citadel three decades later (1989–96).

He was a Fulbright Scholar and served in several economic and financial capacities with the Air Force during his distinguished military career. He and Fisher DeBerry would meet again during DeBerry's tenure at the United States Air Force Academy as head football coach. Watts was the comptroller general of the United States Air Force. They remain close friends.

"Fisher was always a good friend. He and LuAnn are special people who have exemplified everything that is right in college athletics," Watts stated. "And they both go well beyond that with their adherence to their personal principles and great assistance to others in need through their foundation."

The Citadel's loss was Wofford's gain. DeBerry had some wonderful sports moments along the way. His spirited play in football helped his team to win games. He hit a ninth-inning home run to help little NAIA Wofford College beat the University of Kentucky. He realized his love of sports and had honed his skills in coaching during the off-season. He went back to Cheraw and helped coach the high school football team during the summer for fifty dollars a week. It was a job that his former high school football coaches gave him. From that austere beginning, he was honored by the NCAA on May 17, 2011, by being selected to the College Football Hall of Fame. A lot had happened in between.

Fisher DeBerry did a lot of things right.

DeBerry "semi"-moved to the Charleston area in 1987 when he purchased a beach home on Carolina Avenue at the Isle of Palms. He was coaching the Air Force Academy at the time in Colorado Springs, Colorado. He had been to Charleston many times previously and looked to find a quiet place near the beach. The Carolina Avenue purchase gave him and wife LuAnn a sunrise and sunset.

DeBerry got his start by coaching high school football. His role as an assistant and high school teacher progressed. He started his coaching career at Bennettsville High School and then McClenaghan High School in Florence, South Carolina. There, under the tutelage of head coach Jim Wall, DeBerry gained a perspective of work ethic, relationships and organizational skills that would benefit him for his entire career. He'd learned much from coaches Ed Bost, Bob Bell and Jack Summers at Cheraw High School and, later, Jim Brakefield, at Wofford College.

"I had great mentoring early. Jim Brakefield, Conley Snidow and Gene Alexander all took a special interest in me. Coach Brakefield was hard-nosed and tough, but so deeply respected by everyone," DeBerry offered. "Later in my career I was invited to work on his staff. He was a fantastic leader of young men."

With Brakefield at Wofford College in 1968 and 1969 and then at Appalachian State University in the 1970s, DeBerry learned the nuances of the wishbone offense. This offense and its later variations would serve DeBerry throughout his career.

"I also benefitted by learning about wide line splits from Coach Conley Snidow at Wofford College. Coach Brakefield studied the wishbone option system at the University of Texas and added exaggerated line splits we used at Wofford," DeBerry added.

Coach Conley Snidow passed away in 2007 at the age of ninety-one. Jim Brakefield died in 2002. He had coached at both Wofford College and Appalachian State University along with Emory and Henry College.

DeBerry was a defensive secondary coach on a Wofford team that won twenty-two straight games, concluding with a loss in the NAIA national championship game of 1969 versus Texas A & I.

Armed with the tools of success at two institutions, DeBerry gained his big break. Coach Ken Hatfield hired DeBerry away from Appalachian State in 1980 to join him at the United States Air Force Academy in Colorado. DeBerry started as the quarterbacks coach. Hatfield and DeBerry made a great coaching tandem. The success pattern was nearly instant. DeBerry took over as offensive coordinator in 1981. The Falcons averaged winning nine games per year the last two years of his role. This was an astonishing feat for a team adept at recruiting pilots, not NFL players. The results vaulted Hatfield to the A-list of top NCAA coaches. The University of Arkansas, Ken Hatfield's alma mater, hired him away prior to the 1984 season. DeBerry took over and stuck to his basics of a precision option offense and sound defensive strategies.

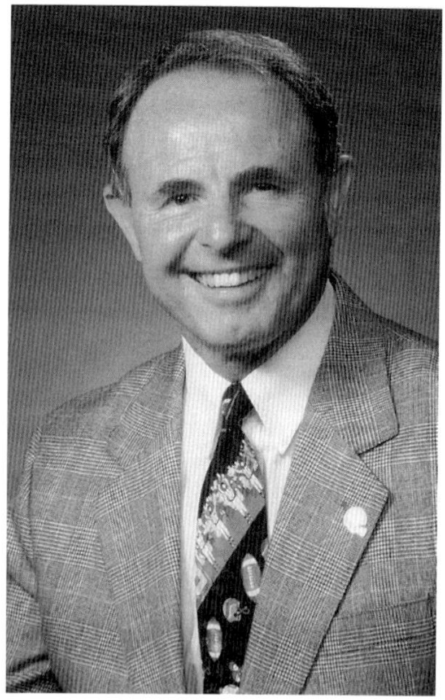

Hall of Fame football coach Fisher DeBerry of Cheraw, South Carolina, now enjoys walks with wife LuAnn from their Isle of Palms beach home. *(LuAnn DeBerry)*

DeBerry's first two years resulted in records of 8-4 and 12-1. In both years, the academy won bowl games (the Independence Bowl over Virginia

Tech and the Bluebonnet Bowl over the University of Texas). The 1985 season vaulted Air Force Academy to the number-four team ranking in all of NCAA football. Fisher DeBerry was named the Bobby Dodd NCAA Coach of the Year. And he'd only just begun. He also received the American Football Association National Coach of the Year. Over his twenty-three seasons as head coach, DeBerry's teams won 169 games. They won three Western Athletic Conference championships, fourteen Commander-in-Chief Trophies (and another tie) as the best interplay record versus the Naval Academy and West Point. They also recorded six NCAA bowl victories. Over his Air Force Academy career, the Falcons won at least eight games eleven times! Those numbers would seem to be at the NCAA Hall of Fame level, especially given that all of his players had signed contracts to pursue careers in the United States Air Force. In fact, they are indeed Hall of Fame statistics. DeBerry was selected to the College Football Hall of Fame in 2011.

"We had some good coaches along the way," DeBerry noted in humility. "I was kinda lucky that we were able to attract good, solid young people, tweak our system, retain coaches and play hard. I have no real regrets, looking back. I enjoyed every single moment of working with our fine administration, the coaches and fostering great relationships with other NCAA coaches along the way."

Those special relationships lasted. He befriended former Florida State University legendary coach Bobby Bowden and Baylor University coach Grant Teaff. He and Kenny Hatfield remained lifelong friends. Opposing Western Athletic Conference head coach LaVell Edwards from Brigham Young University calls often. DeBerry and former Richmond University head coach Dal Shealy have also stayed in touch.

"The coaching fraternity is special," DeBerry stated. "We all understand the mission and what it takes. There are a lot of long hours, and when you're dealing with young people, there are always surprises you didn't count upon. It seems like there is a new circumstance at every practice and every game—an injury, classroom work, personal family concerns, eligibility, media and the like. You have to be able to adapt."

DeBerry made a commitment to the Charleston area by his 1987 purchase on the Isle of Palms. He lives there most of the year—when he's not at his Oklahoma second home near his daughter, Michelle; his son, Joe; and his athletic grandchildren. Grandson Joe Sabatini is a two-sport star of his high school team. He's the varsity quarterback and the baseball team catcher. Granddaughter Jessica is the number-two singles player on that same high school's tennis team. She was 21-2 during the 2011 season. Son Joe

DeBerry was an All-ACC first baseman at Clemson University and drafted by the Cincinnati Reds in third round of the major league draft. He played professional baseball for six years.

DeBerry has rediscovered Charleston from those yesteryear days of his visits from Cheraw.

"Charleston has really changed from my college days and my early coaching years," DeBerry conceded.

"Most of Charleston is new to me," he continued. "We came to the beach for years, and that's the only thing that's stayed the same! Otherwise, LuAnn and I enjoy going downtown. It's like no other place anywhere. Great restaurants…and there are so many other things to do. We could spend all day just in the museum. LuAnn and I just love going down to that playhouse on John Street to see the musicals they perform. They're every bit as good as anything you'd see in New York. Charleston has everything you'd find in a big city and fantastic weather to enjoy as well.

"Heck, I'm the best Chamber of Commerce spokesman Charleston's got!" DeBerry exclaimed with a smile.

Fisher and LuAnn DeBerry are enjoying their forty-sixth year of marriage. That DeBerry ever got a second date with the sweet and lovely LuAnn was a most unlikely circumstance.

"I invited LuAnn to a party with an old friend that was, well, out of sorts and not particularly mannerly," DeBerry recounted. "I was taken with her as soon as I saw her that evening. I felt so bad about my friend's behavior and what she may have then thought of me because of it. I just had to do the right thing and apologize. So I called LuAnn up the next day and made the apology, hoping she would entertain seeing me again and giving me another chance. She was good about it and allowed me to call on her the next evening. From then on I knew something special was going on in my life. I still pinch myself when I think about sharing my life with LuAnn."

Their 1965 wedding was back in Cheraw. In the years following his 2006 retirement from the Air Force Academy, LuAnn has joined him in every chapter of his very active life after football. Together, they have created the Fisher DeBerry Foundation that benefits youth from the difficulties of single-parent households. They have attended perhaps hundreds of local, state and national fundraisers for other charities and causes, most notably the Fellowship of Christian Athletes (FCA).

DeBerry recently put together another fundraiser in Columbia he designated simply as "Coaches Night for Charity." At this fledgling event, DeBerry brought in the head football coaches from six colleges in South

Carolina. The six head coaches addressed the audience about the prospects of the coming season amidst a silent and live auction and other charity-related donations. Each coach selected a charity that benefited by the proceeds of the event. It gave the coaches a chance to interact socially and help others less fortunate as well.

"Our intent is to give back to the state that has given us so much," DeBerry stated. "We're so blessed to have so many fine coaches in this state. And they have been selfless in giving their time to others."

The DeBerrys have exemplified the sentiment by immersing themselves in selfless toil for the benefit of others. They do it because they both agree that it's the right thing.

"I noticed in my last eight years of coaching that I was in more and more single-parent homes. These families struggle. It costs about $165 to send a child to FCA camp. That's all. They get a full week of wholesome activities with others and not only build upon athletic skills but relationship skills and moral centering," DeBerry noted. "Over the last eight years, I suppose we've been able to raise $250,000 to $300,000 that helps a lot of kids in those situations. Many had few opportunities for anything like this and cannot afford extracurricular costs on tiny family household incomes. Eighty-seven percent of these children live with their moms.

"I often wished, growing up in Cheraw, that someone could have done something like that for me," DeBerry mentioned. "So I do it in memory of my mother, who made so many sacrifices for so many years. Besides, it's just the right thing to do, and doing the right thing always makes me feel both humbled and personally happy."

For now, the DeBerrys are devoted to their causes, their grandchildren and each other. They walk the beach together nearly every morning and throw in a few sunsets per week as well. DeBerry calls his good friends Bobby Cremins (the head basketball coach at Appalachian State while DeBerry was coaching football), Cal McCombs (assistant coach at Air Force, now living in Charleston) and Les Robinson (another coaching friend from Sullivan's Island) to meet for a small breakfast and coffee on occasion. Cremins now coaches at the College of Charleston, and Robinson has retired as athletic director at The Citadel. McCombs is now retired after stepping down as head football coach at VMI. They sometimes meet for dinner as well. DeBerry sharpens his still-considerable athletic skills by playing golf (walking with a carry bag, of course) and is frequently in touch with former players and coaches from Cheraw to Wofford to the Air Force Academy.

DeBerry is the epitome of a friend. He cares about people—whatever the race, creed or economic strata. He is devoted to his wife, LuAnn, in ways that are mindful as celebrated in the great works of literature. He is a constant with his two children, Michelle and Joe, and their spouses. Grandchildren are enough reason to have two homes and plenty of time to sit in the stands and enjoy and mentor their victories, trials and setbacks. The DeBerrys are family people through and through. They have Cheraw, South Carolina, running in their veins and are proud of what they have endured for what it taught them and how it enabled them to assist in the achievements of others.

It is a curiosity that one that would meet Fisher DeBerry and smile at first and then smile at last. The first smile is the anticipation of meeting a great Hall of Fame football coach. The last smile is a realization that one has just met an honest-to-goodness humble and decent human being. That lasting impression would infer that DeBerry might just be more interested in your plight than his lifetime of success. He would! That warms you to your bones.

If doing the right thing always had equated to wins, Coach James Fisher DeBerry would have ended his career undefeated.

Keeping Up with Keith Waring

Keith Waring stays busy. His day is considered a business day sometimes on steroids. This Charleston-area real estate developer and investment broker has an electronic calendar in his phone that delineates his deep commitment to others. Though he engineers capital projects for a bevy of investors, his role as a father, grandfather and community citizen is often his most appreciable priority.

Perry Keith Waring was born in Charleston in 1955. He grew up in the area designated as "West of the Ashley." His family roots tap the community of Adams Run, South Carolina. With the growth of the past few decades, Adams Run is nearly West of the Ashley extended. Waring attended St. Andrews Junior High and Middleton High School. He completed his formal education at the University of South Carolina. One of his Waring's treasured friends who rose through all three of those educational backgrounds with Waring was South Carolina House Speaker Bobby Harrell.

"I knew Keith from junior high through college. He is a creative, industrious and well-centered friend," Harrell intimated. "I am not at all surprised by his success at so many levels."

Waring and his wife, Donna, have three children and two grandchildren. The second grandchild was born in May of 2011 and changed Waring's electronic calendar yet again. He stopped everything and dashed to a Columbia, South Carolina, hospital to be there for his daughter Lauren.

It's not like Waring wasn't busy that day and the next. He's always busy. His slim waistline attests to his energy and activity—along with a great gene pool. As a minority, Waring has an appreciable interest in researching local

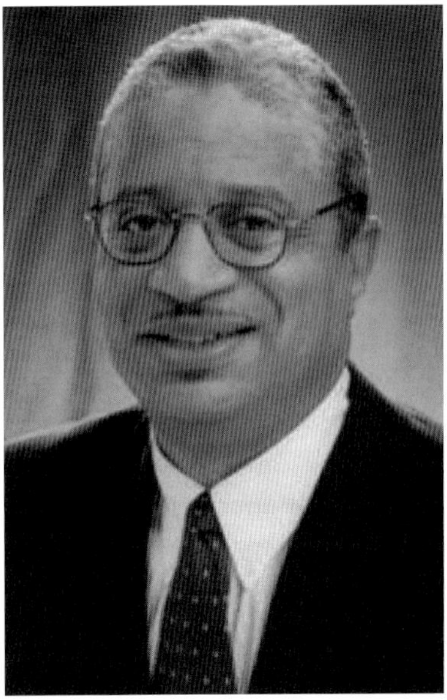

Community volunteer Keith Waring has assisted the Charleston area with his leadership in the approval of a half-cent sales tax to benefit transportation and recreation. *(Donna Waring)*

There was also a societal separation Waring discussed in the mid to late 1960s as a matter of reflection, revelation and historical concern.

"There were two closed societies—black and white," Waring noted. "It is a gift to have lived and seen the transition into one. My parents were active in the civil rights movement. They were lifelong members of the NAACP. As children, we did not want to go to the white school. We passed friends on the way to St. Andrews Junior High [integrated] that were still going to Wallace School [predominantly black]. It was the junior high friends like Bobby Harrell that did not see color and helped those like me to adjust. They did not have to befriend us, but they did so, even when it was unpopular. There was a vocal minority that didn't want us there, but that also changed with time."

Waring is contemplative about the sense of race issues in today's society.

"I'd say it best like this," he revealed. "Even the worst racist out there today thinks he has African American friends. And in another sense, Charleston is worlds ahead of the country as a whole. This is one of the better examples of the blending of race. But it is different nationally. Thurgood Marshall was the first black Supreme Court justice. Today, we only have one black Supreme Court justice, Clarence Thomas. In the year 2011, out of one hundred United States senators, there is no black senator. That's really amazing."

Those are troubling national numbers put in perspective, but by the same sentiment, one could see that Waring did not find an indignity to be touted or taunted. He was simply pointing out the landscape with the intonation that much had been done and there is much to do.

His wife, Donna, graduated from Bishop England High School in 1973. They have three children—Mark, Tracey and Lauren—that they have encouraged to be a part of the burgeoning community spirit that now pervades the Holy City. Waring sees a great future for his children and grandchildren.

It is, at least in part, because he built it to be so.

Knowledge Is Golden

Mallory Factor

There is an old joke about a very recognizable and popular man who went to Rome to visit the pope. The man would be much like Charleston's newest celebrity, Mallory Factor. In the punch line, as the celebrity is standing next to the pope on a balcony overlooking a throng of thousands at the Vatican square, one bystander turns to another and asks, "Who's that man in the white robe standing next to Mallory Factor?"

Well, in fact…three years ago an emissary of the Vatican, Father Mark Haydu, arrived in Charleston as part of an international mission from Pope Benedict XVI. Father Haydu continues to serve the Vatican as the international coordinator of the Patrons of the Arts in the Vatican Museums. As part of his mission, he met scores of Charlestonians in private home settings and public receptions. At these meetings with Charlestonians, Father Haydu discussed the wonderful advances of those great and ageless repositories of world treasures brought to the Vatican across the palette of history. He noted that the Vatican is planning a new fountain, the first since 1753. He invited the ensemble to come to see him and tour the Vatican museums as his guest. He had found the right audience. Of course, Mallory and Elizabeth Factor were not only on the Vatican's guest list—but the Factors had arranged Father Haydu's visit!

Mallory Factor is president of Mallory Factor Inc., an independent merchant bank and financial relations consultancy that he founded in 1976. Factor is a columnist for *Forbes* magazine and also writes and speaks frequently on economic and political topics for cable news stations, leading newspapers and other publications. He also is a member of the Council on Foreign Relations and served as vice chair of the Council's Task Force on Terror Financing.

Factor brought the Vatican to Charleston. And Charlestonians find him as a "cumya" who has endeared himself to the Holy City.

Factor is the cofounder of the Charleston Meeting, an influential political meeting of conservatives in Charleston. The Charleston Meeting is based on the same format as Factor's successful Monday Meeting in New York City, which attracts top political personalities, journalists and business leaders as speakers and participants.

He was recently appointed as the 2011–12 John C. West Professor of International Politics and American Government at The Citadel. He is also a member of the South Carolina Legislative Audit Council, elected by both houses of the legislature.

He is a Tony-nominated Broadway producer and a long-serving trustee of the American Theatre Wing and Brooklyn Academy of Music, both in New York City. Factor also has cultural interests in Charleston. Within a year of arriving in Charleston, he and his wife established a prestigious prize for Southern contemporary art at the Gibbes Museum. The Factor Prize has focused national attention on the Gibbes and the art of the South.

It would seem that Factor is three or four people at once. He is trim, charismatic and smart; impassioned, energetic and friendly. His expertise in his spectrum of endeavors is profound. He has the vibrancy, vitality and vision to gain the respect of an assemblage in sentences metered with his now-famous egg timer. He uses the timer to control the flow of national and international speakers at the incredibly informative Charleston Meeting.

Factor graduated from Wesleyan University and attended Columbia University's law and business schools. His home in Charleston features an intellectual oasis of spouse and progeny: his wife, Elizabeth, and their five children: Cailley, Memorable, Creagh, Merritt and Camden. He is eminently proud of them and their individual successes.

Factor moved his family from a six-floor townhouse on Manhattan's Upper East Side to downtown Charleston in 2006. His national and international connections and prominence dictate that he and his family can live wherever they want to—and that's precisely what they have done. They have chosen Charleston as their home.

"There are so many reasons to come here and to stay here. For us, it is about the warmth of the people, our wonderful climate, our strong cultural tradition and the cuisine. Charleston attracted us because it is an urbane city but with the perfect scale for family life," Factor intimated. "My wife and I used to vacation at Kiawah, and when we were expecting our fourth child we decided to look for an alternative to our fast-paced New York City life. Foremost in our minds was our idea that we wanted a place where our family could flourish and where parents prioritized their family life, all without giving up the cultural opportunities that city life allows. For us, Charleston is that place. The more we live here, the more we embrace Charleston and also the more we want to keep it a secret for the people who live here."

Perhaps not surprisingly, the Factors are raising their five children uniquely. They all speak at least four languages (English, French, Mandarin Chinese and Spanish). The older three have also learned Latin. They don't go to school, but instead are privately tutored in classical history and other subjects. Hey, it worked for the Founding Fathers, why not the Factor children? Several of the children are national champions in French and state champions in mathematics. And his oldest three are only nine, eight and six.

Factor's timely contribution of the Charleston Meeting to the Charleston community is considerable. The discussions of world-related issues through

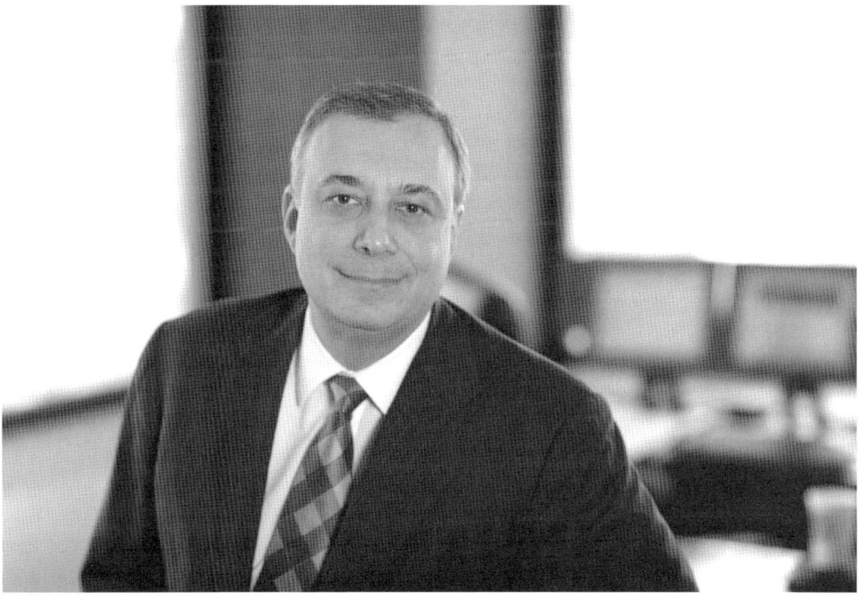

A true Renaissance man, Mallory Factor has made Charleston his home, though he still travels frequently to New York, Washington, D.C., and La Jolla, California. *(Courtesy of Mallory Factor, Inc.)*

invited well-respected speakers are a spellbinding experience of political and cultural awareness. Factor has joined with terrorism expert Mike Smith and retired Marine Corps major general James Livingston to host these monthly events. Livingston is one of only about six dozen current living recipients of the Medal of Honor, the highest award achieved in battle. It is earned. The president of the United States personally presents the Medal of Honor. President Richard M. Nixon performed that honorable function for then Major Livingston.

"I found Mallory Factor to be someone who promoted the idea of making sure people became fully informed on the issues," Livingston stated. "The people that he brings are well versed in the political process and the need for clear leadership at all levels of American life."

Super organizer Andrew Boucher also joined the Charleston Meeting, rounding out a team effort that has been the talk of Charleston. The Charleston Meeting is a permutation from Factor's original concept hosted in New York.

"The New York meeting began with six people who shared a common idea while sitting around my desk almost a decade ago: to change the direction in which our country was heading, to hold on to the values and ideals upon which our country was founded and to ensure that our children and our children's children would have the same opportunities that we had while growing up. The ideals of the Monday Meeting [New York's version] are based on the belief that America is the greatest country on earth—not just part of a global community. We believe that our unique history and founding ideals make America qualitatively different from all other nations on earth, and if we continue to follow these ideals we are capable of lasting greatness," Factor explained.

"From that modest start, the Monday Meeting, a private meeting by invitation only, grew until it was attended by over four hundred people every month. The group includes political donors and rainmakers, corporate leaders, think tank leaders, grass roots organizers and members of the media," Factor revealed. "Over the years, we have had almost every major figure in the conservative movement attend and contribute to the meeting, from William F. Buckley Jr. to Ann Coulter, from Newt Gingrich to Mitt Romney, from Sean Hannity to Mike Huckabee. The meeting is essentially a big tent of conservatives of all stripes who believe in free markets and limited government. The idea is to have, in a single room, all of the people that are needed to accomplish big things—the money people, the organization people, the political leaders and the media. Even though I have since moved here, we still hold the Monday Meeting in New York every month, and it remains very vibrant."

New York has nothing on Charleston.

"When I landed in Charleston, people often came to me and asked me to start a similar meeting here. I was initially skeptical, because I didn't know the political landscape in South Carolina well enough and felt that the meeting would need to take a different form here," Factor explained. "However, after I had lived here for a few years, General James Livingston, Michael Smith and Andrew Boucher came to me and said that they would join me in launching a meeting in Charleston. I agreed, and it started out, even from the very beginning, as a great success. I think the meeting and its participants help us all understand that South Carolina has a unique role in the American political process because of its 'first in the South' role in presidential elections and its interesting political landscape. As soon as I mentioned the Charleston meeting to the speakers at the New York meeting, many of them immediately agreed to come speak here. This showed me that the leaders of our national political movement are interested in what is going on in South Carolina and what people in this state think of their ideas. They are very intrigued to see how they will play in Charleston."

Intrigued? Yes. Surprised? No. The Charleston Meeting has grown from about forty-five initial attendees to two hundred. It is a leadership meeting designed to engage the people in our area with the power, connections and resources to actually make a difference for our state. For this reason, the meeting is by invitation only.

"The Charleston Meeting is now the third-largest meeting of its type in the country after only my meeting in New York City and one in Washington. Further, we now have many of our most important statewide political leaders, donors and grassroots leaders as active participants," Factor pointed out. "It is a big tent here too, and I am amazed and pleased about how well the meeting is working so far."

Factor is concerned with America's future. His profound commitment to his faith and political ideology may not fit others, but it is a beacon of light to him as he proctors his children into the world that this generation improves or, perhaps, impairs.

"Just before I entered college, I read a book called *Capitalism and Freedom*, written in 1962 by Milton Friedman. The work spoke to me and taught me that a nation needs economic freedom to have political freedom. Friedman explained so clearly in his book how big government poses a threat to our fundamental liberties. Now I have the chance to share Friedman's ideas with the next generation. This coming year, I have the honor of being the West Professor of Government at The Citadel, and I look forward to introducing the cadets and graduate students there to many of the great thinkers that started me on my way—Friedman, of course, but also Burke, Hayek, Bastiat and others," Factor said. "These thinkers have even more lessons for the youth of today than they did for me in the late sixties and early seventies when I was a college student, because we are facing far more attacks on our freedom today."

Claude Frederic Bastiat, a French economist from two hundred years ago, merits a quote most apropos to the current political positioning of law to labor—and unions—in the National Labor Relations Board's potential battle with the Boeing Corporation in North Charleston.

"Law cannot organize labor and industry without organizing injustice," Bastiat instructed circa 1840.

Bastiat was a political thinker who has found the most eloquent of followers in modern-day America. It is Mallory Factor that reminds us now of Bastiat's principles and protestations. He is inspired by not only economics and history, but philosophy as well.

"My other inspiration has been my personal belief in the American dream," Factor proposed. "The American dream has come true for me personally. America provided me with so many opportunities that I was able to seize upon with hard work and diligence. It is extremely important to me that these opportunities continue to be there for future generations of Americans.

"There have been many positive influences in my life," Factor continued. "First, like many people in Charleston, my faith in God's law is right up at the top. Charleston is a great place for people of faith, because the idea of relative morality has not really taken hold here—as much as in the big cities and the blue states. When we turn our backs on Judeo-Christian morality in favor of a relative morality in which there is no right and wrong, we lose our moral compass and can no longer steer our country on the right course. Second, my family—my mom, my wife, our children—serve as my foundation and give me the energy, vision and joy to work to make a difference. Third, Ronald Reagan was a huge inspiration for me, because he showed us all that the strength of America is our foundational American values. He showed me the way that a rising tide that will lift all boats, although ironically it was actually John F. Kennedy that coined that phrase."

Being in the center of a political whirlwind is nothing new for Factor. The Factors were at the center of New York Republican political life as a well-known host and hostess. They were even profiled for their political affairs and parties in an extensive spread in *New York* magazine a few years back, and Factor's political endeavors have been covered in numerous publications from the *New York Times* to the *Washington Post*.

"I have been lucky to get to know numerous world leaders, from military commanders to leaders in Congress. One of the highlights was a visit by Baroness Margaret Thatcher, whom I consider (along with Reagan) one of the greatest leaders of the twentieth century," Factor noted. "About eight years ago, we had the opportunity to host Baroness Thatcher at our home for dinner in New York. The only problem was that her trip was scheduled to occur only a few days after the due date for our son, Mem. A good example of how my wife always supports my endeavors is that she convinced me that we should go ahead and plan the dinner, even though it coincided with her due date; she would make it all work out somehow. So, we did, and Baroness Thatcher dined at our house with fifty guests, including various members of the House of Lords and Commons, just two days after my wife and new son came home from the hospital! It proved to be Baroness Thatcher's final trip to the U.S., other than for Reagan's memorial service, and there were a lot of interesting moments that came out of her visit. At one point, I asked her what she thought of Tony Blair, the then prime minister of Britain, and she quickly replied, 'He's like President Clinton, but without the testosterone.' Despite her advanced age, she still had her wit."

The respect he has gained has been throughout the American political theater and into even other walks of life.

"Over the years, I have had the opportunity to spend time with many members of Congress and to form many long-term relationships there with many Republican senators and even several Democratic ones. For four years, I was the senior fellow on the Republican Policy Committee, and I had the opportunity to chair the Chairman of the Joint Chiefs of Staff's Economic Roundtable as well as a jobs summit in the U.S. Capitol," Factor related. "What I have learned most is that our political leaders are just regular people who get confused and have all of these pressures on them. They have trouble knowing who their friends are—and sometimes have trouble picking the right side of an issue. Furthermore, government is so big, unwieldy and downright complicated that even the senators can't get their arms around the issues—especially with the think tanks and lobbyists bombarding them with their own interpretations. The truth is that when you go to Washington, Washington takes you over. Even the most well-meaning public servants get caught up in the power game there. That is one of the big problems with big government."

Coming from those hallways and highways to the quiet and tempered surroundings of Factor's Church Street Charleston home has been therapeutically comforting. He has found a pace that fits his mindset while giving him time to sort the exigencies of the world politic.

"Charleston is so cosmopolitan while remaining friendly and small. It has all of the advantages of a larger place without all of the drawbacks and compromises of large city life. My wife is from the South, and our family loves living in a southern state as well as in one of the thirteen original colonies. In Charleston, history endures, and America's founding values and ideals have not been pushed aside to make room for modernity," Factor posed. "For all of these reasons, we feel so lucky to live here. And now I am looking forward to joining The Citadel community as well and hopefully making a contribution to the corps of cadets."

Factor has joined The Citadel faculty, because he wants to be a part of the value system and critical thinking that the young people have come to The Citadel to experience. There is much material to cover and burgeoning issues that affect not only this generation, but the next as well.

"I am extremely concerned with the United States' debt and how it will impact our children's opportunities," Factor detailed. "With such an enormous level of debt, the United States is losing its independence and is starting to be at the mercy of our creditors. I have been focusing on this issue for a long time. Also, I think our K–12 educational system is failing. Our school system is (wrongly) designed for the benefit of teachers and not for the students that it is supposed to serve. We need to get back to basics and make sure that our children are learning useful skills and essential information in our schools, and that they are learning about the principles on which our great nation was founded. We need everyone in America to be on the same page about saving our nation so that we can face together the dire straits we are in. In Charleston, people understand this, but it is not so clear to the rest of our nation."

If I ever go back to the Vatican, I'm standing next to Mallory Factor.

Remembering My Father

"Bully" McQueeney

My father died on March 24, 2011. We buried him a few days later. In the whirlwind of the responsibilities my dad would have expected me to perform during that trauma, it seemed I had scant time to mourn his passing. Yet I did so intermittently, like the briefness of small showers before a storm. I'm thankful that we had a close relationship. I lament his passing profoundly, like a wind-driven spring tide saturates the marshlands.

He was my best friend.

There is nothing the same on earth during the time that ruefully follows after the loss of a father. Is it the reminder of mortality or the anticipation of the promised life immortal that weighs on the senses? There is such finality mixed with the rawness of deep emotions that remain. And yet my father would not want to cause any expressive discomfort whatsoever. He would either try to put death in perspective or—more likely—humor the situation.

My eight siblings and I followed my mother's lead in tossing a flower into the grave. Mine was a white mum. It had no underlying meaning by its whiteness or variety. It was just a flower from an arrangement that lived from the nourishment of the earth just a few days ago. Like my dad.

The greatest generation that Dad represented is passing from the earth. They did so much to earn everything that my generation inherited. They toiled. They sacrificed. A value system based on honesty, loyalty and responsibility was forged in the fires of deprivation and destruction. They prayed, they persevered and now they are perishing quietly. We will never

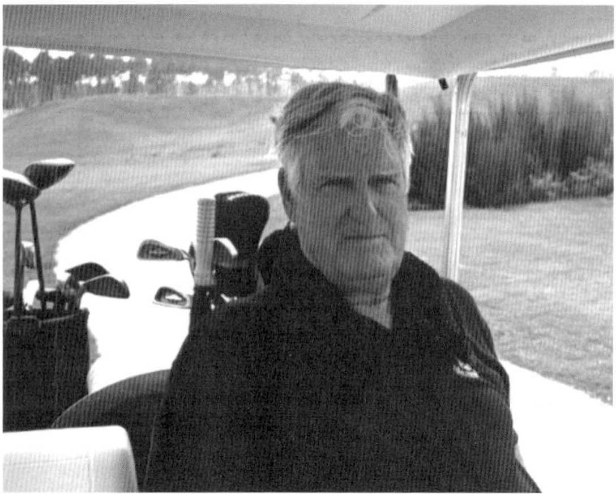

Bully had two passions: The Citadel and golf. Those passions crisscrossed at the Horry County Citadel Club each year. *(Joseph P. McQueeney)*

see this special gift of iron forged and die-cast brotherhood to the soul of humanity again. Dad epitomized this.

He led by example. We got up every Sunday and went to church. There was no option of omission that did not result in corporal punishment. He was both solemn and happy in a pew. It was another home for him. His deep, resonant voice was not given to notes that rose in crescendo. It never dissuaded his vigor for joining in the chorus. This minor malady is, evidently, a genetic flaw passed on to some of his children. The antimelodic gene struck me especially hard.

When Dad got married in 1947, my mother's name changed, and so did his. My mother's thick Charleston drawl never allowed her to phonetically enunciate Dad's given moniker. Instead, "Billy" came out as "Bully." In short time, all of her family and his friends adopted Mom's mispronunciation. "Bully" became the institutional brand. It was an endearing term for the rest of his life. Eventually we all called him by the name Bully.

Bully had every reason to be a failure. His father was a disabled World War I veteran who became an alcoholic. His irresponsible father was further enabled by the blanket compassion of his wife and family. Bully spent parts of his teen years finding my misguided grandfather in taverns or pubs to safely return him home for the evening.

Bully's mother died from a gas-stove accident when he was sixteen. This tragedy left his older sister, Frances, to care for him and his two other siblings. Still his father was nonresponsive to the family needs. The availability of his father's World War I pension check of forty-one dollars was always susceptible to other options than the care of the now-motherless family. If Bully and his brother, Buster, located him in time, they could interrupt tavern rounds to buy family food. Their rented home on Carolina Street was spartan, and rent was paid sporadically. Their desperation survived all the way to the edge of deprivation for want of the essentials a family must have. The two brothers joined the brave masses of young men who served the country amidst a war-strewn globe.

Bully and his older brother, Buster, were inseparable. They worked hard during the Depression performing odd jobs and running errands for nickels and dimes. When the U.S. entry into World War II became imminent, Buster joined the Marine Corps, and in months, Bully joined the navy. Bully was only seventeen. During those war years, the older sister, Frances, married an engineer. They moved to Los Alamos and worked on the famed Manhattan Project. Younger sister Kitty married an Air Force officer prior to the war's end. The Carolina Street household had been shattered into old memories that were only sewn back together erratically upon the infrequent occasions of their geographically hindered reconnections.

That home on Carolina Street has recently been renovated. A few years ago, I took Bully to the house, and he recalled many wonderful stories of the neighborhood. To be sure, it was a small, Catholic enclave that weaved these large families into the fabric of Depression-era Charleston. Bully's best friends, Joe Condon and Lawrence Dodds, were across-the-street neighbors. These three tall and sinewy young men defined the hard times and then later defined their own resiliency. All three went off to World War II without the notion that they would ever return. Their eventual reentry into postwar Charleston brought impact.

Joe Condon managed the growth of urban-to-suburban retail in the Charleston area. He served as president of one of the handful of meteoric Charleston-based establishments—Condon's Department Store. He was a visionary. Joe Condon was part of the epochal resurrection of Charleston from its long, sleepy days of Reconstruction. His family of nine children became next-generation friends, classmates and teammates with the seven Dodds children and the nine McQueeney children. One of his sons, Charlie, was twice elected as state attorney general.

Bully's other best friend from the neighborhood, Lawrence Dodds, became one of the most decorated World War II veterans to return to Charleston. He was awarded three separate silver stars for combat bravery under the direction of General Mark W. Clark during the difficult Italian campaign of 1943. His recorded bravery brought several other citations as well as the Purple Heart. He saved other soldiers by shielding a mine. He carried shrapnel embedded in his body for the remainder of his life. He was the epitome of gallantry, willing to die to save others. Lawrence Dodds's older brother, Johnnie, was a Charleston legend, becoming the mayor and steering father of the beautiful city across the Cooper River, Mount Pleasant. Mount Pleasant is now the fourth-largest city in the state. The Dodds name is synonymous with the vision and ambience of that community.

The post–World War II baby boom had gained healthy results from those Carolina Street beginnings.

There were many others that grew up in the adversity of the Great Depression there, inspiring the dual perspectives of determination and persistence. They had gained something special on Carolina Street that certainly had a measurement in biographical deeds, but more so in the width and depth of their honor, their resourcefulness and their indomitable spirit.

Bully was no different. He grew his family of nine in the boundaries of the Catholic church and the pragmatism of his own experiences. He proctored the children through all the honest and forthright opportunities that the burgeoning Charleston economy would provide. There was discipline, responsibility and education. None lacked attention. And all emulated him.

Bully lived his life immersed in passions. He espoused his likes and dislikes openly. He loved being in crowds, where he seemingly thrived with his robust and gregarious personality. All conversations were built on smiles. He stayed in touch with friends by the old-fashioned methods—postcards and phone calls. He loathed laziness. He had a disdain for complainers. He abhorred people who said one thing and did another. He was never a patient man. In these ways, he was all too human and so very predictable. Yet his goodness was compelling.

He prayed devotedly. He played competitively. He profoundly appreciated friendships. He searched for character over conclusion. He could not allow a meal ticket be paid by another. He never anticipated gratitude after doing something special. It was because it was what he expected of himself. The weight of conscience prevailed over the forces of evil. He knew right and wrong and veered in the correct direction accordingly. The twin villains of rumor and innuendo were given no quarter. He applauded the quality of effort over the quantity of result. Family meant loyalty always. He had an abiding pride in the accomplishment of his children and grandchildren—each of them in their own way. His eyes would light up when they visited. Growing up for us was always a progress towards a potential. As impressionable children, we never looked beyond our own dinner table to find our own idol and champion. He was there nightly to reprimand us, to lift us and to mentor us with profound insight.

In time, Bully mellowed with the completion of his mission. All children were imbued with his commitment to honest work for an honest wage. The unemployment rate of these offspring is and has been zero. They all were guided to the completion of their respective formal education levels.

Bully had persevered through periods of providing thirty-three meals per day against the cycles of a commercial sales industry that did not always cycle back when intense finances were needed. But he and his wife of sixty-four years "made do." His eventually emancipated household brought on their golden years of travel, leisure and prosperity. He had a well-earned respite. In addition to his own travel, his children arranged cruises and even the experience of focused globetrotting. Bully and Charlotte traveled to Rome, Switzerland, Ireland, South Africa and Austria. The Carolina Street kid had arrived. He saw things that his Depression-era childhood would not have forecasted. He made the experience of that travel not only memorable, but also hilarious.

As a son who sat down to write—and eventually perform—a Bully eulogy, it was not lost on me that he lived a long life and that he achieved, mentored and enjoyed. So many of his friends had predeceased him. All of his siblings had died many years earlier, his brother, Buster, having passed last in 1996. Indeed, he was among the last of his golden generation of friends left. Joe Condon had died almost thirty years ago. Lawrence Dodds passed three years ago—nearly to the day. Others had gone as well.

There is no seminal achievement that footnotes history associated with my father. He did not draw a headline or author a byline. He had modest public talents and no appreciable physical attributes other than being tall. Outside of his friends, my mother and my siblings, his opinion was not sought on topical matters. He had no skeletons to expose. He lived within his means, married above his station and earned below his worth. He trusted everyone and left the front door unlocked until the day he died. He never owned a firearm but was adamant that there was a right to do so, provided there was a congruent responsibility. He believed that a child's highest potential was not the responsibility of a teacher. He had an intense regard for the military. He respected the Lenten season in full devotion to its religious meaning. He would not take a drink during Lent. He abhorred discourteous people. He could not bring himself to ever tell a lie. He liked a tall vodka and tonic, especially on hot summer evenings.

Like my father, I would be an unlikely notation source for a specific biblical verse. But because of my father, I sought something appropriate in order to attach my feeling of loss to the powers beyond my comprehension.

It is written in Ecclesiastes (excuse my paraphrase) that there is a season for everything— "for every purpose under heaven." The season that finds me in pensive regard of my father has Charleston's azaleas in bloom. It is the start of baseball season, a rite of passage both Bully and I got excited about. In the week after his passing, the globe's most famous golf tournament, the Masters in Augusta, Georgia, would be played. For more than twenty years, Bully, along with my first cousin, Winn Tutterow, and I had a complicated formula that intensified our interest in this competition. The bet of ten dollars hung in the balance. He usually won by picking someone obscure to pad his points. I even once took him to Augusta to see the Masters. The NCAA men's college basketball national championship is played in the same season. St. Patrick's Day—Bully's favorite day—happens during this uplifting springtime period. Celebrations of the Irish saint transcend the exhilaration of warming flower buds and the sprig of other green shades across the lawns of Charleston. Spring also ushers in the traditions of The Citadel's Corps Day. All is right on earth and in heaven during this season. There is no better time to live, and no worse time to die.

But it is a passing season, and there is "a time to weep, and a time to laugh; a time to mourn, and a time to dance…and a time for peace." Indeed, the season remains. I have laughed and cried and found peace.

We have a lifetime to fulfill the precepts and counseled teachings of our fathers. In time we may edify them by—as much as we dare—becoming like them. I have lived within that sentiment but will not likely ever achieve its promise. Yet, I'll try to reduce all conflict, concern and complication to the denominator of what my father's advice would likely be.

It is good to be my father's son. There is hope.

In the days that followed Dad's passing, I planted two dwarf azaleas upon my father's grave site at St. Lawrence Cemetery. Perhaps Bully will know when I am there to water them. Perhaps my eyes will again moisten. And this season will pass to the next, I suppose. Those azaleas will mark time for me. When they bloom again, it will mark the renewal of another spring season. They will flourish in time. In time, they will wither. The sustenance of earth will provide the meaning for the time between.

May God embrace my father, or at least give him an endearing slap on the back to show him he approved. Give him those strong legs again and a rejuvenated spirit, too. And how about a vodka and tonic with a lime twist? And God, if you're wondering what he really likes, think about getting Bully an early tee time and unlimited mulligans.

Amen.

Epilogue

If you are a convert to the splendid kaleidoscope of life enjoyed by what may be America's most unique community, then the city of Charleston has been a destination. This work aspires to have a recognizable charm for you. It is your chosen way of life amongst the chosen few. Yours is the most highly selected wine of the very best vintage. Sip and savor.

If you are a visitor to this marvelous city, then no accident of transportation has left you at our doorstep. Fortuitously, you came to see us in our habitat. You are our most prized commodity, and we hope to treat you accordingly. Tourism has defined this community over the last forty years like no other economic segment. It is the fervent hope of the author that this work gives you insight into what has been a societal phenomenon. Your glass is on our table to be served. Savor, and then sip!

Should you be that rare commodity that still pervades the foundation of Charleston culture, one of the some sixty thousand pluff-mud natives of the 1940s, 1950s and 1960s, then you are special indeed. You have assisted this community in opening up our homes and our hearts to the world outside—so that they may partake of us—and subsequently spread the good news to others. This book is your life. You own the wine cellar.

The personalities herein are more treasured than our antebellum architecture, more timeless than our sweetgrass baskets and warmer than the swelter of a June day at White Point Garden. They are uniquely themselves and in so many ways ourselves.

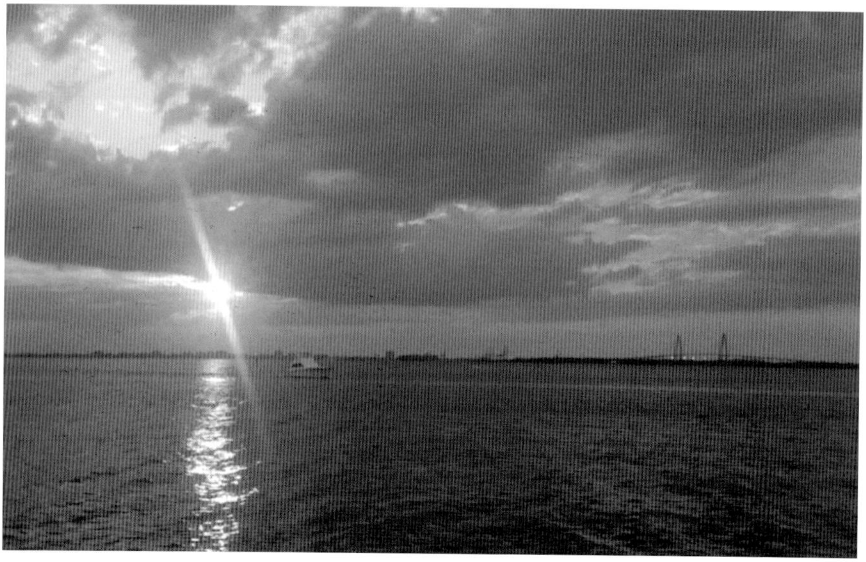

Every trip to places new brings one back to Charleston's hue. *(W. Thomas McQueeney)*

The faces and interwoven relationships of a society transcend all else, generation by generation. Yet the irony remains that the faces bow to the forbearance of time while the buildings and gardens remain essentially the same. It is the people who are timeless.

A Brief Cultural History of Charleston

It was the reasonably friendly Kiawah Indians that allowed the coexistence of a European culture at Charles Towne in 1670.[44] A gift to a commercially hopeful group of supporters to England's King Charles II, the adventurous subjects of the Lords Proprietors settled upon this deep-water port without incident (unless you count a marauding Spanish fleet, a timely hurricane and a large campsite without the benefit of Deep Woods Off! insect repellant). Though wars with the Yemassee Indians interrupted several smallpox and malaria epidemics, the colony remained relatively quiet for a hundred years. That's when Mel Gibson, well…um…ah…Colonel Francis Marion, along with gentlemen like Colonel William Moultrie and Henry Laurens, decided to become free agents and joined the American Revolution. Yes, Charleston had characters throughout its history!

The battle at Fort Sullivan (now Fort Moultrie) was the largest naval battle of the American Revolution. The fact that there was no existing American navy at the time mattered not. It happened nearly a week prior to the signing of the Declaration of Independence, on June 28, 1776.[45] The South Carolina state flag is emblematically commemorative of this winning American battle. Eventually, the colonists prevailed, and the Quaker poster child Ben Franklin made it to the Quaker Oatmeal box even before there was Wheaties. The halcyon days' commercial success beckoned, and the port became the fourth-largest city in America over the next four score and seven years. It supplied the world with tobacco, cotton, rice and indigo. Nobody really knows what indigo is, but there were those in Charleston "dyeing" to market it.

Unfortunately, Charleston also supplied North America with human cargo from Africa by way of the West Indies. This despicable practice found its end in the rubble of the city's worst calamity, the War Between the States (1861–65). The fall was steep, the decline colossal. The natural tragedies of earthquake (1886),[46] fires (1838, 1861)[47] and hurricanes (1880, 1907, 1937, 1989)[48] did nothing but enhance the spirit of the calamity-aware citizenry. They repaired and painted and provided the framework of manner and custom to their young without ostentation. Two, three, four generations crept through the calendar of mankind with enduring heed to values, friendships and service to others. The world would wait on their progeny.

Charlestonians were no one in particular, but everyone in composite. The Anglican Brits became the Episcopal backbone of the community. The French appeared en masse from the 1791 Haitian Revolution.[49] Along with the sailing dosage of Irish, they formed the seeds of Catholicism in the city. The Jewish population came from all points in Europe to enjoy the promised freedoms of the Earl of Shaftsbury's *Fundamental Constitutions of Carolina*, written by none other than his private physician and secretary, John Locke.[50] Charleston enjoyed the second-largest Jewish population in America. The Scots formed the First Scots Church (Presbyterian). The Quakers came and left for Pennsylvania ten years later. It seemed there was a drinking establishment for every dozen citizens in those days. The pub ratio hasn't changed that much! The Germans would become our finest merchants and built a fine Lutheran brotherhood. Even the Greeks came and established a fine, broad base of expertise in several endeavors. They left that ugly wooden horse at Troy. The beginnings of both the American Methodist and Southern Baptist churches can trace lineage to Charleston.[51] It truly became the Holy City as evidenced today by the nearly two hundred churches, most with steeples gracing its low skyline. The ethnicity of the city was diverse but concise. We all grew up on tea, rice and a cornucopia of seafood delicacies.

In so many fortunate ways, the assimilation of the races in Charleston has greatly impacted the benevolent culture of the city. A war that tore apart a country found two peoples with a common thread. Though the aforementioned waves of immigrants have found their respective niches in the many honored societies of Charleston, there can be no mistake that one of the greatest impacts upon Charleston's society is indelibly and importantly African.

The city that stands today is ostensibly the city that Africans built. The Gullah tone in the Charleston dialect is the African inflection that originated in Angola.[52] The rich and delectable cuisine has rudiments in the Ivory Coast, Surinam and Colonial West Africa. We know these tastes in our poultry, our sauces, our fresh seafood and our hominy grits. Often overlooked, the total impact of the African influence on Charleston may be inestimable. The latent influence of African American culture has surfaced in the last thirty to forty years. Kwanzaa is a cultural community festival celebrated the week after Christmas. The Moja Festival has gained wide community support for African art. These worthwhile events showcase both the traditions and the soul of Charleston's burgeoning African American community.

Other cultural influences are nonetheless significant in this, the only English colony in North America that was once a walled city. It is surmised that the aforementioned Kiawah Indians taught us about oysters. The French, Germans, Irish, Greeks, Scots and others gently stirred the great melting pot in Charleston.

It was General Lafayette along with Admiral de Grasse that assisted our fight for independence. The French-lineage General Pierre Gustave Toutant Beauregard actually commanded the troops that fired upon Fort Sumter on April 12, 1861, initiating the great calamity of a four-year war.[53] Amazingly, after thirty hours of bombardment, that battle produced zero casualties. We were even hospitable starting a war. Charleston's most eligible bachelor, General Beauregard, would make for an interesting character for Hollywood should he have lived a century or so later. Is it the French lineage that makes Charleston men suave?

What is a French Huguenot? Some say it's a rope trick invented by a sailor from Marseilles. The Huguenots are a major Protestant Reformation sect of France, much like the Lutherans of Germany or the Calvinists of Switzerland. The French Huguenot Society is the oldest of its type in America.[54] In fact, it is the only one in America.

The Irish have long supplied the framework of Charleston politics from Revolutionary times to the present. A perusal of Charleston street names and buildings would unveil the Irish mayors such as Grace, Morrison and Riley. The Hibernian Society of Charleston (1799) is the oldest benevolent Irish society in America and was founded to assist Irish widows and orphans.[55] It now assists every ethnic area of the community, with fifteen scholarships given annually through its Hibernian Foundation. Its annual St. Patrick's Day speakers read quite honorably with recent orators Vice President Dick Cheney, Senator Joe Biden, Senator John McCain and former Irish Taoiseach Albert Reynolds.

German influence has been anything but subtle. Meeting and King Streets thrived for more than two centuries on the backs of great German merchants and craftsmen. The German Friendly Society, the Arian Society and the German Rifle Club boast some of the finest members of the community to this day. The German Friendly Society has met every Wednesday evening since its inception in 1766. The society held its ten thousandth meeting just a few short years ago.

The English and Scottish societies like the St. Cecelia's and the St. Andrew's Societies have been considered the most elegant of elegant. The St. Cecelia's Ball was a reason for post-Revolutionary Charleston planters to leave their plantations to enjoy a minuet or two. Colonel Francis Marion was said to have broken his ankle escaping from a window at the St. Cecelia's Ball during British occupation (1880–83). There could be no finer opportunity for a Charlestonian to "dress and impress" than to attend either of these very traditional functions. Thinking about going? It is unlikely that the invitation is in the mail!

The Greeks came for a better life and found reasons to stay and multiply. Their merchandising impact—during a period when the corner grocers were mostly Greek entrepreneurs—has spread. They became doctors and athletes, teachers and businessmen. They enhanced Charleston, and Charleston arose from the Greek ingenuity and know-how. The annual Greek Festival is a must-do Charleston event, and the College of Charleston is home to some of the earliest Greek-named fraternities in the country, founded in 1770, before there was a United States of America.

Recent additions to celebrate the arts include Spoleto Festival USA (1977)[56] and the Southeastern Wildlife Exposition (1983).[57] These are quite considerable national and international events. Charlestonians may cite the Spoleto participants as "Spoletians," but the fact is those artsy folks have elevated the arts to an even higher level than ever before. We try to sell them our excess indigo.

The latent influx of Hispanic, Italian and Scandinavian peoples will only make Charleston a better place. They say we are even getting immigrants from Ladson and Goose Creek.

Charleston is rich in the old societies and has even championed the influx of entrepreneurs from the New England states. The New England Society first met in 1819 and counted among its members Samuel F.B. Morse, a portrait artist who became better known for the Morse code. The society never adjourns, so its first meeting is still going on!

The relevance of the cultural history of Charleston past can be seen in the attire, disposition and insight of those who are captured in time for this snapshot of the Charleston community in the middle of our fourth century. This is a proud city—too proud to quit. This is a happy city as well, with laughter in the face of disaster. And it is an enduring city—a lineage of humility, civility and servitude. It is my city. I hope in some way it becomes yours, too.

Notes

1. City of Charleston, S.C., "City of Charleston: The Official Website of the City of Charleston, SC," http://www.charleston-sc.gov.
2. Jonathan H. Poston, *The Buildings of Charleston: A Guide to the City's Architecture* (Columbia: University of South Carolina Press, 1997), 625.
3. U.S. Bureau of the Census, "Table 2: Population of the 24 Urban Places, 1790," http://www.census.gov/population/www/documentation/twps0027/tab02.txt.
4. Earl Black and Merle Black, *The Rise of Southern Republicans* (Cambridge, MA.: Belknap Press of Harvard University Press, 2003), 117.
5. NNDB, "L. Mendel Rivers," Soylent Communications, http://www.nndb.com/people/076/000121710/.
6. Ibid.
7. Naval Historical Center, "Typhoons and Hurricanes: Pacific Typhoon at Okinawa, October 1945," U.S. Department of the Navy, http://www.history.navy.mil/faqs/faq102-6.htm.
8. Donald Williams, David Gleeson, Walter Duane and Jimmy Finnegan, "History of the Charleston St. Patrick's Day Parade," Charleston St. Patrick's Day Parade Committee, Inc., http://www.stpatrickparade.org/history.htm.
9. Pearlstine Distributors, "From 1860 to Today," http://www.pearlstine.net/about_pearlstine/.
10. Medical University of South Carolina, "A Brief History of MUSC," http://www.musc.edu/history.html.
11. Waymarking.com, "Old Charleston Museum, Charleston, S.C.," http://www.waymarking.com/waymarks/WM3M8R_Old_Charleston_Museum_Charleston_SC.
12. Sabin Vaccine Institute, "The Legacy of Albert B. Sabin," http://sabin.org/about-us/history.

13. Mike Brewster, "Bill Veeck: A Baseball Mastermind," Bloomberg BusinessWeek Online, October 27, 2004, http://www.businessweek.com/bwdaily/dnflash/oct2004/nf20041027_3631_db078.htm.
14. Ken Braiterman, "Bill Veeck Did More for Baseball Than Send a Midget Up to Bat," kenbraiterman.com, June 26, 2010, http://kenbraiterman.com/28.
15. *Augusta Chronicle*, "Solomon Blatt," http://chronicle.augusta.com/stories/2000/01/01/op_277078.shtml.
16. "General Mark W. Clark, USA, Ret (1954-1965)," The Citadel, http://www.citadel.edu/citadel-history/presidents/28-clark.html.
17. U.S. Congressman Tim Scott, "Biography," http://timscott.house.gov/Biography/.
18. Brian T. Smith, "ETSU's Jennings, Talford Reflect on Oklahoma's Loss," TriCitiesBlogs.com, March 19, 2009, http://www.tricitiesblogs.com/sports/article/etsus_jennings_talford_reflect_on_oklahoma_loss/21940/.
19. U.S. Geological Survey, "Historic Earthquakes: Charleston, South Carolina; 1886 September 01; 02:51 UTC (local August 31); Magnitude 7.3; Intensity X; Largest Earthquake in South Carolina," U.S. Department of the Interior, http://earthquake.usgs.gov/earthquakes/states/events/1886_09_01.php.
20. "Charleston South Carolina's History with Tropical Systems," HurricaneCity.com, http://www.hurricanecity.com/city/charleston.htm.
21. "Spoleto Festival: 'Il Festival Dei Due Mondi,'" lifeinitaly.com, http://www.lifeinitaly.com/tourism/umbria/spoleto-festival.asp.
22. Town of Mount Pleasant, South Carolina, "Transportation," http://www.townofmountpleasant.com/index.cfm?section=10&page=10.
23. Charleston Inspired, "Military & Federal Installations," Charleston Regional Development Alliance, http://www.crda.org/business/unique_advantages/military_installations.html.
24. Telephone call by author to Charleston Place Hotel, Charleston, SC, August 30, 2011.
25. Linder, Douglas O., "*State v. John Scopes* ('The Monkey Trial')," University of Missouri–Kansas City School of Law, http://law2.umkc.edu/faculty/projects/ftrials/scopes/evolut.htm.
26. Community Management Group, People's Building, http://www.cmgcharleston.com/peoples.htm.
27. Army ROTC, "Palmetto Battalion: Army ROTC," The Citadel, http://www.citadel.edu/armyrotc/.
28. Biographical Dictionary of the United States Congress, "Hollings, Ernest Frederick (1922–)," U.S. Office of the Historian, http://bioguide.congress.gov/scripts/biodisplay.pl?index=h000725.
29. Infoplease Family Education Network, "Gramm-Rudman-Hollings Balanced Budget Act," Pearson Education, http://www.infoplease.com/ce6/history/A0909709.html.

30. Ibid.
31. South Carolina Department of Parks, Recreation and Tourism, "French Huguenot Church," http://www.discoversouthcarolina.com/products/3407.aspx.
32. "Washington Monument," EnchantedLearning.com, http://www.enchantedlearning.com/history/us/monuments/washingtonmonument/.
33. The Reformed Episcopal Church, http://rechurch.org/recus/recweb/index.html.
34. U-S-History.com, "The Protestant Reformation," Online Highways LLC, http://www.u-s-history.com/pages/h1136.html.
35. This Far by Faith, "People of Faith: Denmark Vesey," The Faith Project, Inc., http://www.pbs.org/thisfarbyfaith/people/denmark_vesey.html.
36. *Post and Courier*, Events: Church Anniversary, Evening Post Publishing Company, http://events.postandcourier.com/charleston-sc/events/show/201416425-church-anniversary.
37. Ibid.
38. Eternal Word Television Network, "St. Benezet, or Little Bennet, Patron of Avignon," http://www.ewtn.com/library/mary/benezet.htm.
39. Damerow, Harold, "Avignon Papacy," Union County College, http://faculty.ucc.edu/egh-damerow/avignon papacy.htm.
40. Historic Charleston Foundation, "Our History," http://www.historiccharleston.org/about/history.html.
41. Preservation Society of Charleston, "Founding and Preservation Society History," http://www.preservationsociety.org/who_history.asp.
42. United States Marine Corps, History Division, "Who's Who in Marine Corps History: General Louis Hugh Wilson, Jr.," http://www.tecom.usmc.mil/HD/Whos_Who/Wilson_LH.htm.
43. United States Marine Corps, History Division, "Who's Who in Marine Corps History: General Robert H. Barrow," http://www.tecom.usmc.mil/HD/Whos_Who/Barrow_RH.htm.
44. Charleston County Public Library, "1670–1720: The Proprietors' Fortress," http://www.ccpl.org/content.asp?id=15748&action=detail&catID=5749&parentID=5405.
45. The Patriot Resource, "Battle of Fort Sullivan," PatriotResource.com, http://www.patriotresource.com/amerrev/battles/sullivan.html.
46. U.S. Geological Survey, "Historic Earthquakes" (see n. 17).
47. Brian Hicks, "Charleston at War: Charleston Beaten Down by Great Fire," Charleston Post and Courier, January 30, 2011, http://www.postandcourier.com/news/2011/jan/30/civil-war-150-years-part-eight-of/.
48. HurricaneCity.com, "Charleston South Carolina's History with Tropical Systems" (see n. 20).

49. Bob Corbett, "The Haitian Revolution of 1791–1803: An Historical Essay in Four Parts," Bob Corbett's Home Page, hosted by Webster University, http://www.webster.edu/~corbetre/haiti/history/revolution/revolution1.htm.
50. H.R. Fox Bourne, "John Locke and the Fundamental Constitutions of Carolina," Library4History.org, http://america.library4history.org/VFW-Huguenots-California/COLONIZATION/JOHN-LOCKE.html.
51. First Baptist Church, Charleston, South Carolina, http://archives.charleston.net/org/firstbaptist/.
52. Gullah Net, "Gullah Language," ETV Commission, http://www.knowitall.org/gullahnet/gullah/language.html.
53. "P.G.T. Beauregard," Son of the South, http://www.sonofthesouth.net/leefoundation/General_P_G_T_Beauregard.htm.
54. The Huguenot Society of South Carolina, "History of the Huguenots," http://www.huguenotsociety.org/history_new2.htm.
55. Williams et al., "History of the Charleston St. Patrick's Day Parade."
56. CharlestonLowcountry.com, "Charleston Spoleto Festival USA: History," http://www.charlestonlowcountry.com/specialpages/spoletohistory.html.
57. Southeastern Wildlife Exposition, "General Info," http://www.sewe.com/gen_info.php.

About the Author

W. Thomas McQueeney is a "child of the pluff mud." He is one of six brothers who have graduated from The Citadel. He earned his degree in English in 1974. McQueeney is a 2009 recipient of the Order of the Palmetto, the State of South Carolina's highest award. He chairs the Medal of Honor Bowl and also serves as president of the South Carolina Athletic Hall of Fame. He is an accomplished artist and has authored four other books. *Sunsets Over Charleston* (2012) is the companion volume to this production. He is married, has four children and resides in Mount Pleasant, South Carolina.